GW01314170

ALAN HURNDALL is an award-winning journalist and film maker and has authored four books. He grew up in Camberwell between four pubs, three youth clubs, two scrap metal yards, two doss houses, a doctor, a dentist, a pawn shop, a mini cab office, a chippy, a baker, a dry-cleaners, a launderette and the customary two pie and mash shops.

His parents owned a newspaper kiosk which was also a cover for his dad's illegal bookmaking activities. Among the customers were some of Britain's most notorious gangsters including a Godfather of crime and a train robber or two.

Alan left school at 16 and worked as a news agency runner before enjoying a successful career in newspapers and television, even editing the local newspaper he used to sell and deliver as a paper boy. He is a former Campaigning Journalist of The Year, BAFTA nominee and a Royal Television Society award winner. In later life he taught journalism at university and as a student gained a Masters Degree in Creative Writing. So, starting in Fleet Street and ending at university! His mum would have said this was typical of him - everything arse about face.

Alan is married to Alison and lives near the Peak District in Derbyshire where they provide a taxi service for their grandkids and serve them chicken curry and cake after school on two days a week.

By the same author

NON FICTION
Pottery Cottage
The Invisible Girl
The Crooked Spire Killings

A selection from more than 1,000 reviews of Alan's work

"I love Alan's style of storytelling." - jmw8796
"Best True Crime book I have ever read." - DaveH
"Wonderfully written and in parts brutal." - Mrs J
"It's a must read, and I expect to read it many times." - Sarah Kenneally
"Fantastically written with such care and consideration to the family involved." - Vonnie
"Written with passion. I'm looking forward to reading another Alan Hurndall book." - JJ
"Fantastic writing, Alan Hurndall." - Mrs M. Taylor
"Thank you Alan for a brilliant page turner full of insight." - Karen Smith
"What a read this is. Well done Alan Hurndall." - Mick Ludlam
"Alan had me hooked, staying up until the early hours to find out the next twist." - Anya L
"Alan is a great writer. Can't wait for his next one." - Gemma C
"Alan has a style of writing which draws you in and keeps you wanting to get to the next chapter, and then the next... Dan Brown used to be my favourite author, Alan Hurndall now holds that place." - Glenn Turner

Alan R. Hurndall

THE
KID
FROM
THE
KIOSK

First published 2024

Copyright © Alan Hurndall 2024

The moral right of the author has been asserted.

All rights reserved. Without limiting the rights under copyright reserved above, no part of this publication may be reproduced, stored in or introduced into a retrieval system, or transmitted, in any form or by any means (electronic, mechanical, photocopying, recording or otherwise), without the prior written permission of the copyright owner and any publisher approved by the copyright holder.

ISBN No 9798322488019

Dedicated to my Nan, Dad, Mum and brother Johnny.
Rest in Peace.

Written for my lovely grandchildren. Enjoy discovering your roots kids!

CONTENTS

PREFACE

On the 31st of August 2024 they closed my old primary school.

Thousands of kids started their journeys through life there, paths that led near and far, sometimes across the other side of the world. My secondary school had already bitten the dust. But locking the gates of Comber Grove Junior and Infants for the last time felt like the final nail in the coffin of my childhood.

The house I grew up in is now a petrol station; the kiosk where I served sweets, newspapers and cigarettes from the age of ten was reduced to firewood; the youth clubs where I escaped in the evenings to play table tennis, snooker and Three Card Brag are no longer; the Regal Cinema near Camberwell Green where I booed the villains at Saturday Morning Pictures, Woolies and Kennedy's butchers on the Walworth Road, the pubs where I waited on the doorstep with a glass of R. Whites and a packet of Smith's crisps with their little blue rolled-up salt sachet are all long gone.

Then there's the men that came knocking - the gasman, insurance man, coalman, the Pools man, milkman, the landlord, and the debt collectors. All consigned to history.

As the family sole survivor, the loss of my loved ones inspired me to write this memoir - to create a permanent record of life in the Fifties and Sixties in my little corner of South London. Dad, Mum, Nanny Jane, brother Johnny - now rest in peace leaving the living to remember their lives, their love, and happy times.

It's not a stuffy social history but a loving tribute as seen through the skewed prism of a little boy growing up in a rapidly changing world. The sights, the sounds and smells of my childhood are embedded in my brain. The little things - the bathhouse steam, lugging the damp bagwash home, the pong of chlorine at the swimming baths, the stink of sick and sawdust in the school hall, the stench of ale and tobacco after last night's party.

Colours too - grey (and shrunken) school jumpers, golden Caramac bars, black plimsolls, navy girls' knickers when they did handstands, orange Jubblies, Green Shield Stamps, that rich red Lifebuoy carbolic soap, lemon drops, our yellow kiosk… I could go on for pages.

We're born. We live. And then we die. Our purpose is to make memories. And when I'm sitting in my metaphorical rocking chair smoking my metaphorical pipe and my grandchildren ask me to tell them about the 'Good Old Days,' I can now reply with a knowing smile, 'Read my bloody book.'

ACKNOWLEDGEMENTS

The following is a true story about my early life growing up in Camberwell. Everything recorded here, although seemingly far-fetched in parts, actually happened. Conversations are gleaned from my own memories, from family anecdotes, hand-me-down tales, hazy recollections, gossip and second-hand whispers. However, there are no downright falsehoods. Characters, including my own family, may be unbelievable, but they are real. And may they all rest in peace.

I would particularly like to thank the following for their expert help…

Carole Adams
Tim Peacock
Paul and Emma Millington
John Butterworth
JB Club Press
Southwark Library Archive
London School of Economics
Comber Grove School
Mike Kent
Georgie Allen
The late Glenda Charman
Joe and Joyce Abrahams

Historical Sources
Southwark Archive
A Life At The Chalkface by Mike Kent
The Temple of Youth by John Butterworth and Jenny Waine
Clubland
Cambridge House
White Fang by Jack London
Pardon Me For Living by Geoffrey Green
Gangster's Moll by Marilyn Wisbey
My Manor by Charlie Richardson
The Wrong Side Of The Tracks by Tommy Wisbey
The following Facebook Groups – William Penn; I Grew Up in South East London; Growing Up in the 50s, 60s & 70s; I grew Up In Walworth; South East London Memories; Cockney Sparrows; Camberwell SE5 Friend Finder; Memories of Walworth; Camberwell and Bermondsey; Camberwell Residents Memorial Page; Now and Then Walworth; Camberwell, London; UK Residents 50s, 60s, 70s and 80s; Pie, Mash and Liquor Appreciation.

-1-
The Accident
November 5ᵗʰ 1971. 1.20am.

Darkness.

I'm now coming to, but it's a blurred, confused consciousness. I can't see but I can hear… the hum of muffled voices, the crunch of boots walking on shattered glass, and the whirl of machinery which I'm about to discover is from a fire crew's cutting equipment. Then, in this blackness, a floating, dismembered male voice right next to me. 'This one's dead.' Words that will haunt me forever.

Other senses kick in - the smell of charred rubber, petrol fumes and smoke. And now, at last… sight. I'm staring up at an autumnal sky above some street in South London. It's a clear night. The moon shines. The stars glitter. But they are where the car roof should be. That's been ripped off by a collision or by the cutting gear. I'm trapped in the rear, between buckled seats and twisted metal, and cannot move. My head is in a fixed position looking upwards. My left shoulder is bizarrely both numb and painful. I will later learn that the nerves have been damaged by whiplash. My left knee is at a weird angle from the rest of the leg and is throbbing. My right hand feels warm and wet. I can just about raise it to my eyeline - now I see blood oozing from the webbing between two fingers.

A fireman pumps air into some contraption under my arm and it shifts my shoulder back into place. I can now move my head. Relief. He offers some comforting words but I'm not listening. A line of about eight people stare at me through the lid of what a few minutes ago was a Ford Escort. One of the onlookers recognises me. Andy Gardner. He's the brother of Barry, a former schoolmate. He offers a knowing smile and then says, 'Don't worry Al, you're gonna be all right.' I've been conscious for all of 15 seconds but my brain decides it's all too much. It orders a total shutdown. Everything off… now! I close my eyes and drift back into a blissful, protective sleep.

Darkness.

Another cognitive reboot. Again, sound restores before sight. This time I'm hearing total mayhem. I open my eyes. I'm looking up at the ceiling. Strips of piercing fluorescent light. I'm obviously in some Casualty department, on a trolley, my privacy protected by a green curtain. On the other side I can hear my friend Terry running around hysterically with nurses in obvious pursuit. He's shouting and in tears, 'I've killed him, I've killed him.' It's the stuff of some awful nightmare. But I think therefore I am. I start to unscramble the hell I'm living through. I recall that male voice from earlier, the one I'd heard say 'This one's dead!' I do some grim sums. We'd been to a party and all left in a car, five of us - me, my brother Johnny, my friend Michael, Terry and his girlfriend, my cousin Lorraine.

But who is dead?

With Terry very much alive and blaming himself for killing 'him,' my chilling calculations work out I've lost either my brother or my best mate. And what about poor Lorraine. What's happened to her?

Mum's tortured face appears around the curtain. I ask where I am.

'You're in King's,' she says.

We always call King's College Hospital 'King's.'

'Who is it, Mum? I know someone's dead.' At least that's what I think I said. She'll confide later that I was a rambling mess.

The doctors have told her not to tell me. And she refuses to say, but she can't hide her feelings. She hugs me and fails to hold back tears. I assume it's because we've lost Johnny.

'Who is it? Tell me… *Please.*'

She grimaces and whispers that Lil, Michael's mum, had phoned her at home at 2am. 'We've lost Michael, you'd better get yourself to King's,' she'd said.

I've always been an emotional person, but there are no tears from me here. Just a numbed acceptance of fate. I stare at the ceiling. I feel a jab in my arm and a new warmth coursing through my veins… and once again I escape into the serenity of unconsciousness.

Michael, 3rd left, on holiday with me (far right)

I dream. The umpire at a cricket match is calling me to the wicket but I can't find my bat, my gloves or my pads. I scour the dressing room and reach a fever pitch of panic. Is this a metaphor for impending death? I'll reflect later that the wicket is heaven and the umpire in the white coat is St Peter beckoning me at the Pearly Gates. But I'm certainly not ready to go just yet. It's a vision that will return in future dreams whenever I'm suffering stress.

I awake once more. Into a cliché. A guardian angel is holding my hand and coaxing me out of my slumber. It's her eyes I notice first - deep, dreamy cobalt. Then her striking ginger hair. I'm in a different part of the hospital. In a comfortable bed. In an isolated room. Under observation.

'Hello Alan. How are you feeling?' she says. Out of habit I smile. 'You've been in a road accident but it seems you're okay. You've been very lucky.'

I'm feeling surprisingly calm. Literally laid back. My left leg is now comfortably bound from ankle to thigh, my hand is stitched, and the fireman's supporting brace replaced by extensive bandage. I've slept through all the treatment, peacefully out of it, probably induced by medication. I ask for a condition report on the others but she deflects my question. I will learn later that Michael is in the morgue, Lorraine is in intensive care, Johnny is in theatre and Terry is under sedation.

'Let's get you better. Just concentrate on yourself for now. I've kept my eye on you all night and I'm pleased you seem to be back to normal. We have to watch head injuries very carefully.'

She brings me tea and toast. We talk for ages between blood pressure, temperature and cognitive tests. She warily inquires what happened. I tell her all that I can remember of the previous evening. We'd been to watch my cousin Marilyn sing at a pub in Grove Park. Afterwards we'd been invited back to my uncle's house for sandwiches. Drinks were poured, the record player came on and we'd all danced to Sinatra. Leaving the party into the cold, we'd all jumped into Michael's Ford Escort. He was driving, with Terry and Lorraine cuddling in the front, and Johnny and myself in the back. There were no seat belts. We'd all been in high spirits, but not drunk. We'd begun larking about, running red lights and such. So much so that my brother leaned over from the back and snatched the keys from the ignition. Everything after that was a blank.

It will later transpire that Terry and Michael had swapped seats and Terry had taken over at the wheel. At Nunhead Lane in Peckham he'd lost control on an icy bend and crashed at high speed into a lamp post. Michael had died instantly. Johnny was somehow thrown into a neighbouring garden and Lorraine suffered catastrophic injuries from which she later died.

Beautiful Lorraine died from injuries in the crash

Johnny has broken his jaw and fractured his femur. He will live with a rod through his thigh for the rest of his life.

I'm the lucky one. I've torn the cartilage in my knee which 50 years later will require a knee replacement. I also have a brachial plexus injury. The nerves in my shoulder are hanging together by a thread and in some parts of my arm I register zero on pin-prick nerve tests. Although I'll be paralysed down my left side for three months they will eventually grow back with no long-term damage. It's a rare injury, apparently. A consultant will summon student doctors in so they can witness my examination and treatment.

Except for a few minor face scratches, Terry, remarkably, is unscathed. But there are mental scars. Over the coming months he'll suffer huge guilt and stress, blaming himself for Lorraine and Michael's loss, and his lifeless body will be washed up in The Thames, bringing the fatalities of that terrible night to three.

The only survivors will be me and my brother.

The nurse squeezes my hand, offers condolences, and asks how old I am.

'18,' I say.

'Same age as me,' she says with a smile. I sense a connection. I ask if she's allowed to mix business with pleasure and she blushes. I play the sympathy card and ask her if, when I'm on my feet again, she'll go out with me one night to continue my rehab - an offer that this student nurse doesn't refuse.

We'll go to the Odeon on Camberwell Green and smuggle a Chinese takeaway back to her digs in the nurses' home. And over sweet and sour chicken she'll ask me my life story…

2

Born Lucky

Mum always thanked the Lord for saving her boys. Truth is, I've always been a lucky so-and-so. In life. In love. And so far in health. If I fell overboard into a shark-infested sea my mates would bet that I'd land on the back of a whale, be ferried to safety to a treasure island where they served 24-hour fast food, and be delivered into the bosom of a mermaid.

Not just jammy. Hapless too. I've been rescued off a snowy mountain, retrieved from a swirling sea, salvaged from lethal rocks by a lifeguard and washed up on a windy lake. I've almost choked on a piece of steak, fractured my skull playing cricket, dislocated my shoulder skiing, and have a bolt through my wrist which I broke diving for the ball in goal.

I've been paralysed and plastered, battered and bitten, stitched and scarred. I'm Lucky Jim, Frank Spencer and Mr Bean rolled into one. As I write this, I'm recovering from tripping over a traffic bollard and falling flat on my face into the road in the South of France. I've a sore head, black eye, a cut on my finger and a bruised shoulder.

Accident prone, for sure, but like the heroes at Saturday morning pictures when I was a kid, I'm always saved in the final reel. I've Mum's genes, you see. She could grow flowers in the desert. When we were all skint and facing the bailiffs, she won the jackpot in a national Bingo game. And, no matter how down or out she was, as she always put it, 'I got out of trouble on the last.' This would be celebrated with a song, a Guinness, a beaming smile and a little shimmy. I certainly inherited her optimism.

Dad, on the other hand, was, sadly, more of a loser. In a two-horse race his bet would more than likely trail in third. He was a born pessimist who, if the world was about to end, would race to put a bet on it.

Their fortunes weren't just apparent while living. They were evident at the appointed hour too. After a series of mini strokes, Dad's passing was prolonged and painful, his hospital death rattle so distressing we could only bear to hug him and leave the ward for him to depart the world as he joined it. Struggling.

Mum, however, died in her perfect way… instantly. In a puddle of stout. She collapsed during a knees-up in an East End boozer while singing For Once In My Life staring into the loving gaze of her childhood crush. When I reached the hospital, her hands were still warm. She had a smile etched on her face and was at peace.

As I said earlier, we're born, we live. And then we die. Our purpose is to make memories in between. Ah, yes, memories. I've enjoyed quite a few of those. Mine take root during one historic winter…

***

It's February, 4th 1953. A figure scurries along Camberwell Road, her head down, her body braced against the cold. She's wearing a navy gaberdine coat, a nurse's hat, and a scarf across her face to protect her from the biting air. Her medical bag is heavy, she's breathless, and she leaves a vapour trail of expunged breath in her wake. Someone's called the midwife. And her mission is urgent. To deliver me into the world.

It's been a catastrophic time. For weeks London's been trapped under a blanket of poison. It began just before Christmas when Santa brought a cold front from the North Pole. The mercury dipped lower than a pickpocket on Epsom Downs. Everyone started burning coal to keep warm - not just in homes, but in offices and factories too. The power stations went into overdrive. Every day, thousands of tonnes of smoke, carbon dioxide, hydrochloric acid and sulphur dioxide belched into the air with nowhere to disperse. London stank of rotten eggs. Cattle at Smithfield Market were asphyxiated, their lungs blackened and their innards filled with soot. Cars were abandoned and public transport shut down.

The Great Pea Souper is the stuff of disaster movies, with the clanging chimes of Big Ben, drifting across the River Thames, providing an eerie soundtrack. The yellow mist gets everywhere, creeping under doors, through cracks in the walls, and even into the book covers at the British Library. The toxic cocktail burns nostrils and people keel over unable to breathe. By this Spring the death toll will reach 4,000 Londoners, mostly from bronchitis and pneumonia.

Tonight, thank goodness, the thick stuff has stayed away. But the roads and pavements are still empty. Folk have got used to staying in and wrapping up warm. Mum's waters have broken and my Nan is at her side, offering comfort and mopping her brow. In the tiny basement kitchen, a gaggle of excited sisters are tripping over each other, boiling the same water over and over, in between running upstairs to assure Janie that help will arrive soon. Consumed by another wave of pain, she screams out. 'You were right, Mum. I should never have married the BASTARD!'

The street door opens in a rush. The midwife is Scottish and has a speech impediment. She scours the house looking for the right bedroom.

'What rrroom, what rrroom?' (or did she say 'what wwwwomb, what wwwwomb?') The sisters giggle behind their hands. The birth - Janie's second - is mercifully quick. A little after 9pm, I emerge, a few days earlier than expected, but seemingly healthy. A quick check confirms my bits are all there and I am indeed a boy. The second toe on each foot points in the opposite direction to the others - a bizarre family affliction that will attract strange looks on beaches and pool sides and ensure blisters for life. But it proves at the very least that I am sired by a Hurndall.

I'm born under the winter zodiac sign of Aquarius and rather appropriately share a birthday with the knockabout comedian Norman Wisdom. If you believe these things, my birth sign says I'll be 'progressive, original, independent, humanitarian, temperamental, aloof, even'. The stars also pledge that I'll be fun with friends and will help others, 'but will dislike broken promises and dull or boring conversations'. True dat!

My parents' genes have been mixed mostly in my favour. I'll develop their sense of humour, quick wit and embrace their strong work ethic. I'll inherit some of Mum's storytelling ability, her resolve for fair play, and her conscience (she once traipsed to Carter Street Nick to hand in a purse she found in the street).

Although in childhood I'll happily deprive London Transport and British Rail of revenue without even flinching, I'll not develop Dad's sticky fingers (wink wink, nudge nudge). I'll never actually half-inch anything except as a six year old when a Crunchie will literally land in my lap on Victoria Station. It will fall off the back of a trolley and I won't say a word. And before any guilt factor can kick in, The Numbskulls in my stomach will be already be breaking down the honeycomb and chocolate into an unwholesome gloop. Thankfully, I'll swerve Dad's mean and explosive temper and his health issues - shockingly poor eyesight, ulcerated legs and a bone malformation where the pinkies on both hands bend like a hook.

The gods have decreed that mine will be the golden generation, born at the dawn of the welfare state, with (so far) no more global wars, and opportunity aplenty. We'll shake off the austerity of the Fifties and there'll be revolutions in living standards, music, fashion, science, communications, and medicine.

A blossoming National Health Service will one day save my life - a life that will be blessed, eventful and full of drama. And, to commemorate my birth, the Government has today announced the end of the wartime rationing of sweets. In the morning, new Clean Air Regulations will be published which will free the capital of fog and smog forever.

Sweets AND fresh air! What more can a kid want? Told ya I'm charmed!

Headline on the day I was born

3

Lights Out

Any new arrival is of course a time for celebration and over the next few hours Mum will embrace a line of sisters, brothers, aunts, uncles, cousins, friends, neighbours and general hangers on - the types who can sniff a free drink from miles away. In come bottles of light ale, snowball mixers and cheese rolls, on comes the sturdy old Decca turntable, and out come the scratchy Sinatra and Frankie Laine LPs. My mob are never short of an excuse to party! The house reverberates with singing and dancing. Upstairs, Mum is feeling sore in more ways than one. But among the throng of well-wishers, there's one glaring omission - the father. He's missing in action, somewhere in the grimy backstreets of Soho.

Christened John Hurndall, he's known throughout South London, the West End and the Underworld as 'Lights', although no-one seems to know exactly why. Some assume it's because he had a wartime fruit stall in the Berwick Street always emblazoned in light even during blackouts. Others guess it's because he's light on his feet. Long after his death I will read on an online gambling forum that he used to sell batteries to the bookies at New Cross dog track to light their pitches. Hence Lights! The more cynical offer that it's because he's light fingered. Whatever, it stuck and Lights he is and always will be.

He's been neither seen or heard of for two days now. The smart money is on any one of three places - Waterloo Station selling flowers; in Lonny's gambling den; or in a nearby Turkish Baths having a kip after an all-nighter in the aforesaid establishment.

Dad lives in a secret world. Down a dark Soho alley, in a tiny mews, nestled between bedsits rented by pimps and prostitutes, and above a launderette (incidentally also owned by Lonny). There's no sign or welcoming neon; no membership required, no need to sign in. On a need-to-know basis, only those in the know... well, know. There's even a doorbell code. A camera clocks you as you ring twice - both short bursts - followed by a third, longer ring. Upstairs, Lonny looks up from his Investor's Chronicle and checks the screen. If the face fits, he presses the buzzer to let it in. Strangers are not welcome. They are left waiting on the pavement until they take the hint.

It might reek of tobacco, stale sweat and old men, but there's nothing seedy about this place. The fortunes of war are played out against a kaleidoscope of green baize and black and gold flock wallpaper and in the glow of sparkling chandeliers and an electric Belling. This in contrast to the proprietor who dresses in immaculate sterility. Small and slim, always in black trousers, and a white drip-dry nylon shirt. Elasticated silver armbands hug his neatly rolled-up shirt sleeves.

He greets his regulars with a grin, an offer of tea or coffee and a bacon sandwich - a betrayal of his Jewish roots - but a godsend when you've been out in the cold all day living on your wits. There's a strict no booze policy, save for a swig from a hip-flask here and there. You are here to play cards - rummy usually - and to donate to his investment fund via the commission he charges for the tables, or 'house money' as they call it. Mrs Lonny doesn't exist. They quip he's married only to the concept of making money. His fingers are in a number of pies, including toffee-apple and sarsaparilla stalls at various London markets, rented out as legitimate licensed franchises - permissions gained following generous brown envelope donations to council officials.

The clientèle is a mix of successful businessmen, affluent playboys, cab drivers, scoundrels, thieves, street traders, shopkeepers, and the wealthy retired easing their boredom playing up the fruits of their investments.

They all have their own language: bastardised Cockney rhyming slang, only ever using the first word of the rhyme. Hair is *Barnet* (hair), ears are *Donalds* (Peers), eyes are *minces* (mince pies), teeth are *Hampsteads* (Heath), neck is *Gregory* (Peck). If someone is coming up behind you'd better watch your *hay* (haystack). It's the same with numbers. One to ten are: a *sov; bottle* (two); *carpet* (three); *rouf,* (four backwards); *ching,* (five); *half a stretch,* (six); *neves,* (seven backwards); a *TH,* (that's eight); *clothes line* (nine); and *cockle and hen* (ten). Twenty is an *apple* (apple core, score); 25 *a pony;* 500 *a monkey;* and, *a grand,* or a *long 'un,* is 1,000.

They never bother with names either. Most London landmarks are a generic noun. Oxford Street, *'the Street';* Trafalgar Square, *'the Square';* Covent Garden, *'the Garden';* and Petticoat Lane, or East Lane market, *'the Lane'.* Camberwell Green is *'the Green'* and any gambling club the *'spiel'.* The River Thames is simply *'the Water'.*

In tonight are Ernie, who owns two fruit shops in the Edgeware Road; Mad Paddy, the most brazen shoplifter in London, who once rolled up a mink carpet in Harrods dressed in brown 'corner shop' overalls to give the appearance he was from the store's warehouse; Terry the Dip, fresh from the rush-hour at Oxford Circus Underground station; Joey the Smudge, who takes 'photos' of tourists for extortionate prices without film in his camera; the Colonel, a retired Army officer from Kent; and Mad Mike who eats and sleeps in his taxi.

And then there's dear old Lights, hooked on a hedonistic lifestyle of horses, greyhounds, cards, and snooker where, because of his poor eyesight, you only have to put him in the long grass to win. Except for one famous occasion when he'd insisted on playing the best player in a Soho snooker hall for an 'apple core' (score) - provided he was given thirty points start. By the time they'd reached the colours, Lights' lead had dwindled to just a few. With all the colours still on the table, defeat was inevitable. Suddenly, all hell broke loose. Fighting broke out between rival gangs and the hall was plunged into darkness. When order was restored and the lights came back on, mysteriously all the colours except the final black had disappeared. And that was perched conveniently over the middle pocket. It was Dad's shot.

'Black,' he said with a straight face.

He's spent today selling flowers on Waterloo Station concourse. During the war he made a living flogging single red roses to lovelorn servicemen arriving from bases and ports in the south. When the hostilities finished, he extended the business to selling bunches of flowers. His customers are mostly male office workers on their way home to their wives and girlfriends. It requires mingling with hordes of rush-hour passengers and nifty footwork dodging British Rail officials and the Transport Police. Most evenings he sells out.

Once, a well-to-do woman approached draped in mink. He was down to his last few blooms. In a condescending voice she rudely demanded a bunch of flowers to take home. She only had a ten-pound note. And he would have to like it or lump it.

'Certainly, madam... Wait here and I'll go and get change.' With that, Lights vanished, leaving the poor woman holding the last of the flowers and standing over a pile of empty cardboard boxes. He went straight to the gambling club.

'How's it going, Lights?'

'Very well... I've just sold the business.'

***

Waterloo Station in the 50s

So, on my birth night the phone interrupts play. When this happens, everything freezes. The number is private but it might be anyone - the Old Bill, the taxman, or a disgruntled victim of some villainy. Worse, someone's wife or a girlfriend. Lonny allows it to ring several times. Lights, with a six o'clock shadow, and the proverbial John Player's fag gleaming in the corner of his mouth, looks up from his cards and peers through his bottle-end specs. He signals a 'cut throat' sign. He is definitely not here. There's a 'thumbs down' too from the others. Lonny pauses for absolute hush and lifts the receiver.

'Hello.' The school can hear a female voice, like Olive Oil in Popeye. Lonny puts on his caring tone.

'No, he ain't here, love. Let me just ask around to find out if anyone's seen him.' Lonny puts his hand over the receiver and shouts loudly despite the fact that the men are only a few feet away.

'Anyone seen Lights?'

Like a hunted fox Dad stays still and silent.

There's more gabbled conversation down the blower. 'OK, Janie, if I see him, I'll tell him straight away,' says Lonny. He puts the receiver down and looks Lights straight in the eye. 'She knows you're here. She says you're a lying bastard, it's time you got a proper job and hopes you go under a bus.'

Lights is unfazed.

'Charming. Maybe she wants me to train as a mechanic.' The school collapses in laughter.

But Lonny now gets serious. 'Lights, you'd better go, mate... you've had a little boy.' To give dad his due, he's on his feet in a flash. The others throw a quid or two on the table, enough for a cab home, and for him to stop off for a peace offering.

He arrives home with bottles of her favourite tipple. But the knees-up is over. All that's left are the empties, the stink of stale booze and cigarette smoke, and a few dried-out rolls. If he expects a medal for coming home, he's wrong.

'Where the fuck have you been? You ought to be ashamed of yourself.'

He studies the sleeping beauty in his cot for a moment, pours his wife a Guinness and slips into bed next to her. He may be boracic lint but tonight he's contrite and comfortable and back on his own turf. Tomorrow is always another day.

'Night, love,' he whispers, daring to cuddle up. The silence is deafening.

'The boy's beautiful, by the way. What we calling him?' he inquires.

The cold shoulder treatment often lasts for weeks. But not tonight. A thaw is on the way. And after the required few minutes of reticence she responds.

'I quite like, well... Alan.'

'Nice.'

And that's his last word. Shattered by his physical exertions at the railway station, the highs and lows of the club, and the emotional rush of the evening, he sleeps sweetly and snores loudly, never once waking up - even when the newborn cries out for more of that magic mix of momma's colostrum and milk stout.

Night, night, you old bastard. Forgiven. As always.

4

Camberwell Beauties

The day after I'm born, two men walk into a pub in Cambridge and make a remarkable announcement to the incredulous barmaid.

'We've just discovered the secret of life.' As chat up lines go, they aren't bad. But they are in fact true. Watson and Crick are not fictional Victorian detectives as their names might suggest, but scientists who've come up with the answer to one of nature's most fundamental questions - how do living things reproduce themselves? They've worked out the structure of a chemical that makes up our genes and passes hereditary characteristics. It has an instantly forgettable name, deoxyribonucleic acid, but DNA, as it is known, will be liquid gold to mankind and whole industries of medics, lawyers, crime writers and detectives, who will find they can suddenly solve cases simply through examining a single strand of hair retrieved from a crime scene.

I've been thinking about my own genetic make-up - who I am and where I came from - the sort of questions you ask when you've put a few miles on the clock. After the remains of my cradle cap disappeared and the jaundiced skin regained its natural colour, it was agreed that I'd done rather well on the gene front, managing to avoid most of Dad's aesthetic deficiencies (except for the aforesaid wonky toes) while inheriting Mum's physical characteristics of neutral blandness, illuminated by a bubbly personality and a twinkle in the eye. And from somewhere I've gained a mop of blonde hair which will stay with me until I am seven.

Ah, but what about your genealogy, I hear you say. In just a few clicks we can all now discover that our great, great, grandfather's mother's aunt's brother founded Outer Mongolia, or was once Lord of Luton. With the records of many institutions now digitalised, the process is much easier, particularly if your family served in the armed forces, or studied at Oxford etc. But if they were ordinary common or garden people then it's a bit more complicated. This is of course all a thin excuse to mask the fact that so far I have failed miserably to trace a single blood relative before the year 1849 when John Falder Hurndall married Martha Wheable Boyce.

According to the genealogy site Ancestry, the name Hurndall probably derives from a lost unidentified place, bizarrely in Bucks, a combo of Old English "hyrne" (angle corner) and "dael" (valley). The Hurndall name can be found in the US and Canada, but mostly in the UK, and in London in particular. Wikipedia reports notable people with the surname as Frank Brereton Hurndall, a famous English polo player, the actor Richard Hurndall, who played Doctor Who in a special episode to mark the 20th anniversary of the long-running BBC science fiction series, and Tom Hurndall, a photographer and activist who was shot in the head in the

Gaza Strip by an Israel Defence Forces sniper during a protest against the Israeli occupation of the Palestinian territories. None of these are relatives.

You see, our family lore isn't recorded in bound archives, or in ancient texts. You certainly won't find our history on the shelves of the British Library, although I suspect there might be a few mentions of one or two individuals in the cobwebbed files of Scotland Yard. We only have rather dubious and highly subjective verbal accounts of what was said and remembered at any given time, boasted and bragged about in booze and, like fishermen's tales, exaggerated and handed down as gospel from one generation to the next.

What I do know is that my roots sprouted in the slums. My parents amassed at least 17 siblings between them, families ravaged by war and the 'white plague' of tuberculosis. They came from 'Sarf' London - and the Camberwell area in particular. Cockneys in character, if not in strict 'Bow Bells' folklore, from the manor that proudly produced those knights of the realm, Charles Spencer Chaplin, and a lad called Maurice Micklewhite, a.k.a Michael Caine. International footballers and cops and robbers made headlines too - a murderous godfather of crime, some of Britain's most ruthless gangsters, at least three train robbers, Australia's first lady of organised crime, and one of Europe's finest policemen - Detective Inspector Jack Whicher, one of the founders of Scotland Yard. The good, the bad and the ugly.

Sons of Camberwell - Charlie Chaplin and Michael Caine

Camberwell Green 1750 and the Camberwell Beauty

Camberwell is squeezed between two old Roman roads. Its ancient ground has yielded the skeletons of prehistoric creatures and stone-age flints. Chaucer's mediaeval pilgrims stopped for a pint on the Old Kent Road. And in a different age, Roman Centurions might have dropped by our kiosk for a smoke on the way to Londinium.

It was once a posh, leafy village of green fields, commercial gardens, stucco villas and ornamental cottages, famous for its springs. A horse-drawn carriage left for Charing Cross twice a day to transport merchants, lawyers and politicians four miles to The City. It even had a butterfly named after it - the beautiful dark-claret Camberwell Beauty. It has a history of markets, music halls, pubs and theatres and the famous fair on Camberwell Green - dating back more than 500 years. My ancestors probably worked that fair. Every August, thousands arrived on carts and donkeys for three days of debauchery. The Green was a rowdy cacophony of people, all 'dust, heat, smells and bother', teeming with stalls selling oysters, pickled salmon, fried plaice, and gingerbread. There were performing animals, people with bizarre deformities, plays, pickpockets, jugglers, magicians, and 'extras' from ladies around the back.

The event wasn't without crime, even tragedy. One year, a magician who professed to be descended from the magi of Persia was performing a puppet show. In the last scene he introduced a battle between Lucifer, the keeper of Hell, and Napoleon's dad. As the king was conveying the effigy of the Corsican to the region of fire, an unlucky boy blew up a sausage-pan backstage. Bonaparte's catastrophe was attended by real fire as the flames caught the hangings of the booth. The poor magician died in the inferno. A shocking albeit spectacular finale. Some of the crowd applauded, thinking it was all part of the act.

The local middle-classes hated the event and everything it stood for. '*For three days the residents of Camberwell are compelled to witness disgusting and demoralising scenes which they are powerless to prevent.*' They won. They persuaded the parish authorities to buy the Green and to close the fair for good.

But huge change was afoot. The slums of central London were gradually demolished for commercial properties. And the advent of the railway increased demand for housing as folk could live further afield from their workplace. London's creeping poverty expanded outwards, pushing the wealthy further afield. The grand homes were sold and demolished as speculative building firms bought up land and built rows of terraced estates for the masses. Most were assembled for profit, with no inside toilets or bathrooms, built for multiple occupation with rent paid to rich landlords.

From a few thousand nobles, in 1800, Camberwell's population grew to nearly a quarter of a million by 1900. Rural Camberwell had morphed into a metropolitan suburb. And here my story starts. In one street in particular. My great grandad lived there, my grandad and grandmother born there, my Nan met her future husband there, and my mother, and aunts and uncles were brought up there…

***

It's a wet wintry day just before the year 1900. A horse-drawn taxi arrives in a rundown quarter of Camberwell called Hollington Street. A police sergeant appears out of the gloom. He is Feader Sziemanonwicz, the son of a Russian Pole and an English mother, stationed at Carter Street station in Walworth, and this day acting as minder to a very special guest. The sergeant holds out an umbrella as an immaculately-dressed gentleman emerges from the carriage. He is middle-aged, already grey, with wispy hair and a full white beard. He wears a tweed jacket, a winged collar and tie underneath a silk waistcoat, laced Plus Twos, knee-high socks, and expensive polished brogue shoes - not ideal footwear for this neighbourhood.

Salubrious it certainly isn't. Behind them, a train chugs wearily by on its way to Charing Cross, pumping steam into the leaden sky, momentarily muffling the clank of metal ringing out from the totters' yards under the railway arches. The place reeks of decay. Rotting rubbish floats in the puddles, horse manure forms a smelly mush on the cobbled road, windows are boarded up and water pours down the walls from leaking gutters. Behind the threadbare curtains the posh bloke and a copper raise curiosity and suspicion. The inhabitants watch as this imposter reaches inside his briefcase for his notebook and quill. The children, playing barefoot in the freezing rain, stop and stare as the stranger begins taking notes.

In fact, the intruder is a friend, not foe, and one of the greatest men of Victorian Britain. This is the philanthropist and social reformer Charles Booth. And he is on a remarkable mission to help London's poor. Without any commission other than his own, the wealthy shipowner from Liverpool has devised, organised and funded one of the most comprehensive and scientific surveys of London life that has ever been undertaken.

Social reformer Charles Booth

It's estimated that a quarter of the capital's population live in extreme poverty, but nobody knows for certain. So to find out, Booth and his team of researchers are traipsing the whole of London noting the conditions people live in. More than 120 years on from this drab day, delving in the archives of the London School of Economics, I will find copies of his notes, the ink from his elegant, spidery handwriting smudged by the rain.

Of Hollington Street he records... *'Three-storey yellow brick houses. All doors open. Some flowers. Fearful mess in street. Bread, meat, paper, veg, old tins; heavy rain but street full of children. Bare feet. Most windows and doors broken and blocked with boards or stuffed with brown paper. Inhabitants Irish Cockneys, general labourers; much overcrowding; many turned out when sanitary inspector went round 12 months ago, but now returned. Narrow backyards, no gardens; drunk, very rough, wifebeating, assaults, but not criminal, no thieves, housebreakers or prostitutes, but maybe a few tax dodgers...'*

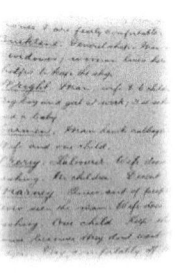

Booth's notes

Only half the kids here go to school. Comber Grove, where I was to attend 60 years later, reports a *'wretched neighbourhood, proverbial for its depravity and ignorance'.* Following his inspection, Booth walks to the local mission, St Michael and All Angels, in Wyndham Road, the scene of riots half a century previously. A Chartist rally for workers' rights on Kennington Common had been attended by thousands of people. Fearing trouble, nearly 4000 policemen were called in. A group of 500 demonstrators, armed with staves of barrels, sticks and palings, broke off and fought with police near Hollington Street. Among those brought to trial were Charles Lee, a gipsy, and an unemployed seaman called David Duffy, a *'man of colour',* known to police as a beggar in the Southwark Mint where he went about *'without shirt, shoe, or stocking'.*

He interviews Sister Harriett who makes it her business to know what's going on in her patch, chronicling every house and its occupants. Booth writes of the good Sister... *'she is an elderly woman and seems in a hurry to get the interview over. The sister supervisor comes in and enquires how long it is going to take...'* She reports to Booth that most of the street is multiple occupancy and owned by private landlords. The tenants are carpenters, hawkers, shoesmiths, a fish curer, labourers, cabmen, even a cricket ball manufacturer. The houses are all six-roomed, two rooms per floor, and house several families in packed conditions with no inside toilet, just an outhouse in the back yard. Sister Harriett not only knows most of the people, but their business and private lives too, keeping an eye on the way they bring up their kids, noting their drinking habits and whether or not they attend church.

At No.1 - the very house where my mother will grow up - a family called Redgrove live with several children. He's a shoemaker and his wife, a dressmaker. Two other families lodge there. Next door is the landlord of houses 1-23, who lives with his wife: they are *'very comfortable'*, although in a back room on the top floor are two widows, *'very poor, but decent, honest people'*.

On the ground floor of No. 5 are the Webbs, and their three children. He is a *'cripple'*, but works as a cheesemonger and rings the bell at church. His eldest daughter is a charlady and *'a bad sort of girl'*. In a backroom lives a single man who is also disabled. He's respectable and makes toys for a living but is similarly destitute. On the first floor are the Grahams, a fish curer and his hawker wife and their three children, with two other families in the house. At No. 7 are the Penmans and their seven children. He works in a mineral waterworks. They abstain from alcohol and are *'extremely poor'*. In a first-floor backroom at No. 11, is a young woman with one child whose husband is said to be in India. Sister Harriett describes her as *'almost starving'*. At No. 13 resides a pensioned soldier who spends most of the day drinking. He used to sweep a crossing *'but now his wife does it'*.

Some couples have as many as ten kids. A mother refuses to send her children to school because they are ragged. At No. 25, in a back room, are the Archers. Mr Archer lives there with his wife and five children and are *'a bad lot'*. The old man is in prison for robbery. The boy used to go out with his father and was implicated. The wife makes paper bags which she sells for fourpence halfpenny per 1,000.

Booth's survey reveals that 30 per cent of people in London live in poverty - earning less than a pound a week. He even lodges with London's working classes as part of his research, noting how the change of diet wreaks havoc with his stomach. He draws up a 'poverty map' where he assigns a colour to every street according to the conditions he observes. The rich avenues are yellow. These are where the upper crust live, with their fine homes and servants' quarters. The middle-class houses he colours red, and the poor blue. At the very bottom of the scale are the black streets, where even the rats run scared.

But what about Hollington Street? You guessed it - dark blue with a black line, deemed one of the capital's worst streets. *'These are the lowest class consisting of occasional labourers, street sellers, loafers, criminals and semi-criminals. Theirs is the life of savages, with vicissitudes of extreme hardship and their only luxury is drink.'*

Stirred by Booth's findings, the Camberwell clergy demand action. The Vestry Committee report that *'The overcrowding in this district, and the sad state in which the inhabitants have for many years been compelled to subsist, have been a source of the deepest pain to the clergy and others brought into contact with the poor people dwelling in this neglected area. Such a state of things cannot be conducive to public morality, nor be advantageous to the public health. The neighbourhood is a black spot in the midst of a comparatively well-to-do, well-ordered Parish. It is the despair of the clergy, who find it impossible to put any permanent social order into a body of people continually shifting, and continually recruited by the incoming of fresh elements of evil or distress.'*

Camberwell Borough Council begin secretly buying up properties in and around Hollington Street, to improve living conditions for the next generation. Among the new families is my great grandad, Harry 'the broom hawker' Shaw, his wife Jane (née Fry) and their three young kids. My Nan, Jane Elizabeth, is their eldest. The 1911 census records the Shaws living at 21 Hollington Street. By then he is 38 and has fathered seven children, but one has died.

My Nan plays with a little girl called Tilly Twiss, the daughter of a bricklayer, who lives at No. 57. The playmates take very different career paths. At fifteen Nan is already out working as a servant and living with a wealthy family in nearby Westmoreland Road. Tilly leaves school at 12 to work in a Camberwell sweatshop, toiling 12 hours a day, six days a week. Still in her teens, she turns to prostitution, working The Strand. At the age of 16 she falls in love with a 'client,' 24-year-old 'Big Jim' James Devine, an Australian soldier and small time criminal. They marry around the corner from Hollington Street at the Church of the Sacred Heart in Wyndham Road. They produce two children, a daughter stillborn, and a son whom she leaves behind when, aged 19, she boards the boat to Sydney with her man.

By the time she is 25, Tilly will amass 70 convictions for offensive behaviour, foul language and prostitution, and will be jailed for a razor attack on a man. She'll become a vicious, fiery madam whom the Australian label the Queen of the Night. But she's more than a street girl. She has a savvy business brain too. Living off immoral earnings, i.e. running a brothel, is illegal. But she realises the law only applies to men, not women. She takes advantage of the anomaly and builds an empire of whore houses. At the height of her career she owns more than 30 brothels, a fleet of cars and properties around Sydney, and runs drug and grog rackets. She becomes the first lady of organised crime and Australia's most notorious female criminal, even boasting that she owns more diamonds than the Queen of England. A criminal career conceived, honed and crafted in Hollington Street.

Hollington Street and Tilly Devine (née Twiss)

A young print worker called George Hill - my grandfather - moves into 15 Hollington Street and takes a shine to the pretty teenage girl Jane Shaw a few doors along. When war is declared George, like thousands of young men up and down the country, signs up to fight the Kaiser. But before he leaves for the battlefields, he and Jane marry - at St John the Divine Church in Kennington on August 1915. At the time he is 28. She is 19 and has been promoted from a live-in maid to the cook for a wealthy family in Westmoreland Road.

Grandad Hill (far left)

Catastrophically he inhales poison gas and is sent back to England suffering from lung damage. He resumes working as a packer in the print, and they rent several rooms at No.1 Hollington Street, but his condition will eventually claim his life. The cause of death is pulmonary tubercle - hard nodules in the lungs - as a result of gas poisoning. My mother Jane is one of six kids - aged between two and 13 - left fatherless by the death of their dad on New Year's Day, 1932. Nell is the oldest, with my mum Jane, 12. Then comes George, named after his dad, Gladys, Albert and Irene, the youngest who will never remember her father.

Mum as a baby with older sister Nell

Mum (far right) at the seaside with Nell and baby George

	6	7
	Cause of death	Signature, description and residence of informant
...an	I (a). Pulmonary Tubercle (b). Gas Poisoning (in War) no P.M Certified by F. Joyce M.B.	J. E. Hill Widow of deceased. Present at the death 1 Hollington Street

My grandad's death certificate

Nan has to fight for a meagre war widow's pension which she supplements with two or three jobs. The burden of care is placed on Nell and my Mum who, although reasonably bright scholars, are obliged to leave school at 14 to put food on the family table. Nan does a sterling job bringing up her family single-handed. They are well fed, well turned out and well-mannered and encouraged with their schoolwork where they are all competent at writing, reading and arithmetic. The older kids have jobs in the home and muck in accordingly. Nell does all the sewing; Janie feeds the younger ones, while George and Albert have to butter the morning rolls after their Mum arrives home from overnight office-cleaning. They even have a piano which they all play, with Nell in particular excelling at 'singalong' party songs. The Hill boys are allowed to earn extra pennies from the older men by acting as lookouts for any 'Old Bill' during street corner gambling sessions such as 'pitch and toss'. Mum's first job is working as an office girl in the small printers in Camberwell Road where her dad had worked. In a nutshell they are poor, but happy; free of class angst, all have a wicked sense of humour, and are driven by a proud widowed matriarch who puts her family before herself at every turn.

The Hill family - Rene, Mum, Gladys, Nell, George and Albert. RIP

Fifty years on from Booth, stopping off on the way to school, I will watch my mother's family home disappear as wrecking balls bulldoze Hollington Street as part of a council slum clearance programme. The street will be wiped from the map forever, the molecules of my ancestors - their DNA - buried beneath new tower blocks.

Booth paved the way for social reform, the welfare state, improved schooling, free school meals and state pensions - a revolution that will one day enable a young working-class lad like me to break free from the shackles of deprivation to carve out an exciting career, and to travel the world.

So thank you Mr Booth.

5

Hopping Mad

After my grandad's death, days out for a single parent and six kids are, of course, out of the question. However, the family enjoys working holidays every September, joining the exodus of 200,000 Londoners to the hop fields of Kent. For three weeks they pick hops destined for the brewing industry. It's hard work, but fun.

Waiting for the confirmation letters from the farm in Headcorn is agony. Friends and neighbours have got theirs. *Have we been left out?* Finally, the postman delivers the good news and preparations can begin. On the given day, in exchange for 'petrol' money for the horse, a friendly totter rolls up at Hollington Street with a pony and trap to ferry the Hills to London Bridge station, complete with a mountain of clothing for all weathers, cooking utensils, bedding, and provisions.

British Rail lays on 'Hopping Specials'. Many folk sleep at the station all night to get the first train at 4am to ensure they're ready to start earning as soon as possible. The poor old ticket inspectors are led a merry dance. Some families buy only a few tickets, shuffling between them, ordering the kids to hide under the seats, and nipping to various parts of the train to avoid the 'snapper'.

At the other end, farmers collect their workforce on tractors and trucks. The accommodation is very basic - a three metre square hut made of breeze block with a corrugated iron roof. There's no electricity. Lighting is provided by candles or little gas lamps. Water is via a standpipe and sanitation provided by a dedicated toilet block, usually with an earth closet. There's generally a dedicated cookhouse. Some pickers make their homes into little palaces, with lace table cloths, best china and frilly curtains. A few enterprising souls manage to somehow transport proper iron-frames and mattresses but most beds are knocked up from spare wood. Many kip on the floor - on straw donated by the farms.

The fields are divided into rows of hop vines which grow on a network of six-metre poles connected to each other by string. Once the hops reach the top, they grow laterally. Pickers are paid according to the weight of hops in the bins. On that first day the bins are laid out at the beginning of each row. Families compete to see who fills them the fastest. Everyone works hard, pulling or cutting the vines down, stripping the leaves and separating the hops. Measurers come round with mobile scales, watching for strokes like hiding stones in the bin to boost weight and of course, earnings.

At the end of the day, arms ache and clothes and hands are stained yellow from the sap. After a scrub and grub, the evenings turn into one big party around the fire, with accordions and wash boards used for skiffle. Village pubs do a roaring trade too. Pilfering is rife and they charge a shilling deposit on glasses. If you're mug enough to put your drink down it's sure to be whisked away and cashed in by someone else.

Many years later I will join the family exodus - and hate every minute of it. Perhaps I'd been mollycoddled. The cold, the wet, the smells, the grime, the rats, the living conditions. I will even have to wear Wellington boots! One image will never leave my mind. Families put out pots of jam to deliberately attract wasps - the idea being that they're more interested in sucking sugar from jar than stinging us. Once lured in, the wasps can never get out and by the end of the day scores have died and gone to heaven in a sea of sweetness - their perished yellow and black jackets providing a colourful contrast to their strawberry grave.

Mum (second from right) hop picking with relatives and friends

***

Mum attends Hopping with her family throughout her childhood and teenage years. One day her mum's brother, Uncle Tommy Shaw, turns up at Headcorn with a younger accomplice, who's immediately made to feel welcome. Tommy's a real ducker and diver, street bookie and street seller, particularly in the flower game. His friend is tall, over six feet, with horn-rimmed glasses and wispy, combed-back hair. He's good company, generous, and polite, and everybody likes him. His name's John, but Tommy introduces him as - you've guessed it - Lights.

As is usual, Janie is making people laugh around the bonfire. She adores a sing-song. Everyone has a 'number' they're required to perform at parties. Hers is Sleepy Time Gal, which was released when she was a little girl. She's a marvellous raconteur and storyteller. It doesn't matter that everyone has heard the same old stories before. A plain Jane in looks perhaps, but not in character. She's fun, street-smart, but quite naïve about certain facts of life. When puberty arrived, she hadn't a clue what was happening, and thought she was bleeding to death. If anyone asks her if she's all right she always replies, 'Well, I was last month.'

Mum (left) the life and soul of every party

Her favourite story is when a young suitor took her to the pictures when she was fresh out of school. After the cinema lights went down, the lad put his arm around her and she giggled. Then he moved his hands to her knee, and she giggled more. His hands moved to her chest and she giggled again.

'Why do you keep laughing?' he said.

She replied, 'If you're after my sweets, they're in my pocket.'

Lights takes an interest. She's younger, and much smaller than him. Back in London, they start going out. They become an item at family parties and other gatherings. He wines and dines her at pubs and clubs, takes her horse and dog racing, and on trips away to places like Blackpool, Bournemouth and Brighton.

Booted and suited – even at the beach!

Knowing he'd been in trouble with the law, albeit for minor offences, my Nan tries to warn her off. Mum always boasts about herself that she's 'honest as the day is long'. No matter what their background - toffs, tramps or thieves - she always sees the good in people. 'I speak as I find,' she always says, loftily.

She believes she can change her man for the better. But if she's chalk, he's cheese. She's positive in outlook, always on an even keel. He's on cloud nine when he's up, but crashes down to earth when things go wrong.

He'd certainly had a tough upbringing. He was one of at least 11 kids, but he was never sure exactly how many. Several of his siblings died young of tuberculosis, which afflicted so many families in that era. One died shortly after birth, two died when toddlers, and a fourth, sister Irene, succumbed to TB at the age of 23.

He was born in 1917, amid considerable deprivation - so bad he refuses ever to discuss it. Most of his family are profoundly deaf, and whilst Lights himself has good hearing, via extraordinary large 'lugholes', he has very poor eyesight and is forced to wear 'bottle-end' specs his whole life. He was sent to a special school for the blind and partially sighted in Neate Street, Camberwell which meant he had very little formal education. But his afflictions, physical and emotional, mask a sharp wit and quick-thinking intelligence. He once pleaded to a Magistrate to take pity on him because the only reason he was caught was because of his poor eyesight - he didn't see the Old Bill coming!

John and Janie met 'down Hopping'

He comes from a long line of 'Johns'. I discover that his grandfather John was born in the East End but moved to South London around the turn of the century. The 1901 Census reveals his grandfather to be 28, married and working as a printer's assistant. His grandmother Louisa Hurndall (née Bollam, my great grandmother) was 27 and originally from Battersea. She died in her thirties.

At that time they had three children: seven-year-old John (Lights' father and my grandad) and younger sisters Ellen and Martha. After working initially as a bottle washer, Lights' dad followed his father into the print and in 1913, married Elizabeth Jane Snelgrove from a family of South London costermongers. They started a family straight away. Lights came along in 1917. His mother died young after bearing at least 11 children.

Janie and Lights were brought up in a manor steeped in street-selling tradition, and came from a long line of 'costermongers', a term used to describe hawkers in general. Mum's grandfather sold brooms, relatives ran flower stalls, while Dad's mother, who died in middle age, was from a family of street sellers who plied fruit and veg on the streets and markets of London. In short, the street game is in their blood.

Costermongers hold an historic status in the folklore of London, existing back to the 16th century; they are mentioned in Shakespeare plays. They met a need for rapid food distribution from the wholesale markets - Covent Garden for flowers; Smithfield for meat; Spitalfields for fruit and veg; Billingsgate for fish. Operating from carts or market stalls, costermongers would attract custom with loud chants. They had a running battle with the authorities who wanted them banished from the streets, but the public enjoyed their colourful personalities, sales patter and of course, the lure of bargain prices from sometimes 'hooky' goods.

Their hostility to authority - particularly the police - is legendary. They gained an unsavoury reputation which according to a slang dictionary written in 1860 derived from *'low habits, general improvidence, love of gambling, total want of education and their use of peculiar language'*. Nothing much has changed there, then.

On his marriage certificate, Lights lists his profession as 'greengrocer'. As a hawker, he flirts with the law, running market stalls or selling goods out of suitcases on street corners. This is all perfectly legal if you disregard little legal niceties such as the Misrepresentation of Goods Act, Trading Without a Licence, Handling Stolen Goods, Obstructing the Highway, Obstructing the Pavement, and any health and safety regulations. Oh, and check the true source of those goods.

6

The World At War

Having lost their father to the Great War, the next global conflict brings more misery to Mum's family. London comes under relentless bombardment. The fire service will later estimate that in an eight-month period from June 1940, 30,000 bombs fell on Greater London. The Luftwaffe sometimes drop as much as 500 tons of bombs a night. The raids become known as the Blitz, short for Blitzkrieg.

The first night takes everyone by surprise. Mum is 19 and employed on the production line of the Oxo factory on the South Bank, the glow from its distinctive three-letter red neon extinguished by the blackout. She's heading out after the night shift when the bombs fall. The staff are nearly all young women. It's chaos. Some flee across Hungerford Bridge to the north side, but when another bomb falls there, they rush back to the south, only to run into workers escaping more explosions there. Many are stranded on the bridge in panic. A burly copper lifts two sisters and carries them, one under each arm, into the tube station at The Embankment. When the dust settles Janie hears that one of her best friends has been killed.

Mum (far right) with her Oxo girls

Over a quarter of a million Londoners are made homeless. To that extent Hollington Street is lucky, remaining largely unscathed. In an archive of World War Two memories gathered by the BBC someone called Tony Baker will recall as a child seeing a bomb hitting the Samuel Jones paper mills in Southampton Way. The mills burned for two years! A nearby peanut factory had been turned into a munitions works and that too was struck by the Luftwaffe. He will remember dust carts passing his home piled high with bodies. Another time he sees a German bomber machine-gunning rescuers trying to reach people injured in a blast.

Janie and Nell continue to live at home but spend many hours in communal Anderson Shelters, bedding-down in the Underground, singing anti-Hitler songs to keep spirits alive, and making new friends along the way. During one blackout, Mum is nearly arrested. On her way to the bomb shelter her torch goes on the blink and she starts shaking it. Suddenly, it bursts into life, sending a beam into the night sky.

A warden appears from the shadows, accusing her of flashing to the enemy. *'I've never flashed at anyone in my life,'* she tells him. Charmed by her cheek, he lets her off with a warning.

Lights is called up to join the Army but escapes active service because of his poor eyesight. One day I will ask him about his role in the war and he will reply, 'I got the DCM, on special order from the Queen.'

'What's a DCM, dad?'

'Don't Come Monday,' he will answer.

Dad's military career didn't last long

The government orders the evacuation of thousands of children to the countryside. One can only imagine Nan's anguish having to wave her young ones goodbye outside the town hall, wondering where they are going, who will be looking after them, indeed the horrific fear she might never see them again. The two youngest, Albert and Irene, 13 and 11, end up in separate accommodation near the Cornwall coast. Letters discovered in my uncle's loft soon after the millennium reveals the love between a family divided by war. A letter home from Albert in 1941 sees him in good spirits and enjoying life in the country.

Dear Mum. Thank you very much for the three shillings you sent me and the lovely parcel. I gave Ron (his cousin) a packet of sweets and he said thank you. Thanks also for the drawing books. I gave Ron one of those too. Give my love to George and Gladys (his siblings). Haymaking is here again mum, and you ought to see me leading and driving the horses. Reminds me of Hopping, it is better in fact. I have some carrots, broad beans and peas, radishes, shallots, and you will have a parcel in three or four weeks, my own garden, own grown ('ere you are ladies, all fresh, ha ha.) Well, mum, don't forget two shillings and bike. Cheerio, love from Albert. xxxxxx

Elder brother George, 19, has moved to Blackpool to study to become a surveyor. He's also registered for military service, requesting the Navy. Earning money as a pupil draughtsman, he sends food, money and gifts to his little brother and sister, noting in his diary, *'Must send Albert some cash. He's broke.'* He sends thirty shillings. He also sends the same amount every month back home to Camberwell. The war might have separated them all. But they write to each other frequently - with reminders of why separation is necessary. George records in his diary - *'letter from mum with news of house being blitzed. Sister Gladys cut. Nine killed in Horsman Street by flying bomb.'*

Mum (centre back) with sister Nell (far right) and her husband George Slater

Rene, 12, writes a letter to George.

Trebant Cottage, Blue Rock, Lanreath, Cornwall, May 3, 1942. My dearest George. Many thanks for your most welcome letter we got. I hope that everybody is quite well where you are lodging, including yourself of course. Everybody is quite alright here at the present. I suppose you have got a girl (don't blame you, ha, ha). Today the weather is very hot and I am getting nice and brown. How is the weather in Blackpool? I hope it is nice. Janie is thinking of coming down to see us when she gets her next holidays and we are all looking forward to seeing her. It makes a nice change for her to stay in the lovely countryside for a change, also the rest will do her good. It will be nice if you could come to see us. It will be nice when we are all together again after this blessed war is over. Sorry it is only a short letter, more rabbit next time. I remain your ever-loving sister. Irene xxxxxxxxxxxx

In the same envelope is a letter from brother Albert, staying with a Mrs Shepherd at 'Willacombe' Lanreath.

Dear George. Thanks very much for your welcome letter. Also 2½d stamp. I hope you are keeping well and that your cold is better. Give my love and regards to the people you are living with. Well, brother, I am keeping very well, thank you. It would be proper if you could manage to come down and visit us. If you do come down, remember to bring your camera as mother forgot it when she came down. Still, I daresay lots of people would have forgot it, as mother came home from work at six and had to catch the train at 10pm and had to get the girls tea etc.

Well, George, since you asked me what force I prefer to go in, I shall say now, the Air Force. How is the weather at Blackpool? Lovely, I hope, as it is here. But the farmers would not say no to a shower of rain. It would do a splendid lot of good to the seeds and crops. You told me in your letter that you go to dances. Well, I do too and have great fun doing the foxtrot, waltz and polyglide etc.

I'm going to take your tip about jobs. Mr Rundle (our teacher) says that I ought to get a good job. Well I hope so. Mum bought me a fountain pen and here I am writing with it. It is a British make called Burnham. It is 14ct gold, and I like it very much. It's got a gold clip and lever, also two gold rings around the lid. I expect you understand. I wish you all the best of luck with your exams. Well, George, the time now is 2pm Sunday afternoon and the weather makes me feel lazy. Hoping to see you soon. Will close with heaps of love, your ever-loving brother, Albert.

As Albert is writing, George is taking a break from his studies to see Mickey Rooney and Judy Garland in Babes on Broadway at the Odeon in Blackpool. Sure enough, three weeks later, having finished his exams in science, geometry and construction, he takes the train to Cornwall to visit his estranged siblings. In his diary he records that the journey is '*very scenic*'. He arrives at Looe at 10pm where Albert has been waiting for three and a half hours. He meets his landlady, Mrs Shepherd, and sees '*my darling' Rene, and her friend Lilian (I think Lilian loves me)*'.

He also reports that Albert is already talking in a funny accent, although his sister isn't. He's having a great time, including going rabbit shooting. After three days of fun George heads to London, taking three of the dead rabbits with him. He records that Rene is '*very upset saying goodbye*'.

However, two months later she's in much better spirits.

Dear George. Thank you very much for your lovely parcel which was the torch. I liked it very much. Well, George, it was quite all right that you didn't send me it before. We are all keeping well. I hope you are too. We are having lovely weather here and I had a letter from Mum today and she said she was going hop-picking next week.

Albert came over this morning and I will give him your new address soon. He told me he only had threepence for all he was worth. I gave him one of my tuppenny halfpenny stamps. I couldn't do any more. He says he likes his new billet very much. He lives very close to me and will go to the same school. Well, George, I hope you will excuse the pencil as I can write much quicker. I showed Albert my torch and he liked it very much. I am glad you like the place where you are staying. Will you excuse this funny old writing, as I daresay you can understand it.

Janie, Nellie, Aunt Jess, Louis Hobbs and Shirley are all coming down to see us in September. They are staying for three days. It will be nice to see them all again. Me, Lilian, Hilda, and Dorothy all went to Looe yesterday and went in the sea. We did enjoy ourselves. A London woman and her little girl went with us. She's from Clapham, quite near Camberwell. She knows Camberwell Green and all the other places. So it is very nice to be near someone who has come from London, isn't it!

Well George, I must say my arm is aching, so cheerio 'til next time. Give my love to Ben and his parents. I know I don't know them, but still, never mind. Give them my love, anyway. Goodbye. Love from your loving sister Rene. xxxxxxx

The end of the war is of course a time for great celebration. With the Allies advancing on Germany, and the Nazis in retreat, the end is nigh for Hitler. The sense of anticipation is extreme. On May 5th 1945, three days before VE Day, Mum writes to both her brothers.

Dear George and Albert. Please excuse me for not writing earlier, as I honestly have gone right off letter writing. I'm not so good as I used to be in my young days, ha ha. I really must thank you for my telegram. I was so surprised to receive one from you two hardworking boys. Although I have been rather long-winded since receiving your telegram, please don't think that I don't appreciate it as I do very much. It is so thoughtful when one is far away.

*How are you feeling now that you are sober? (or are you?) I bet you won't get like that again in a hurry, no matter who comes home. I really felt very sorry for you. Now, perhaps next time you are told your head will be bad by your sisters, you will take notice, ha ha. Now Albert, the luck in the war since you have been away has changed, don't you think? Every minute gets more exciting. Believe me, the wireless is never off. Waiting all the time for an 'important announcement.' Everything seems exciting here at home. These days, any minute waiting for a telegram from Georgie Slater (*her sister's husband, being held in a German Prisoner of War camp*) and preparing flags etc for VE and V plus one days, ha ha. We honestly cannot believe the news is so grand. I would like to see you two for VE Day, it will be so nice altogether as we all were the first day of the war. (Mother's gas mask on upside down, ha ha) Granny looks far better these days with no worry of rockets etc. She takes her corset off now, ha ha. When we heard the news of Hitler's death we flew round to Gran at 11 o'clock at night,(me, Nellie, Gladys, Rene). I told her she can go in the first coach. She had to laugh, she completed those smashing names she always called him. Well G and B, I am in work and time is short. Try to let us have a line from you, Sherbert, and here's hoping to see you on VE Day when it comes. Bye, bye TTFN, see you soon, love Janie and all at home. xxxxxx*

Sure enough, they all get together to celebrate the end of the war. George writes in his diary... *May 7th 1945. GERMANY DEFEATED! Unconditional surrender. Travelled home at night.*

May 8th VE DAY. Saw Churchill four times in Westminster. What a marvellous time. Saw the King and Queen at Buckingham Palace with Gladys. VE DAY + 1 Churchill speaks. VE Day + 2 Built chicken shed. Beer shortage in London. Nellie's George (the POW) expected home any minute.

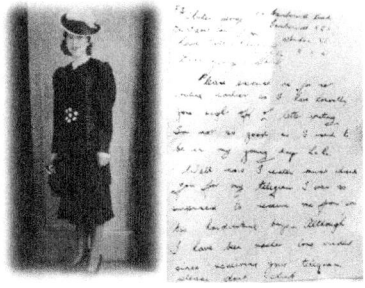

Mum's letter to brothers Albert and George, whom she refers to as 'Chicken George'

At last, life can get back to normal. The loss of their father. War. Evacuation. It might have destroyed many a poor soul. But, like plenty of Londoners, they fought adversity with laughter and love, forming a unique family spirit which bonds them for the rest of their lives. And talking of bonding...

7

Til Death Do Us Part

Less than a month after the end of the war - on October 20th 1945 to be precise - on a sunny and dry autumn morning, a group of Cockneys gather at one of Camberwell's most historic buildings, the grand church of St Giles, a stone's throw from Camberwell Green. They are here to attend the marriage of my parents, Jane Louisa Hill, 25, and 28-year-old John Richard Hurndall - Janie and Lights. An honest, God-fearing, forgiving, funny, caring, larger-than-life soul, in union with a witty, generous, street-trader. In the absence of her father, Janie is given away by her brother George, and the best man is her uncle Tommy Shaw, the man who introduced them. It has all the trappings of a traditional wedding - four bridesmaids in dresses, hair garlands and shoes, all matching. The guests, mostly family, all look happy and smart. Not many know or care about the history of the place. A church of some description has stood here for more than 1,000 years. Named after St Giles, the patron saint of the poor, the building has remained largely unaltered for more than 100 years, although some of the stained-glass windows, destroyed by bombs, are boarded-up ready for replacement.

Till Death Do Us Part

The photos are taken in black and white but will be colourised later and will rest proudly on my piano for decades. The bride, auburn hair and sparkly blue eyes, is in traditional white and carrying a bunch of crimson carnations, her favourite flower. She stands at around 5ft 5ins tall. She's not as slim as she once was, has slightly protruding teeth, and bags under her eyes - the result of a partying lifestyle. Dad stands upright and formal, towering over his partner. He's wearing a navy pin-stripe suit with huge regal lapels. His only colour is a cream button-hole flower pinned above a silk top-pocket handkerchief to match his silver tie. There are only a few years between them, but he looks a good ten years older than his bride. His hollowed face and wire-framed glasses could put him in line for a movie part as a Nazi SS officer. His hair is slicked back by extravagant swathes of cream. He wears a forced smile which fails to hide a line of decaying teeth that are not long for this world, soon be extracted in one fell swoop at his insistence and replaced by dentures.

***

This happy day signals the start of 40 years of good times, bad times, break-ups and make-ups, laughter and tears. They will never be boring. She will leave him several times with us kids in tow, but despite rumours of another woman, they will stick to their marriage vows and remain together *'til death do us part'*.

They set up home in a rented house in Fentiman Road, Kennington, near the Oval Cricket Ground. Britain is gradually getting back on its feet after the War. The docks, which employed many south Londoners, were devastated, along with commercial districts and the historic heart of The City. Janie is still working at Oxo, but at weekends helps her old man selling in the street. They work as a team selling flowers and other bits and bobs at markets, with Lights anxious to show off his experience in the street game, offering advice to his bride on what to buy and how to sell. What he fails to appreciate is her own sales instinct, inherited from generations of hawkers. The Street Game is in her DNA too. That first Christmas, on the hunt for ideas, they visit a fancy goods warehouse off Petticoat Lane. They're looking for items to sell over the festive period. On the top shelf of the vast store, she notices a display of brightly-coloured plastic toys.

'What are those?' she says to the owner, Henry Cohen, who happens to be a friend of theirs who lives in Streatham.

'Toy trumpets from Hong Kong. Nobody wants 'em,' Henry says.

'I reckon they'd make a good Christmas toy,' says Janie. Lights jumps in with a patronising sermon.

'You don't wanna bother with effing toy trumpets. Who's gonna buy them?'

After much argument, she finally gets her way and persuades Henry to let her have a quantity on sale or return. That way if they bomb, she will at least get their outlay money back. Janie fills a holdall and takes several hundred to Rye Lane in Peckham. She's quite musical and somehow contrives snippets of tunes from the three notes available, walking down the high street literally blowing her trumpet.

41

The response is phenomenal. Everyone wants them as a novelty and she sells out within half an hour. Lights dismisses it all as a fluke. But she goes back to the warehouse and buys the whole stock. She visits different high streets and is again knocked over by eager punters. Henry knows he's on to a winner and imports more. Lights swallows his pride and gets in on the act. Between them they are responsible for a trumpet craze all over London. Mum's shrewd investment pays for weeks of the highlife - Christmas, the races, greyhounds, West End shows, nights away, and a delayed summer honeymoon - all first-class - to Brighton with the importer Henry Cohen and his glamorous wife Mary.

With the Cohens and their daughter

The flip side to this 'boom or bust' existence is his habit of disappearing for days, particularly when money is in his pocket. He inevitably arrives home skint. She always gives him hell, but always forgives, though never forgets.

The phone goes in the middle of the night. It's a nurse in a casualty department somewhere in the East End. He's been on some venture or other and broken a rib in a crash whilst traveling as a passenger in a lorry. He's asked the nurse to ring home… just so he can avoid a verbal volley from Mum for his absence.

A typical make-up tactic is to phone home with a raft of apologies asking her to meet him for a drink in a local pub.

'I've had a touch,' he will say. 'Put on your best dress.' One day he tells her to jump in a cab and go to a particular backstreet pub where he says there'll be 'two G' waiting for her to collect at the bar. *A couple of grand!* That's handy. Mum swallows her pride and on arrival the Guv'nor automatically pours her a drink.

'Where's the money?,' she demands.

'What money?'

'I'm supposed to collect two G,' she says.

'I'm pouring one now. He's ordered you two Guinnesses.'

Dad and his mates watch this play out from the adjoining public bar in fits of laughter.

Almost three years after their wedding, Janie gives birth to their first son, naturally called John, or Johnny. It is May 1948. It's the end of their working double act for a while. She's now a full time mum. She has to put up with him not coming home, either 'working' away, going to the races, or gambling all night in Soho spiels, then sleeping it off in Turkish Baths. Once, just before I was born, he goes up the road in his bedroom slippers and comes home two months later - via a spell in Oxford Prison.

So, as you already know, I come along in 1953. Janie and Lights press on with raising us boys, enjoying emotional highs and sinking lows due mostly to the haphazard nature of their way of life. While she mostly looks after us, he rises to the responsibility of being the main breadwinner. His life equation is simple. People equal money, and lots of people equal lots of money. And he isn't short of ideas.

The Cup Final a few months after my birth - between Blackpool and Bolton - is a case in point. The final is seen as a celebration by the Football Association with tickets distributed through the game to county officials and dignitaries. Real fans only get a fraction of the 100,000 distribution and will pay anything to see their teams at Wembley. It means a lucrative few days of buying and selling.

On every Cup Final eve, Dad touts tickets at The Regent's Palace Hotel, opposite the Eros statue in Piccadilly Circus - the unofficial nerve centre of the black market. Then on the morning of the match he will lug boxes of flags and rosettes onto the Tube to the stadium. He usually slips a stallholder a backhander to look after the motherlode so he can be mobile among the crowds and target the coaches crammed with excited fans. One of his tactics is to board supporters' buses as they pull up, thus blocking the exit gangway so that no-one can get off until they've at least inspected his wares. And if they don't fancy a rosette then maybe they'll want to buy or sell a ticket for the match?

The following month, Lights enjoys one of his biggest paydays - the Coronation. They are both arch royalists and no wonder. It's the country's biggest celebration since the ending of the war. Three million people travel to London to witness her crowning glory. Guns salute, fireworks light up the sky, and crowds cheer. Lights decides that his offering to her millions of loyal subjects are little paper Union Jacks superimposed with a picture of the smiling young Monarch. They cost next to nothing to buy wholesale, but he suitably inflates the price to match the nation's buoyant mood.

Everyone wants a souvenir and something to wave - and the pennies yield pounds. He's even out the night before, selling to the thousands camped out on the streets. On the day itself he's everywhere - outside Westminster Abbey, where more than 8,000 guests, including Prime Ministers and Heads of State from around the world are assembled; at Buckingham Palace where crowds strain on tip toe to catch a glimpse of the golden state coach; and along the route, where Her Majesty waves regally to the masses who in turn wave Lights' flags.

8

Home Sweet Home

Mum struggles to cope with her husband's prolonged absences. With a new toddler and in desperate need of support, she moves us all back in with her mum. Nanny Jane lives in Camberwell Road, between the Elephant and Castle and Camberwell Green, a house known to all the family as '104'. Nan's six kids have married and flown the nest and she's alone so it makes economic and practical sense.

***

Home is a grand four-storey Victorian terrace rented from the Bloomfields, a wealthy local Jewish family. John Bloomfield owns the whole row of ten tall houses sandwiched between his petrol station further up the road and his car showroom on the corner of Bethwin Road.

104 next to a car showroom

Facilities-wise, we want for nothing. Within 600 yards are four pubs, a café, three youth clubs, two scrap metal yards, two doss houses, a doctor, a dentist, a pawn broker, a mini cab office, a chippy, a baker, a dry-cleaners, launderette, and one of the biggest green spaces in London. Further up the road is a cinema, a washhouse, two public swimming pools, a police station, East Street market and of course two pie and mash shops.

It is a lovely spacious house, with six rooms and access to an attic which has been taken over by new tenants - roosting pigeons. It has an arched entrance, a huge front door with an old-fashioned metal knocker, and two coal cellars. Entry is on the first-floor level. We live on the lower floors, and Nanny Jane occupies the rest. There's no central heating and no bathroom. We have an outside toilet out back which is only used in extremis. The inside loo faces directly on to the staircase. The

44

door latch never works and if you are going up the stairs there's a good chance of seeing a family member going about their business smiling down at you.

We are growing up amid a noisy little cocktail of domestic and industrial pollution. Out front - traffic fumes, the continuous hum of cars and buses; out back - the shrill of machinery and the rumble of trains. The house is freezing. We rarely sleep with the window open. Johnny and I have an electric blanket. We're forbidden to sleep with it switched on but every now and then we forget and wake up roasting. Our bedroom faces the railway line. When the train stops people often wave so the net curtains are permanently drawn to prevent any Peeping Toms spying on our bits.

Watching Johnny play cowboys and Indians

Life revolves around the basement kitchen, with its dangling 150 watt light bulb and lino which is curled up at the edges and mopped once a week with bleach. We may just as well be living in one room. We cook there, eat there, wash there, bathe there, and watch TV there on our rented box from British Relay. Dad, slumped in his Parker Knoll upright, with his fag parked permanently in the corner of his mouth, sometimes even sleeps there. In one corner is the gas oven with a chip pan on the hob permanently filled with Cookeen either in a solid state or semi congealed according to the temperature. The odour of hot fat and tobacco impregnates our hair and clothes, and even our bedroom immediately above. It's like living in a chippy.

In the other corner is a giant cream-coloured Frigidaire, purchased after a touch on the horses. No one knows how to adjust the temperature which means the Anchor butter pack is permanently in a rock hard state. It's then placed by the fire until it becomes runny, for toast or sarnies, then put back to freeze again, forever changing colour. The other mainstay of the fridge is a long-dated pack of Stork margarine. Mum would rather die than allow 'marge' on our bread so it's only there for baking, a rare occurrence - hence its long date.

On top of the fridge rests Dad's beloved Bakelite transistor radio. With the precision of a safe-cracker, he has spent an age setting the dial to the medium-wave Home Service, marking the exact point in black Biro. No-one is allowed to even touch it. I once make the mistake of tuning it to Radio Luxembourg for the Top 20. He goes on at me for weeks. Mum calls him a *Sophie Tucker* (rucker).

The kitchen dresser takes up most of the wall. It's green with plastic sliding windows and drawers for cutlery, plus a small pull-down facility to cut and butter bread. There's always a crusty bloomer from Hassells on the chopping board surrounded by bread crumbs and a carving knife which some bloke sharpens on the doorstep every month or so.

In the corner is the workhorse Ascot water heater over a posh stainless steel sink unit. It's shaped like a rocket, white with a silver conical top. It lights with a *WUMP!* It provides hot water for washing up, bathing, and washing down the sides. Mum washes her hair in the sink via a rubber shower attachment which is always slipping off the taps. She screams out with shampoo in her eyes for someone to re-attach the hose.

In the cupboard underneath is her Mild Green Fairy Liquid, Persil, Brillo pads and Domestos. She's very fussy about brands. Never Omo or Daz, nor those cheaper supermarket bottles of pop and mixers. Always Pepsi, Coke or Schweppes and Palmolive soap except at Christmas when we use up the posh bars of Cussons Imperial Leather we receive as gifts.

In winter the room is one big biohazard. We burn coal in the grate to keep warm: it is replenished daily from the cellar. It is dark, dingy and dirty in there. Johnny swears he once saw a rat but I suspect it's to get out of filling the coal bucket so I pretend I saw one too. The coal is occasionally supplemented by free fuel - what are known as 'tarry blocks', right outside our house. The main roads had been constructed with a layer of wooden blocks heavily preserved with bitumen and creosote. Over time they've became impregnated with oil from the motor traffic and burn brightly. But they give off lethal fumes. Both parents smoke, and the kitchen is filled with a fug of tobacco and coal fumes. When I pass I shall donate my lungs to medical science.

Outside our house: families scramble for 'tarry blocks' to burn

There is no bathroom. If anyone fancies a soak they have to either walk to Camberwell Baths a mile away, or bring the tin bath in from the yard. This is a real drag. It's always full of leaves or spiders and takes ages to fill from the Ascot, supplemented by pots and pans of water boiled on the gas stove. Then of course it needs emptying, taking ages to ladle the water into the sink, clear and dry the bath with towels, and carry it back to the yard. It's a marathon. If the adults want a bath we have to get lost or go upstairs to torment our Nan. It's all very basic.

The only other downstairs living area is the 'front room', unheated, cold and damp, and used solely for family parties, the only time anyone is allowed to put the electric fire on. It has an orange light underneath a plastic fascia of logs to give the illusion of a glowing fire. There's an old piano, which I play chopsticks on in summer, and a radiogram - a combined radio and record player. The room also serves as a storeroom for any bits of gear that come Dad's way.

The Japanese cocktail cabinet is a case in point. One night, two men in a van deliver this elegant (but completely impractical) piece of furniture. It's jet black with images of Geisha girls beautifully carved on the outside. The inside is immaculate - highly-polished walnut and glass shelves extending in all directions like some origami creation - and lights that come on automatically when you open the lid or the doors. It literally reeks of class. The smell permeates the whole of the downstairs. As a piece of craftsmanship it's sublime, and was probably designed for the gentry to store spirits and exotic drinks, served no doubt by a butler. But during its six months in the Hurndall household it will remain largely empty, except to store Mum's bottles of stout which she prefers at room temperature. Even Dad admits it looks out of place alongside the room's other bit of furniture - a giant cheap and nasty sideboard, four feet high on 'gold' bowed legs. The back is mirrored and the drawers fronted with white quilted imitation leather which is in fact plastic stuffed with material which looks suspiciously like cotton wool. It is hideous, but makes a great goal for indoor football.

The house is blessed with a front garden the length of a tennis court and a rear yard of equal size. Both remain spectacularly untended and unattended. All we have is a rusty old gardening fork which is never used. The front garden is 'protected' by an old rotting picket fence whose uprights point in every direction except the vertical. The nails holding the fence together have long since rusted but like a guardsman on sentry duty it stubbornly refuses to fall down whatever the weather. In summer the garden becomes a small meadow, the grass growing two feet high and producing seedheads in the shape of little arrows which stick to our clothes and make great darts.

Every August Dad pays cider money to a down and out from the 'kip house' - a Seaman's Mission a few doors along - to dig up the garden and burn the grass and weeds. It creates huge plumes of smoke which play havoc with the traffic on the main road. The clear up reveals a litter mound of lost tennis balls, fag packets and drink cans, along with whatever else has been blown here or discarded.

Me hiding in the front 'garden'

In the rear, Nan keeps chickens. They terrorise the back yard making it out of bounds to me and my brother. My job is to retrieve the eggs from their coop at the bottom. It stinks and I hate it. Fortunately, they aren't particularly productive. They are probably driven to distraction by the screeching of metal from the aluminium factory only a few yards away. In summer the workmen open the factory doors to allow air in. We can see them in their protective face shields creating huge sparks as they finish the metal on their machines, sending the chickens into a frenzy. Over time, one by one the birds keel over, no doubt scared to death of the noise and the fumes. It is a blessing for everyone. We feast on roast chicken and chicken stew for weeks. And if they'd pecked a little deeper they might have set off a German unexploded wartime bomb nestling a few yards from my bedroom window! It will be thirty years before it's discovered - during demolition of the site. It's a good job nobody used that gardening fork. We could have all been blown to smithereens…

Some of the earliest pictures of me

Our one and only holiday together – a weekend in a caravan

With Johnny now at school, I have Mum's sole attention, taking me on day trips to the outdoor pool at Kennington Park, on pony rides, and to places like Trafalgar Square to feed the pigeons, always followed by a roll and a pat of butter in Lyons Corner House. I accompany her to places like the hairdressers, where she has a regular perm. While she sits in her curlers under those huge oval-shaped dryers, I sit beside her pretending I'm in a space ship and stuffing myself with push-up lollies, Lucky Dip Sherbert Fountains, Black Jacks, Fruit Salads, and pretend to smoke sweet cigarettes. The ladies say how sweet I am, making a fuss and annoyingly pulling my cheek.

At Christmas she takes us both to Jones and Higgins department store in Peckham to see Father Christmas. I'm wary of the fat old Santa with his white beard and refuse to sit on his lap. Never mind, he tells me, what would I like for Christmas? A fort, I reply, the first thing that comes into my head just to escape out of there. My wish is granted but it will never be built. I'm not at all interested in building or making things.

With Christmas approaching, Lights has to look for other potential earners. He's Camberwell's Del Boy long before the character will even be born. Lights and Mum's uncle Tommy Shaw buy a gross of chicks to sell at East Lane market. They store them in Nan's freezing cold attic overnight. Next day, climbing the stairs to the loft, Lights suddenly stops in his tracks, obviously concerned.

'What's the matter?' asks Tommy.

'I can't hear 144 squeaks, Tom.'

Sure enough, the poor things have perished in the cold.

A mate of his has heard about a forest somewhere near East Grinstead which is laden with Christmas trees. You can help yourself! Yep, money growing on trees! They buy some hand saws and rope, and pull in a mate with a lorry to transport the produce to London. The trees are worth quite a few quid in London markets in the run-up to the festive period. Lights goes to work selling them while the tree fellers continue refilling the production line. It seems too good to be true… and it is.

Midway through the third day, the felling party are enjoying a flask of tea and cheese rolls, when a bloke turns up brandishing a shotgun. It's the estate gamekeeper, and minutes later they hear the wail of police sirens: it turns out that the forest is owned by some wealthy duke. Everyone on site is arrested. Lights' mate spends Christmas in Pentonville serving six months for theft. Absent from the crime scene, Dad escapes arrest, but visits his mate in jail over Christmas. And of course sends money to his mate's distraught wife.

A wannabe jockey and a day out with Johnnie to Trafalgar square

9

Here is The Newsbox

My parents' entrepreneurial roots are sprouting - they're buying their own business. In the garden of our home is a kiosk run by a woman called Winnie who rents it from our landlords. She confesses to Mum she's had enough, and offers her first shout to take over the lease. For £150 it can be hers.

'What do you think, John? You think we can make a go of it?'

Dad remains silent, his head buried in the Sporting Life. But his indifference is a sign that he approves. It's also his insurance for the inevitable blame game should the venture go tits up. Through a combination of begging and borrowing, they scrape the money together. News of this latest gamble is met by sighs and open mouths by Mum's extended family. Giving Lights access to a daily supply of ready money is like inviting foxes into a chicken coop and expecting them not to help themselves to supper.

Whatever, The Hurndalls are in business! The Newsbox, as it's called, is basically a wooden shack painted bright yellow. It's isolated from neighbouring buildings, but has its own electricity supply. No-one quite knows where the wires lead or who pays the bill. Lights lives up to his name, boosting the lighting so that the kiosk glows like a lighthouse in the dark winter afternoons and fog. He knows from his market experience that you need a crowd to create a buzz so he extends the roof across a section of the pavement to enable customers to chat or wait for the bus out of the rain.

Accounts are set up with all the main tobacco, sweet and newspaper suppliers - the likes of John Player, Gallagher, Cadbury's, Rowntrees, Trebor, and John Menzies. We sell magazines, comics, sweets and tobacco, all the dailies, and the local South London Press, the South London Observer and the SE London Mercury. The best seller is the working-class bible The Daily Mirror. We stock a single copy of the Times, reserved for our GP Dr McManus whose surgery is opposite. He collects it every day along with 40 Senior Service and gives Dad, who coughs his lungs up every morning, impromptu medical advice. Like, give up smoking!

The kiosk is given a makeover. Dad orders new signage - NEWS OF THE WORLD, PLAYERS PLEASE, OLD HOLBORN. He gets in newspaper billboards with their teasing headlines - **MAN HURT IN CAMBERWELL BLAZE** - only to find that someone has burned their hand on a chip pan.

They start on a wave of enthusiasm, seven days a week from 6.30am until 7pm, taking it in turns to open and lock up and serving together during rush hours. The estates down Bethwin Road are expanding with more and more high-rise flats and we're the first port of call on the main road for a paper and a packet of fags for the bus into work. The clientèle is almost totally white working-class - 'straight goers' Dad calls them, meaning people who've never fallen foul of the law - dockers, printers, shop workers, labourers, factory women, busmen, postmen, secretaries, office girls, mechanics. There isn't a lawyer, an accountant or a surgeon in sight.

Mum always makes herself presentable. Indoors it's rollers and turban. But in the kiosk it's curls and rouge lippy. Dad wears a collar and tie and flat cap but during cold snaps covers up in a brown 'warehouseman' work coat. In its splendid isolation, the kiosk gets hot and stuffy in summer and becomes a frozen igloo in winter. They have a little fan to stop the chocolate melting and a portable heater to stop their feet from going numb from cold.

The Sabbath afternoon is their only break together. Opposite is a drinking club run by their friend Bertie Cochrane, Mum's early heartthrob. After Nan's Sunday roast, they let their hair down there around the juke-box and piano. They start on brown ale and Guinness but often 'get the flavour' and progress to shorts, arriving home pissed as farts and going straight to bed. One evening I open the street door and see Dad paying a taxi driver.

'Oh, did you go on somewhere?' asks Nan.

'Nah, the soppy bastard forgot where he was and flagged down a cab,' Mum slurs. It is the shortest taxi ride in history - a 'U' turn, from one side of the road to the other, all of 15 yards. And, generous as ever, particularly in booze, Lights tips the driver. Getting drunk unleashes Mum's deep-rooted anger at her old man's behaviour and triggers bitter rows and tears. But she blames 'mothers' ruin' - the gin rather than her suppressed feelings.

When Dad gets pissed we hide. He's the most amicable and amorous drunk in the world, smothering us with wet extravagant kisses, an overwhelming smell of whiskey, and squeezing us to death in the process. But he always pays a price for getting sloshed. While he drifts into a stupor, Mum creeps in and weeds his pockets, stashing away any leftover money for rainy days. He awakes with a sore head in the morning swearing he's been 'buzzed'. And he's right!

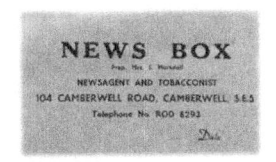

The letterhead shows Mum as proprietor

Mum's bought a rusty old pram to transport fags and sweets. It's stored under a tarpaulin behind the kiosk. It's robust, with small wheels and Formica seats that fold flat for shopping. She pushes me along Walworth Road, with me pointing the way like Rommel.

They need somewhere to store the stock. Easy… our bedroom. The room had once been one long grand hall. The family all had their wedding receptions there. It was so popular that people asked if they could use it for weddings and wakes. For example, the local gangster Freddie Foreman and his wife Maureen celebrated their nuptials there. Regardless of who they are, or what they've done, Mum is always eager to help out. Somewhere along the way someone has installed dividing doors which can be opened or closed as desired. This is now Mum and Dad's bedroom with us on the other side of the partition. They often row late into the night. We hide under the sheets to try to shut out the words of war from the other side of the partition, and the occasional crash of missiles - including a chamber pot and its liquid content.

My aunt Gladys' wedding reception taken from our bedroom

We sleep in Willy Wonka land. Every inch is occupied by cardboard boxes of sweets and cigarettes stored on a giant wooden rack that reaches to the high ceiling – 200 Woodbines and Player's Weights packs, tins of Old Holborn and Golden Virginia roll-up tobacco, mountains of Smarties, Mars Bars, Flakes, Polos, Fruit Gums, Fruit Pastilles and Trebor mints. The displays of Crunchies and Bounty bars are a temptation but I'll never touch a single bar. Johnny has ordered me not to steal, although I do find a half-eaten bar of Cadbury's under his pillow.

10

Three Parents!

Nan is now a surrogate parent, taking over much of the cooking and caring duties. A single parent for much of her life, she's made of stern stuff. During the war an unfortunate Luftwaffe pilot had to bale out over Camberwell after being hit by anti-aircraft fire. His parachute took an age to float down in the wind and Nan was among a growing army of angry women chasing through the streets with frying pans to give him what for. Luckily for him the police got there first.

We eat well. After all, she was a live-in cook for a wealthy insurance agent and his family. She operates a strict rota of what to eat on certain days of the week. Dad always ensures she has enough money for the biggest joints and leanest meat. Sundays are always a traditional Sunday roast with all the trimmings. Mondays are leftover cold meat day and further leftovers are made into pies or stews for the rest of the week supplemented by fresh vegetables and crunchy roasted spuds basted in lard. Shepherds Pie and Toad in The Hole are my faves.

Fridays is Fish and Chip Night and on Sunday teatime if Dad's 'holding' he sometimes puts Johnny in a cab to Barneys or Tubby Isaac at Aldgate for jellied eels and seafood. Woe betide him if he comes back with portions laden with eel tails. If Dad's been out boozing he'll cut himself huge 'doorstop' slices of Hovis which he smothers in dripping and salt. Quite often after a binge he'll sick it all up, blaming his stomach.

Nan takes me shopping to Jones and Higgins. Some of my parents' industrial language is clearly rubbing off: I stare out the window of the No. 12 bus repeatedly uttering the F word. Nan clips me around the ear. 'But Nan, I didn't say bollocks!' The highlight of the week is going with her to Arments in Westmoreland Road, one of London's oldest pie and mash shops. It dates back to the First World War when Walworth had the highest density in London and there was much deprivation. Pie and mash is cheap, convenient, filling and tasty, and served if required with stewed eels and liquor made from parsley sauce and juice from the eels.

The shop has a distinct sanitised décor - white glazed tiled walls and marble-top tables - and the staff dress in white too. I lick my lips waiting in the queue watching the theatre of preparing, baking and serving behind the counter - the piemakers in their chef hats, and burn-stained aprons going about their business with lightning speed, cutting pastry, filling the moulds, adding the minced meat, and sliding the huge baking trays into the ovens. The freshly-cooked pies are hurried to the counter where servers spoon dollops of mash and ladle the liquor onto your plate.

I learn early on that choosing the seat is essential. You don't want to be sat opposite some nutter, or a pensioner with their false teeth on the table, or be squeezed against the wall by an overweight adult. On the tables are supplies of salt, pepper and vinegar, including bottles with floating red things that I will later learn are chillies. Nan teaches me to always check that the condiments are screwed on tight. A popular prank among kids is to loosen or unscrew the lids and watch through the window as some poor sod pours a mountain of salt on their food or drowns their meal with vinegar. There is a ritual about how you eat your meal. Some can't wait and steam straight in. Others flip the pie over and cut a cross in the pastry to allow the salt, pepper and vinegar to seep into the meat juices.

Once, the whole shop stopped and went silent. Staff bowed their heads and customers stood up at their tables. Mum being hard of hearing asked the woman next to her in the queue what was going on.

'Arments is Dead,' the woman whispered. Well, that's what Mum thought she'd heard. She gave the sign of the cross and passed on her condolences to the staff saying what a gentleman the old man had been.

'No… it's *Armistice* Day,' the server laughed.

***

Growing up, there's much for a young boy to observe, particularly Dad. He is the man whom everybody loves but would never want to live with, a puzzling mass of extravagance, contradictions and compulsions. He's a screenwriter's dream and is part of local folklore. Except you couldn't make him up. He possesses the charm of comedy screen character Alfie, the wit of Del Boy, the bigotry of Alf Garnet, and he rants like moany old Steptoe.

He buys ten when one will do, particularly at Christmas when he arrives with enough fruit and veg to last until Easter, including exotic figs and dates that no-one will ever eat. He can be happy and generous, but bad-tempered and mean-spirited, all within in the timespan of a five-furlong sprint. Johnny's mates don't know where they stand with him. One day he's saying how nice it is to see them, treating them to free chocolate, the next telling them to fuck off because they're getting in the way of customers.

Mum defuses her old man's mood swings and foibles with humour. She makes everyone laugh and is a fine letter writer. Several times in their relationship she gets him off a jail sentence by sending heart-rending despatches to the court begging the magistrate or judge to give him one last chance.

She never forgets a family birthday and always includes a merry quip in the card. Her nieces and nephews are particularly fond of her. She has a wealth of sayings. 'You'll get us in Carey Street,' she will utter in the face of any risky venture. I will learn later that Carey Street was the home of the London bankruptcy court. Her language is fruity but not coarse. Someone a bit slow is either 'soppy bollocks', 'silly as arseholes', or 'nutty as a fruit cake'. If they're mean, they're 'tight as arseholes'; if thin, 'skinny as a rake'; if unwashed, they're 'soapy'. She once sarcastically nicknamed me 'Talky Joe' for refusing to indulge in conversation. 'Don't let the

55

grass grow under your feet' is when she's trying to get us off our backsides and do something positive. 'Use yer loaf' when we've slipped up; 'yer eyes are too big for your belly' when we can't eat all our seconds. But the advice most heard from her, particularly in adversity, is 'the Lord leads the way'. She never goes to Church though, except for weddings and funerals. But she's convinced she's being guided through any trials and tribulations by some heavenly spirit.

***

I watch fascinated as my father goes through his daily ritual of getting ready. His day begins bringing up phlegm in the toilet. He'll never give up smoking because he says it makes him cough and helps him clear the mucus off his chest! Great logic!

His spindly frame appears in the kitchen in Long Johns (aptly named), having already liberally applied Germolene antiseptic cream and bandages to his ulcerated legs. Every morning, out comes the black Kiwi (not that Cherry Blossom rubbish) to polish his brogues (army-style spit and polish) until he can see his face in them. As far as he is concerned, anyone with dirty shoes is a tramp.

Then it's a wet shave at the sink, murdering the same Perry Como number every day. Shaving is a pantomime. The only brand acceptable is Wilkinson Sword, carefully sliding each individually-wrapped blade out its little white plastic container. If he cuts himself, which is frequent, the blade is always blamed and discarded immediately. His face often carries the scars of attrition - little nicks covered by tissues or toilet paper. After washing his face, he cleans his ears with a matchstick, and styles his hair. The Brylcream is applied extravagantly, leaving a thick deposit of cream in the teeth of the comb. The pillows, headboard and fabric of his easy-chair will bear those grease marks forever.

Next, the dentures. Before I was born, he'd got toothache and insisted the dentist take all his teeth out in one go - a classic example of his all-or-nothing personality. The false teeth are soaked in Steradent overnight and rinsed through with tap water before putting them in for the day (although they are always taken out at meal times and wrapped in a folded hanky). They are props for comic effect too. Once while sitting in a market café his Tony nephew revealed he was getting engaged.

'Congratulations. Have you got her a ring yet?'

'No...'

Dad produced his hanky from his jacket and offered it under the table.

'See if this suits you,' he said, looking over his shoulder conspiratorially for any prying eyes. My poor cousin slowly opened the hanky... only to set eyes not on a glittering sparkler but a full set of discoloured dentures.

After meals he'll often be sick. Whether this is because of a dodgy stomach or some eating disorder, who knows? However, it does allow him to keep amazingly slim.

Dad's always immaculately turned out. Never, never, in jeans or shorts. Whenever he has a 'touch' he raids the West End for made-to-measure suits in Saville Row or shirts from Jermyn Street, buying in quantity to see him through lean times. His shirts are collarless and only ever white, and the suits only navy pinstripe, with the same wide lapels whatever the fashion. They are kept in his wardrobe amid a mountain of mothballs. You can smell the aroma from the hall. Later we will discover that although they no doubt see off flying insects, they also pose serious health risks for children ingesting fumes from the chemicals and will be banned.

Dad has a seemingly endless supply of studded collars accompanied by a silk 'Peckham' (Peckham Rye, tie) from Harvie and Hudson near The Strand. Shirts are laundered (not washed) at a dry-cleaners at Camberwell Green. The term 'belt and braces' can be coined about him - he always wears both. Finally, a grease-stained chequered flat cap completes the Andy Capp look, accompanied by the obligatory fag in the corner of his mouth and the Sporting Life folded in his outside pocket. He is now ready to face the day.

He is a forty a day man, John Player finest Virginia Navy Cut. Having started at the age of thirteen, during his lifetime he will probably get through a million cigarettes. There's no ceremonial lighting up, or taking a deep drag and wallowing in that first nicotine hit. No, the fag is parked in the corner of his mouth for every waking hour, glowing like a lighthouse on every breath. He's an expert managing ash, allowing it to form just enough for it never to collapse, so he can then lift the ashtray to his chin without ever needing to take the fag out his mouth.

If smoking is one obsession, the news is another. He listens to bulletins on TV and radio over and over. The dial is fixed to the BBC's Home Service particularly its new morning programme called Today. His favourite presenters will always be Jack de Manio, famous for his on-air gaffes, and the straight-talking Montague 'Monty' Modlyn, one of the few Cockney voices in broadcasting.

De Manio's career nearly crashed when at the end of a major feature, The Land of the Niger, which was broadcast worldwide to mark a Royal visit to Nigeria, he carelessly announced it as *The Land of the Nigger*. Modlyn, the son of a Lambeth Jewish tailor, had little respect for the rich and famous. He once asked the Ugandan dictator Idi Amin live on air *'How many people have you murdered?'* to which Amin responded *'You very cheeky man!'* Monty was delighted. His autobiography was entitled *Pardon My Cheek* and he even adopted a theme song…

Pardon my cheek, and the way I speak, but no matter where I go
To common or gentry, I talk element'ry
In the only way I know.

11

The old school tie

The journey to Comber Grove Junior and Infants School is roughly half a mile on a path trodden by my family for over a hundred years. My great grandmother, great grandad, Nan, mother, aunts and uncles and of course my brother have all attended. But that long tradition is to end with me. I will be the last. And so on this sunny morning in 1958, holding hands with Mum, I follow in their footsteps to begin my education.

It isn't the most salubrious of walks. Out of the door, onto the main arterial road into central London; a swift right into Bethwin Road, past the slaughterhouse, with its pungent odour of rotting carcasses, and the grinding of the metal factory which backs onto our rear garden; under the railway bridge where the pigeons roost and secrete their ugly deposits on the pavements below; left at Crown Street, where Dad's mate Peggy has his scrap metal yard; and the railway arches where they're always ringing and revving car engines. There's no pavement here. You tiptoe on the road through the manure, shattered glass and burned-out cars; past Hollington Street, now going under the hammer; onto Wyndham Road, where some of Britain's most notorious gangsters, the Richardson brothers, grew up over their mother's sweet shop, and where the Lollipop lady sees us across the road to Comber Grove.

Decay on the walk to school

Halfway there … Crown Street

The institution dates back to 1810 when a wealthy do-gooder, with the support of churches, opened a small school in a cottage nearby. At that time most of the local six-and-seven-year-olds went out to work. The Education Act in 1870 decreed that every child should go to school. The government paid for the construction of new buildings, but parents had to pay for lessons.

My great grandfather was probably one of the first pupils. It was one of the first Board Schools to be opened in Camberwell and attracted a lot of attention. On the first day 500 children turned up supervised by just the Head, two assistant mistresses and four probationers. There was no central heating, and seats near the coal fire were at a premium. In those days the classrooms were small, with the pupils squashed together - if only to keep warm. Lighting was provided by dim gas lamps.

In the first week, several parents complained that their children had had their caps nicked. The mistresses lectured the children about the wickedness of taking things which were not their own. Then one of the teachers had a mutton chop, turnips and a large bag of biscuits stolen from the staff room. Under questioning, two sisters, Louise and Alice Morgan, admitted they'd taken them home to feed their family. Their mother went to the school and said she couldn't understand it because the girls were well fed. She promised to report the matter to the girls' father.

Things began to settle down. A report by inspectors in 1878, around about the time my great grandmother went there, declared the infants' section in a *'hopeful and satisfactory state'* with the children orderly and cheerful with good passes in elementary subjects.

In those days it was called Leipsic Road School, after the German city. There were a number of German street names locally - Ulric Road and Blucher Road, named after a famous German general. However, the First World War stirred up a lot of anti-German hostility. Just a few doors along from my future home in Camberwell Road, a bread shop owned by a family named Schultz was firebombed in the middle of the night. The poor baker and his family had to flee the district. Xenophobia was rife then. A plumber's mate was fined 40s for smashing up a hairdresser's shop in Wyndham Road. The barber was Polish.

The council purged anything sounding remotely German and the name Leipsic Road was consigned to history. The politicians decided that Thomas Comber, a local lad who became a missionary in Africa, was a much safer bet. So, Leipsic became Comber, and Road became Grove. To celebrate, the London County Council gave the rebranded Comber Grove School a new building too - a three-storey affair of London stock brick with an overhanging slate roof and decent sized playgrounds.

Comber Grove School in 2023

The school was next door to a munitions factory providing ammo for the war effort. At 2pm on July 25th 1916 one of the workers lit a sly fag and BANG! - an almighty explosion that was heard for miles. All that was left of the whole building was a portion of wall and the chimney. Fire spread 50 yards 'like a galloping horse', according to one fireman. Three workers died from appalling burns, including a 20-year-old woman. Many more suffered burns or were trapped under rubble. Debris hit the school building and landed in the playground, but luckily everyone was inside and escaped injury. Frantic parents scaled the school gates to ensure their offspring were okay. The factory was eventually razed and a block of flats built on the site.

After the end of that war, the school settled down to a more normal life. Camberwell was still a poor area. And with many of the children's fathers having died in the war, many found this new era tough. The living and working conditions led to strikes throughout the country. In 1926 the kids were sent home early because of riots along Camberwell Road. The school found new ways to help. Most families did not have a bathroom, but under a new bathing scheme the council arranged for pupils to be taken to Church Street baths for a hot bath. Comber Grove also excelled in boxing. Two pupils won the Schoolboy Boxing Championships of Great Britain - a feat repeated a year later. And, in an example of the sexism of the times, the girls were taught and encouraged in gardening, particularly the cultivation of daffodils.

***

I look up at this imposing building as I wait nervously to be called in. It has the aura of a prison rather than a school. The whistle goes and it's time to wave goodbye. We both have a wobble. Some of the kids are wailing, others have to be forcefully pulled from their mothers' arms. We are led to our ground floor reception class, and past the grey concrete stairs, wondering what and where they lead to - and there's that distinctive smell: a cocktail of polish, sawdust and sick.

We sit at individual desks, in straight rows, each with an ink well. There are 40 or so of us. We all look similar - white, and dressed in the same shorts and dresses bought from Whitehall Clothiers just up the road from our house. Apart from one or two exceptions there is no apparent poverty, although one lad has to wear his brother's hand-me-down boots even though they are a far bigger size. He refuses to take them off, creating havoc with his female partners trying to do country dancing. Roughly a third of the class enjoy free school meals. Mum wouldn't dream of applying, viewing it as a sign of being on the breadline, something she is determined to leave behind. She is a great respecter of authority and status. I suppose she'll be classed as a working-class Tory. The reason she votes Conservative is because in her mind they represent money and class and dress smarter than 'that scruffy Labour lot'.

The teacher stands in front of a blackboard at the front of the class with a box of chalk. Later a cane will be added to the tools of the trade. Rote learning is the order of the day. We chant tables and use set text books. Everyone learns the same thing at the same time. Those who can't keep up are labelled 'thickoes'. It isn't long before I can do simple arithmetic and read and write, even mastering my first 'essay.' It consists of precisely 13 words, in that helter-skelter scrawl of all young kids, and written in my blue little schoolbook. *'I want to eat pie and mash for the rest of my life.'* I get a tick from the teacher, but a ticking off from Mum.

'How dare you show us up! They'll think we're skint,' she says.

However, I am certainly on track with that first piece of writing. The shop premises will later earn a Blue Plaque for its place in South London folklore and even have neighbouring flats named after it, Arment House.

My first school photo - angelic five-year-old

In the playground I learn never to go in goal on the other side of the toilets. Some of the older lads can actually pee over the wall and you risk a golden shower. I also discover the hand-me-down rituals of marbles, cannon, cap guns, cap rockets, splits, conkers, pea shooting and British Bulldog. We watch the girls play hopscotch, Cats' Cradle and skipping where as many as ten jump in and out of a huge rope singing songs we all think are new but date back to Victorian times. *One potata, two potata, three potata more…*

Our real playground is far away from the prying eyes of teachers. Whole streets are being razed to make way for tower blocks, hailed by their architects and politicians as 'homes in the sky'. The thud of the wrecking ball and crashing cascade of bricks are the soundtrack to my walk to and from school. We call them bombsites. But bulldozers rather than bombs have flattened them.

Whole streets bulldozed

Entry is strictly forbidden to anyone. But the demolition teams only work until 4pm - and not at all at weekends. So, after school we sneak into the coolest - and most dangerous - playground around. It is perfect for water fights, making guns with sticks and going 'underground' in rodent-infested basements. If the Germans don't get you the rats will. We play 'dares' in half-demolished houses, climb and jump from open staircases, build dens out of bricks and rusty guttering, and inch 20 feet high along steel girders like tightrope walkers. Some of the enterprising older boys go searching for lead to sell in the scrap yards. Deep in the ruins, one girl finds a velvet box with ear-rings and a bracelet. We spend many a fruitless hour searching among the rubble and old furniture for more jewellery. The only limits are our imagination, bravery and stupidity. And I'm about to encounter my first of several visits to King's College Hospital near Camberwell Green.

Demolition sites make cool playgrounds

We find a discarded wardrobe and create a platform from planks of wood to make it easy to climb on top. Nearby is an old mattress with some of its rusty springs protruding. We lug it across the mud until it's directly beneath the wardrobe. We now have the perfect trampoline. We take it in turns to scale up, then jump six or seven feet down, and spring into the air with a star jump. What can possibly go wrong? Well, nothing until my turn. I stand on the summit and pick my spot to avoid the springs which even us daredevil idiots know can go right through your plimsoll if you land on one. I leap into the air… **'Geronimo!'**

With pinpoint accuracy, I land safely on the required spot - but somehow gain far more spring than the previous kids. I freefall through the air and sail straight through a window pane abandoned on the rubble. My hands break my fall… but a shard of glass is embedded in my right palm. Blood is spurting out. I rise to my feet, examine the injury - and promptly faint. One of the lads runs to get his dad who happens to be caretaker of the local secondary school. He brings me round, wraps the wound in a towel, and drives me to Casualty.

The approach on Denmark Hill appears familiar. And then I realise. It's the hospital used in the opening titles of a medical soap opera on ITV called Emergency Ward 10. I'm being admitted to the most famous hospital in Britain! I look around expecting to glimpse the pin-up star of the series, Nurse Carole Young. Another nurse, a real one - not quite as pretty as the actress Jill Browne - extracts the fragments with a tweezer under a magnifying glass. I almost faint again, but my mate's dad talks about football to distract me. I'm given a tetanus jab and three stitches and allowed home. I greet Mum full of beans, waving my bandaged hand to divert a telling off. But I'm banned from bombsites for ever.

I'm skinny, fit and probably the quickest runner in the infants. Footballs are banned after a girl got hit in the face. We can only play with a tennis ball - a pain, but there's no doubt it's helping me develop balls skills. It's football, football, football every playtime, an experience not without hazard as we chase the ball between the girls' skipping ropes and games of hopscotch, inconveniently chalked out in the middle of our pitch. Occasionally the sexes play together - kiss chase, which the girls seem to like more than the boys, and Tin Tan Tommy when the seeker rattles a tin and you have to hide and get 'home' before being found and shouted out. *'Tin Tan Tommy I see Alan in the shelter.'*

It seems only days. But I'm back in King's. I've challenged the other kids to a running game I've devised. You run up and down the playground touching the walls for the whole of playtime. They shoot schoolkids, don't they? The last boy standing wins. A few drop out exhausted but a few of us carry on even though we are reduced to snail's pace. Two minutes before the whistle I trip a yard from the wall and headbutt the London brick. Immediately, an egg appears on my forehead and I've cut my eye. One of the teachers takes me to Casualty where I'm X-rayed, given another tetanus injection, and bandaged up. I am slightly concussed but there's no lasting damage. However, I shall bear a slightly misshaped forehead forever.

12

On The Telly

It is the Spring of 1960 and in the creative corridors of TV land, a television producer called Michael Ingram has an idea that will make me and my mates household faces across the nation. Or so we think.

He wants to make a 'fly on the wall' documentary - a series of 15-minute peeps - into life in a typical London street. It will imaginatively be called *Our Street*. But where? And which one? With his researcher Jaquemine Charrott-Lodwidge, who fought for the French resistance during the war, he burrows through 500 miles of boroughs to try to find... well, an ordinary street. The criteria is simple. It has to be short to cope with filming a dozen or so families; away from the noise of any main roads; preferably a cul-de-sac to reduce through-traffic; neither rich or very poor; and contain a pub and a grocer's shop - somewhere for the people to meet and talk.

They've given themselves a week. It's now Thursday and they are tearing their hair out. They decide to start again. And perhaps be a little less fussy. In their offices in Vauxhall Bridge Road, they decide to head back to the Mile End Road. On Camberwell New Road they take a detour to avoid Camberwell Green and get lost in a maze of terraced streets. And, in a haystack of backstreets behind our school, they stumble on their needle!

Our Street – the one chosen for TV

One of my classmates, 'John West' (or Fishy, as we call him) lives there, and in the next week or two will feature prominently, even embarrassingly filmed being bathed by his mum in a 'baby' bath in their front room.

It also happens to be his birthday and the production team put on a birthday party filmed at St Michael's School in Wyndham Road. John's cousin is a lad called Martin Vernon, whose dad is the caretaker. The notion of deprivation has gone out of the window. There are party hats, streamers, cakes, sandwiches, pop, balloons and games, all provided by the budget.

The street's requisite corner shop

Magazine article on 'Our Street'

There are three giant cameras all on rostrums. Before filming begins the director briefs us all NOT to look at any camera at any stage. If we do, we won't be on TV because he wants everything to appear as natural as possible. But curiosity kills me and I ignore him, diligently tracking which camera is recording by searching for their red light.

The programme creates a real buzz. *When will it be broadcast? Which of us will be in it?* Come transmission, the director is proved right. While the other partygoers point themselves out with glee and celebrate being the next John Wayne or Elizabeth Taylor, I do not appear in a single close up, just a fleeting two-second wide shot of kids around the table seemingly enjoying themselves.

Me enjoying the party (facing far right)

It isn't all plain sailing for the production team. The location is right in the heart of 'totter' land. And certainly no place to leave a roll of valuable electric cable lying around on the pavement unattended. It was here a minute ago! But nobody can find it. Cue lots of local faces shrugging their shoulders and looking the other way. They'll never discover where it's gone, but it is stripped and sold before anyone can shout 'ACTION!' The director also discovers just how savvy these totters can be. He asks for a shot of a traditional rag and bone man on his pony and cart.

'Sure, Guv'nor... that'll be a tenner for the horse feed.'

Years later a Roller will one day pull up at those same railway arches. A scruffy looking bloke with long hair will emerge with a smile and ask if he can get up on the horse and cart for a promotional picture. He will hand over twenty quid.

'... er, don't I know you? Your face is familiar!'

'Possibly. My name's David Bowie. And I make records.'

The Our Street series is well received. One critic writes: '... *the results are praiseworthy, being neither smart nor coy, arty nor shapeless. Nothing very staggering is likely to emerge, but this is an honest and straightforward attempt to hold up a not-too-distorting mirror in the television-set in the corner.'*

-13-
Nanny Jane

Since the death of her husband between the wars, Nan has stayed stubbornly single, surrounded by her six offspring and 15 grandchildren which she considers her life. There's been the occasional man friend, or cheeky flirt with men in the pub, but nothing permanent. However, a partner has arrived on the scene from almost nowhere. His name is Bill Wallace from a respected South London family. Bill looks much older than Nan, and is shorter, muscular and bald. We never do ask, but we assume he's lost his wife and is looking for female companionship.

Nan and Bill at Leysdown

Bill is very generous to me and Johnny. On one occasion he takes us to the Oval - an excursion which becomes the source of much hilarity between my brother and I. Poor old Bill is blind in one eye. He can hardly see the play in the middle and whenever he hears the 'crack' of leather on willow we pretend the ball is heading our way in the air and scream for him to take cover. Every time Bill ducks under the seats, scared stiff he is going to be hit by this lethal missile. 'Where's that gone?' Where's that gone?' is his constant refrain. His fears are confirmed when one batsman hits a six which lands a few feet away and we all genuinely dive out the way.

***

Nan has announced that she has purchased a holiday chalet on the south east coast, at Leysdown-on-Sea on the Isle of Sheppey. She and Bill go most weekends, travelling on the Green Line to Sheerness and then on by local bus. But now it's the school holidays and she's invited me and Johnny to go with them for a few days.

We pack several balls and a tennis racket and set off early by taxi to Liverpool Grove to board the charabanc for Sheerness. It's only 50-odd miles but the journey through South London, Kent and over rickety rackety bridges takes three hours. Then at Sheerness there is more to-ing and fro-ing on public transport to get to our destination. We arrive mid-morning to see acres of identical chalets stretching onto the green horizon. We haul our luggage across the fields until we find number 96, a yellow and white affair in need of a fresh lick of paint. Inside, it's cold and dank and badly in need of airing, despite the fact that they've become regular visitors. There is no electricity but there is Calor gas for cooking.

Leysdown-on-Sea sounds grand and we can't wait to explore. We have our cozzies and money burning a hole in our pockets. Our only restriction is an instruction not to talk to any strangers and certainly not get in anyone's car.

Nan, Bill and me

We walk the makeshift gravel track to the main road, past fields of holiday villages and chalets, numerous fish and chips shops and burger bars. Pretty soon the smell of frying oil is replaced by the distinctive salty air of the sea. We follow our noses to the seafront. But any hopes of spending a day on the beach are dashed there and then. It's full of shingle and broken shells. There is absolutely no-one swimming or frolicking in the water. We take our sandals off for a paddle. Walking in bare feet is painful enough but they are about to go numb. The water, part of the English Channel, is freezing.

The Medway Riviera - Leysdown-on-Sea

The beach might be a no-no, but the place is alive with amusement arcades. Our money doesn't last long, the slot machines swallowing up all our coins. But there's hope for the future. We become expert in knowing how far back to take the firing trigger which sends the ball spinning to the winning cups. This will prove lucrative in the years to come.

We return to the chalet - or so we think. At the entrance to the site we race each other home. However, as we run past one chalet, a Jack Russell terrier leaps out of nowhere and sinks his teeth into my right calf. I collapse, distraught and in tears. The woman owner runs out to see what the fuss is about and tells me it's my fault for scaring the dog and that we shouldn't be running anyway. Johnny says I might have rabies and rushes back to get help. Nan and Bill arrive to find me snivelling on a garden chair, the dog secured on a lead a few yards away. It is deemed that I need stitches and another holidaymaker offers to take me and Nan in his car to the local hospital. I have four stitches plus yet another tetanus injection. I'm still an infant yet have now been treated in hospital three times. It's also the beginning of a hate/hate relationship with dogs.

We get back to find Bill and Johnny sitting outside. They've been there two hours. In the chaos of the dog incident Bill has locked his keys in the chalet.

'I'm waiting to get in with your key,' he tells Nan.

'But I left mine on the table.'

We are locked out. But there is an open toilet window - and I'm the only one small enough to squeeze in.

We're locked out. Alan to the rescue!

That evening they take us to the clubhouse, with a stage and a live band. Nan says the vibe reminds her of Hopping - hundreds of Cockneys from South and East London having a knees up. Word reaches us that there's a kids' talent show later and that our names are on the list. There is a tradition in our family to perform at parties but I am genuinely petrified at having to sing in front of hundreds of strangers. I go AWOL, hiding in the dark between chalets. A search party is formed. I can hear them calling but I think it's to go on stage. In the end they find me crying in the dark and I'm given a reprieve.

After a certain time, kids aren't allowed inside but we can stand at the door drinking copious Pepsis. It's late. And they've had enough. We all roll home, Bill and Nan tipsy, me limping with a stitched leg, and Johnny high from sugar overload. Bill starts singing his favourite song…

All over Italy they know his concertina
Poppa Piccolino, Poppa Piccolino,
He plays so prettily to every signorina,
Poppa Piccolino from sunny Italy.

In his inebriated state, Bill's version is different every time, muddling up all those Ps so much the song becomes a slurring meaningless mess. They've remembered their keys - but there's still the business of lighting the lamp. We watch as half-blind Bill fumbles in the dark and goes through a box of matches. He's either striking them so hard they snap, or taking too long to reach the lamp and burning his finger in the process. We snigger but Nan is visibly frustrated. We sense if we weren't here her language would be quite fruity. We sleep on a makeshift bed. The walls are wafer-thin and we have to whisper so as not to disturb them. We hear them giggling well into the night. Leysdown and Bill make Nan very happy.

Hooky Bookie

Dad has developed a new and rather lucrative sideline - taking bets over the counter. Normally to place a wager away from the track you have to have an account with a 'turf accountant' – no, not people who count grass, but legitimate licensed bookmakers who are rather picky about who they do business with. It means illegal street bookies flourish. One is a paper seller called Titchy who pedals the manor on his bike selling the evening editions and settling the bets. His shout can be heard from a mile away. *"WOOOAAAHHH."*

Now Lights, under the cover of The Newsbox, has become one too. Wagers are handed over in an envelope. It's good for business in that people placing bets feel obliged to actually buy stuff, even if it's only a tube of Spangles.

Someone once said that bookmaking is a licence to print money. True, but only up to a point. Occasionally the punter is successful. Dad is a brilliant and generous winner. But when he loses… well, as Sinatra says when Basie strikes up the band, run for cover!

He commands sole use of the kitchen table, calculating winnings with a ready-reckoner pocket book. I'm only a child and while I haven't a clue about fractions and long division, I already know what doubles, trebles, and accumulators are, even Yankees!

He has two columns, not headed Profit or Loss, but C for Cop, the other B for Blue. He checks the deficit column over and over again, hoping perhaps that somehow it might magically change. Arriving home from school it's vital to make a quiet entrance to see how the land lies. If the B column is longer than the C, you scarper quick. Although to be fair, you can tell straight away. A warm and pleasant 'Hello son. How was school?' means that life for Lights that day has been good.

Whenever racing is on the telly Dad pays special attention to the horses which he stands to lose money on. Inside the final furlong he inches closer and closer to the set, his hands on the screen, desperately trying to hold them back and screaming blue murder at them.

Another cliff-hanger is when he phones James Lane turf accountants for the results of races that aren't on the box. He puts on a posh voice and gives a false name and some random account number… 'Mr Bennett here, 16423, can I have the result of the 3 o'clock at Epsom please.' We know within seconds if he's won or lost - either a smirk of satisfaction, a polite thank you and a gentle replacement of the receiver, or interrogation about the starting price, any non-runners, if there was an objection to the winner, and if they've weighed in. The receiver is then slammed down.

***

It is May 1961, and the government has decided to legalise betting shops. Bookies have to apply for a licence at the local courthouse. Around 10,000 shops open in the first six months, all quietly and efficiently processed. However, Dad's application makes the national newspapers. Two days before the new legislation the Daily Mirror page seven lead story headline is 'EX-CRIMINALS ARE GIVEN PERMITS TO BE BOOKIES'. The story runs… *'Three men with criminal records were granted permits yesterday to take bets from the public. The permits were granted by the Newington Betting Licenses Committee at Southwark Town Hall in London.*

The chairman, Mr Basil Aldous, said: We have heard previous convictions described as honourable scars. We do not consider they merit that description. And we wish it to be firmly understood that we will not consider renewing the licenses of these people if they infringe the law in the next year.'

The article goes on… *'It was said of John Hurndall that he had convictions for theft and had served gaol sentences of six months hard labour, three months and a month. Hurndall said, 'When I was young I was quite foolish but it is eight years now since I did wrong.'*

Read All About It - Dad in court

A similar article makes the front page lead of the South London Observer. It is the first I've heard of Dad's criminal past and I go cold with shame reading it in the shop, hiding copies from view.

However, Dad has been successful, and he will keep the licence in a drawer in his wardrobe along with his birth certificate. He hopes one day to open his own shop. I sense some friction with my uncle Tommy Shaw who has his own betting shop just up the road and doesn't appreciate the thought of Dad treading on his toes.

Lights carries on taking bets at The Newsbox, even though this is against the new law which requires a number of conditions for betting offices, including blacking out the entrance, something of course that isn't possible for a newspaper kiosk!

Legal betting shops have become a new magnet for Dad. He takes his list of bets with him and checks their progress in running. Most shops have live commentaries of every race and a screens for televised meetings.

As wily as ever, he spots a flaw in their systems which enables him to enjoy every gambler's dream - betting on certain winners! Many small shops can only afford just a skeleton staff - someone on the counter taking the money, a settler in a back office, and a 'boardman' who scribbles the results and starting prices on a black or white board. Bets are written out on slips and processed at the counter. On Bank Holidays there are sometimes a dozen meetings. Betting shops are packed and the pace becomes hectic. Punters like to leave it until the last second to place their bets, hoping to get the best price about a horse or greyhound and they tend to rush the counter in a crowd.

Dad begins a scam whereby late in the afternoon, just before the start of a race, he places a multiple bet of, say, three horses, knowing that one of them has already won, selected for its big price. The bet is three singles, three doubles and a treble. Harassed staff are often too busy to check bets against races earlier in the day. When they accept his bet, he's already assured of a lucrative single - and more, if either or both the other horses actually come in. Quite often when he collects his winnings the staff are suspicious but have no proof of the time he placed his bet. They've started banning him and he has to travel further afield to different manors.

His 'after time' racket ends when shops bring in machines which photograph the bet and record the precise second it is placed. Staff can now check this against the official 'off' time. Undeterred, most afternoons you'll find him legitimately playing up the morning's kiosk takings - a habit which is destined to lead us all to Mum's lamented 'Carey Street'.

-15-
She's Leaving Home

When they first opened the Newsbox, Janie and Lights shared duties. However, Mum now manages the books and ordering of stock. But the burden of standing and serving six days a week is beginning to fall mostly upon her shoulders. Dad is obsessed with his bookmaking and betting operation and sometimes goes racing himself. In winter, with the earlier starts, he can get back to help in the evening rush but gradually he's letting her down more and more. Frequently instead of coming home he goes to the dog track, and then to gamble some more at the club. Sometimes he's off the scene for days.

Mum has clearly had enough. It's the school holidays now. And she is about to take it literally. She's packed her cases and told him she's leaving home - taking us boys in tow. We watch anxiously as she throws the kiosk keys at him. She must have planned it for weeks, because she has quite a bit of ready money in her purse, the proceeds of weeding his pockets when he's drunk.

She hails a taxi and we throw in our stuff.

'Victoria Station, please mate,' she says. We haven't a clue where we're going, although she'd insisted we dress smart. She's sporting a floral dress, Johnny's in a sleeveless jumper over a shirt, with long trousers, and I'm wearing shorts and a formal shirt. We are both adorned in bow ties at her insistence.

At Victoria, we look after the luggage while she queues at the booking office. She returns with the tickets.

'Right, follow me.' We lug the cases to the platform. But this is no ordinary train. It's a Pullman, in cream and brown livery, an exclusive refreshment-only service. The waiters wear matching uniforms, every table is laid out with knives and forks and condiments, with a little personal lamp. We've never seen anything like it.

'Where we going, Mum?'

'Brighton.'

The train is due to leave at ten but we're early. She instructs Johnny to go and buy her a Sporting Life. I fret and sweat, fearing the train might pull away without him. It's such a relief to see his beaming face emerge into the carriage carrying the paper. As the train chugs out of the station, a waiter arrives at the table.

'Right, what's it to be boys?'

'Are we allowed scrambled egg on toast, Mum?'

'Of course, anything you like.'

Full steam ahead on the Pullman

As we thunder through the suburbs to the Sussex coast, we enjoy the best meal we can remember, including Pepsis and all the biscuits we want. An hour after setting off, we arrive at Brighton. The station concourse is packed with people in smart suits carrying binoculars. Janie is no fool. It's the start of the Brighton festival - three days of horse racing beside the sea. We join the queue for a taxi. But we aren't going to the track just yet.

'Grand Hotel, please,' she says to the driver.

'Certainly madam.'

We pull up on the seafront outside this huge, posh Victorian hotel, one of the most expensive in town. If she really is leaving home, she's certainly doing it in style. The foyer is really classy, all velvet and chandeliers. She's pre-booked a first-floor family room overlooking the seafront with a double bed and two singles. We're holidaying in five-star luxury and loving every minute. We can never normally afford such opulence but we sense this is her way to get back at him for all those lonely days and nights. I glimpse an occasional tear in her eyes. The porter takes our cases to the room. In no time, we are on the bus to the racecourse, rolling the Sussex downs which are looking resplendent in the August sunshine.

Janie loves a gamble, and loves to dress up each year for Royal Ascot. She simply idolises Lester Piggott, whose career she's followed from the start. He rode his first winner at the age of 12 to become one of the greatest jockeys of all time. Who can possibly envisage that one day I will be his guest of honour at The Lesters Awards, the racing industry's 'Oscars'.

We collect fistfuls of discarded betting cards on the lawns. It's my first horse racing experience and I've quickly become hooked on the theatre of it all - studying the horses as they parade in the Paddock, the colours of the jockeys' silks, the shouts of the bookmakers as the horses go down to the start, the roar of the crowd inside the final furlong. I cheekily sneak behind the scenes. No-one seems bothered with this seven-year-old in shorts wandering inside forbidden areas like the paddock and the unsaddling enclosure. I hover within earshot of connections, listening to the trainers' pre-race instructions and the excuses from frustrated jockeys as they dismount after a race.

Me and mum at Brighton

The smartest putters on the seafront!

The next day is again sunny and hot. Before racing she takes us to play pitch and putt on the front. Afterwards, sweating and desperate for a cold drink, we go into a little café next door.

'Right, boys what do you want?' she asks.

'Pepsi…'

'Me too…'

The man opens the fridge and pulls out a single bottle of Pepsi Cola, opens it, and puts it on the counter.

'That's the last one, I'm afraid,' he says. With that Johnny snatches the bottle from the counter, declaring that since he's the eldest, it's therefore his.

'No it ain't,' I shout, and grab the bottle from him. We engage in a rowdy tug of war, during which the bottle flies through the air and smashes to the ground, spraying frothy liquid and broken glass over the café floor. We've never seen Mum so ashamed and angry.

But worse is to come. Back at the hotel, suitably scolded, she sends us to the room to clean up. To calm down, she orders herself a pot of tea and sits alone in the lounge reading the newspaper.

Unfortunately the row over the Pepsi continues… first in the room and then spilling out into the corridor. At the top of the famous elegant staircase we fight. We bear-hug each other and roll down the twisting staircase still scrapping. At the bottom, a porter emerges and separates us. Mum witnesses it all but hides behind her paper, distancing herself and hoping that no-one will notice that these vagabonds actually belong to her. After a few moments she eventually gets up and asks if we are all right. She gives us a 'caring' rub of our heads, disguising a tug of our earlobes, causing us to wince in pain.

We rolled down the stairs of The Grand in a bear hug

Outside, whilst we stand silent and contrite, she cries her eyes out. Her world has fallen apart. Her husband has let her down, and now her kids have shown her up beyond measure, having learned none of the good manners she's always tried to drum into them. And instead of going to the races she checks out. We go home on the train - a regular British Rail service this time, the Pullman adventure consigned to history.

Before the scrap… posing at a litter bin

16

Good Old Sport

Aristotle said *'Give me a child until he is seven and I will show you the man.'* For me, at least, he's right. Growing up in and around the kiosk, I'll become hooked on news, learning and absorbing more and more as the world changes day by day. Newspapers are Britain's main source of information and we sell more copies per capita than anywhere else in the world. In the next decade or so I'll witness developments in the Cold War, the Space Race, the Berlin Wall, and the Cuban Missile Crisis which will take the world to the brink of Armageddon. The daily headlines will reflect world conflict - in Vietnam and at home in Northern Ireland; disasters like the tragedy of Aberfan when a mud slide kills 116 children and 28 adults at a village school. Culturally too, I'll see massive change particularly in fashion and music. Crooners will morph into Country, Rock into Roll. Move over Bing and Ella here come the Beatles and Elvis. I'll be at the birth of the James Bond movies, BBC-2, colour TV, motorways, the mini car and the mini skirt. All chronicled daily in the tabloids and broadsheets.

I'm learning the lyrics of every Top Twenty song through the Record Song Book. I also get to read comics for free. They arrive in bundles each week ready to be saved for customers to pick up or be delivered on the paper round. I have a sneak read beforehand so effectively our punters are getting second-hand goods. The choice is vast. I don't go much on the more text-laden adventure publications such as the Eagle or the Hotspur. I prefer the simpler and more entertaining comic strips of the Beano, the Dandy, Beezer and Topper. How much of my early impressionable character is being moulded by the deeds and antics of Roger the Dodger and Dennis the Menace?

Dennis is the archetypal badly-behaved schoolboy. The recurring storylines glorify his reign of terror and bullying of 'softies' (effeminate, well-behaved lads like Walter the Softy). And it's true I'm starting to pick on such kids at school. Roger meanwhile gets through life by avoiding responsibility and his parents' rules, or simply making chores easier, with the help of his 'dodge' book.

Then there's Winker Watson, the school wrangler, constantly playing tricks and avoiding unpleasant school activities. I mimic one of his pranks by 'accidentally' spilling invisible ink down the gleaming white shirt of a fellow pupil. He starts crying at the horrendous blue stains and I say 'Don't worry, it's invisible. It'll disappear!' It does - but leaves a lemon stain ingrained in the fabric rendering it unwearable. My mum has to buy the boy a new shirt and she is not best pleased. I even try a Winker-type scam on the comic publishers! Buster comic has a humour section where if you make him laugh with a gag you win a pound. For a year I copy out the published jokes in a notebook and after a suitable time lag post them back to the comic as my own work. But the joke is on me. They never once publish any of the recycled entries and I waste pounds of my pocket money on stamps. I figure they must have some wizened editor with a memory like Dumbo the elephant.

Other characters I like are Minnie the Minx, a wild tomboy version of Dennis the Menace and carrying the same catapult in her pocket and dressed in an identical red and black hooped jersey. Then there's the Wild West's Desperate Dan, the world's strongest man, who feasts on cow pie, is able to lift a cow with one hand and sports a beard so tough he shaves with a blowtorch. The Numskulls, the adventures of tiny human-like technicians who live inside people, running and maintaining their bodies and minds, will live with me forever. Dining out in later life I will imagine the brain controller ringing down to the stomach team warning that an avalanche of pasta and wine is about to descend on them and to get in extra men with shovels. And, bizarrely, even invading my head during sex... at the critical moment the brain numskulls releasing the blood-flow valve thus sending the signal to the procreation team to crank up the weapon and prepare to fire.

But it's not just boys' comics. With a hint of voyeurism I flick through Bunty and Judy and notice a completely different editorial agenda. Their content is more mature wholesome adventures and girl-next-door stories touching on fashion and teen idols. There are cookery tips and cut-out patterns for dolls clothes. Boys are expected to be rough and tough. Swotting is for cissies, while girls are encouraged to be gentle and creative. To what extent is my inevitable boyhood sexism being fashioned by such stereotyping? One customer orders Jackie, aimed at teenage girls, carrying pull-out pictures of pop stars and discussing matters that are 'below the waist'. Certainly, the letter pages are an eye-opener to this nine-year-old as to how the bodies of the other half work. Baffled and appalled, I'm having my first rudimentary sex-education.

Sport has become a consuming passion. Aided by unfettered access to The Sporting Life, statistics are an obsession - scanning the tables of the winning jockeys, who's trained the most winners, which owner has won the most money, the batting and bowling averages, and of course the football league and county cricket championship tables. I take advantage of special offers from the comics and magazines to make my own football league tables - cardboard ladders where you can slot any team to make them top or bottom of the table. I know the colours of virtually every team in the Football League and some away strips too.

The Grand National is another fixation. Dad tells me about the Queen Mother's horse Devon Loch, who when I was three slipped up yards from the winning line when looking the certain winner. 'Bent as a nine bob note,' he says. He trusts nobody outside his circle and sees conspiracies in everything. But sometimes he's proved right. Nicolaus Silver has just become the first grey horse in living memory to win the National. And there's a dramatic story about that. Before the race his stable had heard rumours of a doping plot so switched another grey into the horse box overnight. It's turned out that the substitute animal has indeed been 'got at' and will never race again.

I know every winner dating back to the war - Mr What, Oxo (who Mum backed because she used to work there) and Merryman etc; the names of each fence - Becher's Brook, The Canal Turn, Valentine's Brook, and The Chair in front of the stands. I've even memorised the height and the depth of drop of them all on the landing side. I play the fool, pretending to ride the winner on the kitchen chair using string for reins, a cushion for a saddle and a stick for a whip. To look the part I wear my brother's school cap. Mum thinks all this is hilarious and I acknowledge her applause by doffing my cap to the imagined gallery on the way back to the 'weighing room' - my bedroom.

My imagination has no limits. If I'm not scoring the winning goal in the Cup Final, I'm hitting the winning runs at Lords, bowing to the crowd who are going frantic. Cricket has become a great love. We live just a mile or so from the what is the home of Surrey County Cricket Club and the host of Test Matches against the likes of Australia and the West Indies, collecting the autographs of Ritchie Benaud and Gary Sobers. Extraordinary to think that one day I will play there and score a hundred. This is a golden era for Surrey who, along with Yorkshire, are dominating the County Championship.

We walk through the backstreets with our sarnies and drinks in our bags and arrive at the bustling ground. People are streaming out of The Oval tube station. Johnny calls bunking-in 'jibbing'. And The Oval is, as he terms it, 'a walk over', with doddery old men on the gate. We wait for the opposition bus and when they open the main gate, we blindside the harassed gateman and slip in the ground on the other side of the vehicle.

I will never forget the thrill of seeing that wide expanse of green for the first time, then sitting on the grass between the stands and the boundary edge; the players in their cream flannels; how fast they bowl and how hard they hit the ball with a resounding 'thwack' as leather hits willow. During the lunch interval we explore behind the scenes… bunking into the pavilion, and sneaking right to the top of the stand behind the bowler's arm. It's a magical view. You can see beyond the famous gasholder right across the London skyline to Big Ben.

I revel in heroes and heroism and scour the back pages for the stories behind the headlines. It's the beginning of the age of personality and some of the finest sports men and women emerge in this era - people like the Surrey and England batsman Ken Barrington, the fiery fast bowler Freddie Truman, and the shy, quiet assassin Lester Piggott who with late runs hunts opponents down in the final furlong and overtakes them on the line.

It is the golden age of commentators too. Peter O'Sullevan, in horse racing, Dan Maskell's 'ooh I say' understated tennis commentaries, Murray Walker's high-octane description of motor sport. On the radio, John Arlott dreams up phrases that transport me straight to the wicket, and Eamonn Andrews who brings boxing alive for this young lad listening under the bed covers.

Like most young kids, football is my main love. And I'm ready to go to my first match. But there's no-one to take me. Johnny, who's now at secondary school, is having none of it. I mean, who wants to have their little brother tagging along, cramping their style? He finds me irritating. I've learned a number of advertising jingles from the telly and sing them all the time, delivered in a whiny voice to wind him up, especially at meal times.

'Mum… Johnny's going off round the world.
A million housewives every day
Pick up a tin of beans and say Beanz Meanz Heinz.'

His favourite punishment is to chase me around the house and pin me down on the floor, his weight preventing me from moving. He hovers over me and dribbles, sucking the spit back in just before it drops to my face. Often he's too late and I get a gob full.

'MUM!!!!!'

He punches me for being a snitch and then I say without realising the irony. 'I'm telling… You just called me a snitch.'

However, I won't be silenced. There's a novelty song doing the rounds called Football Crazy sung by two Scottish blokes. I put my own spin on the lyrics.

'Oh, I'm football crazy
I'm football mad
And I've never seen a football match
And that makes me very sad.
And it would take a dozen skinnies
My kit to wash and scrub
Since Johnny became a supporter
Of some terrible football club.'

Eventually the pressure pays off and he agrees to take me to a match, but only after shrewdly negotiating extra pocket money for the cost and added responsibility of having me on his plate. He decides we'll go to Dulwich Hamlet, a semi-professional team who play in the Isthmian League. He blags five bob from the till for the fares and our admission and, if there's enough money left, a snack at half time. Before leaving he lays down the rules.

'Keep schtum. And don't tell Mum and Dad anything that goes off. Understand?' I nod my head in agreement.

Hamlet play in a small stadium at Dog Kennel Hill, East Dulwich, a 15-minute bus ride from our house. A 176 will take us straight there. However, we get on the first bus that comes along going in the direction of Camberwell Green. He insists we go upstairs even though it's just half a mile tops. After two or three stops the conductor appears.

'Two halves for the Elephant and Castle, please,' says John. Now, even I know that the Elephant is in completely the opposite direction to Camberwell Green but obey his orders to act dumb and not say a word.

'You're going the wrong way, son. The Elephant is back there,' the ticket man says, pointing backwards.

'Oh, no. Quick Al. We need to get off.' Johnny rings the bell and we're off at the next stop. Without paying. We've had a free ride to Camberwell Green. We wait ten minutes or so for the 176 which will take us directly to the ground. We go upstairs again. We pass King's College Hospital and the Salvation Army Centre and then the ticket guy appears again. Johnny employs the same ruse.

'Two halves for Camberwell Green, please.'

'Wrong way,' he says. This time he rings the bell and we disembark. I've now sussed that travelling on the top deck gives us precious extra travelling time and distance before the conductor can bothered to climb the stairs. Out of sight is out of mind.

The ground is only five minutes walk from our premature disembarkation. For a small club there's a surprisingly good gate and I attempt to join the queue at the turnstile. John pulls me back.

'No… follow me.' I trail him to the neighbouring rugby field. We climb a bank until we reach the perimeter of the football ground. There's a wrought-iron fence too tall to climb. But someone has conveniently bent the metal supports wide enough for small frames to squeeze through. We are both in the ground. And we haven't spent a penny!

'Come on, fancy something to eat?' he says. We queue for a Pepsi and a pie. And he's still got a large chunk of the five bob left!

The Hamlet take the field in the strangest kit I've ever seen. Blue and pink SQUARES! How can I ever support these! The match itself, against Tooting and

Mitcham, is rubbish, a boring 0-0. Their goalie, a bloke called Alex Stepney, keeps Hamlet at bay. Not even a goal on my spectator debut. I joke we should ask for our money back. It will be my first and last visit there.

The way home is another freebie. He wants to walk down Camberwell's poshest street - Camberwell Grove, a long tree-lined avenue of grand houses. It's downhill all the way to The Green where we hop on another 'wrong bus' home. Everyone's backed a winner - our parents that we've arrived back safely and not run into trouble; I've had my first expedition with my brother; and he has made a nice little profit. He says he'll take me again.

The invitation comes just a few days later. No doubt spurred by his money-making venture to Dulwich Hamlet, we go to Millwall. We hop on and off buses to The Den, situated off the Old Kent Road. They are playing Workington in the fourth division - a few grades up from Hamlet, but with proper full-time footballers. It's the start of a lengthy relationship with The Lions, as they're called. I will get to know the players' strengths and foibles. Reg Davies, the goalie who it is rumoured has once served time, and who has a propensity to come out at corners and accidentally land a punch on the opposing centre forward on the chin; the cultured skills of wing-half Dave Harper; the Irish Brady brothers at the heart of defence; John 'Skidmore' Gilchrist, a dour former Scottish soldier; winger Joe Broadfoot who skins fullbacks for fun, and who once played a one-two off the perimeter wall to beat an opponent and neither the ref nor linesman spotted that the ball had gone out of play.

Millwall win 5-0. Two days later they have another home game, against Barrow. I run home from school ready for my first night match and it's pouring with rain. Johnny and I want to stand behind the goal that Millwall are attacking but we take cover under the stand. The rain stops and we go down directly behind the goal and shout obscenities at the Barrow goalie. At the final whistle we 'run on' through the mud and puddles. I catch up with their keeper and taunt him rudely about his mistake, calling him butter fingers and adding an expletive or two. Unfortunately, I'm not quick enough running away. He trips me up, sending me sprawling through the mud.

'Serves you right, lad,' he says as he jogs to the dressing room. He's certainly got his revenge and his team-mates love every minute of it too. I go home crying and filthy.

Johnny and I are now constant companions to sports events. Mum and Dad are always generous with pocket money, happy that we're actually going places and not hanging around the streets. I have to watch my step though. My teenage brother loves playing tricks and rejoices in seeing me in tears from one of his pranks.

He takes me to my first Speedway meeting. It's at New Cross stadium, backing on to The Den. You can see Millwall's floodlights from the track, one of the tightest in England and nicknamed the 'Frying Pan'. Dad warns us it's a dangerous sport and I'm to stand well back. There are no brakes. He tells us about a rider called Tom Farndon who was killed after crashing through the air and landing over the track perimeter during a race.

It's the home of the New Cross Rangers in their livery colours of orange and black.

'They're no mugs,' says Johnny. 'They've got Barry Briggs, a world champion, and Split Waterman, a runner up,' he says. Now suddenly I'm a speedway expert.

We arrive well in time for the first race. Johnny scours the stadium perimeter looking for an unlocked door. Only when he's satisfied there's absolutely no other way in than via the turnstiles will we pay. We go inside. Before the riders take to the track he buys me a pie and a drink and tells me to stand on the start line to get the full experience. I'm surprised there's no one else on what must be the prime viewing spot. The riders, two from each team, take their positions at the starting gate. Any second now the bikes will go full throttle, the tape will fly, and in an explosion of noise and excitement my first speedway race will be underway. There's a crescendo of revving, the wire goes up and the bikes zoom away creating a plume of dust. But I've made a schoolboy error. I'm now covered head to waist in black soot and cinder. My tea has turned to a sand soup and the pie is covered in grit. Both are inedible. The fans all around me are wetting themselves. I look around for Johnny. He's safely standing ten yards back laughing his head off. I've been well and truly stitched.

We become regulars. New Cross are in the National League and one of the top teams in the country. Briggs and Waterman become our heroes. But our speedway craze won't last. The team will be disbanded, the greyhounds will stop running and the stadium will be demolished. After retirement, Split Waterman will be convicted of gold smuggling and firearms offences with supposed links to the Kray Twins. For such a daredevil rider he will however live to a ripe old age, before passing away in his Spanish villa four years short of his century.

***

Lights is one of South London's faces. He's friendly with hundreds of faces from growing up in Camberwell, running flower and fruit stalls at markets; the kiosk; taking bets, and old lags from prison. There are often favours to be repaid, debts to be honoured.

It's mid-September, a Wednesday night. I arrive home from school as Dad comes off the phone. He casually asks if I fancy going to the Spurs game tonight. I think he's joking. Tottenham are England's best team and he is always ribbing me about Millwall 'not being worth two bob'. However, he's serious. One of his mates, Bob Wilson, has six season tickets and one of the men can't go. Do I want to use

84

the ticket? 'Not half!' He tells me to snatch some tea and to wrap up warm. Bob is picking me up at half five.

Spurs are the English champions and are in this year's European Cup. Last week they played the Polish champions Gornik Zabrze, a hostile, bruising affair. Spurs had been 4-0 down but made a rally with two late goals. Then a crunching tackle by their hardman Dave Mackay had angered the opposition and the crowd. At one point the Spurs players feared for their safety.

Uncle Bob, as I now must call him, picks me up dead on time, and I squeeze politely into the back of his van between three strangers. As we trundle through the London traffic I realise I've never been north of the river and don't even know where Tottenham is.

Outside the stadium is bedlam. The gates are already locked but with our season-tickets, access is easy. These must surely be the best seats in the house - high above the halfway line and cushioned! The atmosphere is electric and the noise goes up more decibels when Les Allen hits the bar after only 30 seconds. The ground erupts when Spurs take the lead on the night through a Blanchflower penalty. After half an hour they are level on aggregate from a Cliff Jones header. The football is fast flowing. Spurs are running riot. They win 8-1 - and this will remain one of the finest performances by a British club in Europe. The 64,000 crowd sing Glory, Glory Hallelujah and Spurs Go Marching On. Never mind lowly Dulwich Hamlet and Millwall. I've witnessed a vintage display of world class football.

One of our party, Pete, has a familiar face. But I can't place him and it's nagged away at me all night. At the Elephant he's dropped off and we all say goodnight. As the car pulls away Bob says to me, 'Do you know who that was?' I shake my head. 'It's Peter Cook, the comedian, you know Pete and Dud?' Of course! Every time the duo are on telly I will think of that 'glory glory' night and how I'd brushed shoulders with one of Britain's great comics. I get home and in bed boast to Johnny about my experience.

'8-1! And I met Peter Cook.'

'Yeah, sure you did.'

Spurs in Europe

Wrestling is our next joint venture - at Camberwell Baths and Manor Place Baths where in winter they cover the main swimming pool with wooden flooring and stage boxing and wrestling. Johnny first takes me to see his PE teacher in action who is also a professional wrestler. Local Camberwell lad and villain of the ring is Mick McManus who becomes a huge star of the sport which has its own slot on Saturday afternoons on ITV.

But our favourite is Billy Two Rivers, the first real life 'injun' I've ever seen outside cowboy and indian films. This is proper. Warpaint in the flesh. In colour too. Two Rivers was born on an Indian reservation near Quebec. He's a great showman, sporting a Mohawk hairstyle and a feathered headdress. After entering the ring he performs a war dance and scares us kids shitless circling the ring making an Indian war cry, his hands cupped to his mouth…

Wooh, wooh, wooh, wooh echoes around the hall.

17

Hit and Run

After another week away in Leysdown, Nan and Bill journey home. Approaching Camberwell Green they rise from their seats. They are weary from travel and the conductor helps them off with their bags. They need to get another bus back to 104 - the last leg of a three-hour journey. It is late and traffic is light. But as Nanny Jane crosses the road she is knocked down by a car.

King's College Hospital is just up the road and she's taken by ambulance in a coma. An X-ray reveals a fractured skull. It appears at first that she might in time make a recovery. However, a few days later the phone rings at home. It is Mum's brother, Uncle George. I watch as Mum's demeanour changes in just a few seconds. It is obvious it's bad news. She puts the phone down and bursts into tears.

'My mum's had a relapse,' she blurts out to no-one in particular. I don't know what the word means but I know enough to realise it's serious. The bruising has damaged her brain and she is now critically ill. She's been transferred to Cane Hill Hospital in Coulsdon, Surrey, a specialist centre for brain injuries.

Maybe she realises how life-threatening her condition is because she requests for me to visit her. The hospital building is isolated in the countryside in wooded grounds inside a brick boundary and looks scary even from the outside. I hold Mum's hand walking to the ward, passing a few psychiatric patients shouting and screaming in the corridors which frightens me to death. But nothing prepares me for the shock of seeing my beloved Nan. I don't recognise her. She looks 20 years older than her 66 years. She has no teeth in and her grey hair stands on end as if she is suffering an electric shock. She's conscious, but seems out of it, staring at the ceiling, in her own distorted world.

But as soon as she sees me her face changes. She always calls me her favourite grandchild I suppose because we lived in the same house.

'Oh… my darling Alan's here,' she shouts at the top of her voice. The very tone reveals her brain damage. It's screechy. And VERY loud. She becomes excitable and manic. 'Give us a hug, I'm so pleased to see you.'

To my eternal shame I just can't. I'm scared. I stay rooted to the spot hanging onto Mum for dear life. This nine-year-old just can't deal with what has happened, process where I am, and what I'm seeing. This isn't my Nan. The Nan I knew has gone, replaced by some strange demented person. All I can do is force a shy smile.

Nan dies two days later on the 20th September 1962. Her death certificate records that she developed bronchopneumonia *following cerebral contusion and fracture of the skull, injuries sustained when struck by a private motor car whilst crossing a public highway*. A subsequent inquest returns a verdict of accidental death, although there were rumours that the woman driving the car had been drinking.

Jane Elizabeth Hill, widow of George Joseph Hill, mother of six, and grandmother of 15, the Matriarch of the family, has left us. My mother will cry for days, yet as much as I dearly loved her, I cannot shed a tear. To me, it's just something that has happened, a horror story to be filed away in the back of my mind for protection. Maybe I had silently grieved seeing her that day in hospital.

In family tradition, she is laid out in an open coffin in her bedroom. Over the next few days streams of visitors come to pay their respects. Curiosity nags away at me. And, inquisitive as ever, I want to see what a dead body looks like. It is night time and in the darkness I creep up to her room. I stand outside her bedroom door for what seems like an age, bracing myself for what I am about to witness, summoning up the courage to go in. A pungent odour hits me as I open the door. Mum will explain later it is embalming fluid used to preserve the body.

I tip-toe towards her. She is perfectly still. Asleep. Serene. At peace from the tormented soul I'd seen in that psychiatric hospital. I stare at her for possibly two or three minutes, waiting for her to move, to wake up and shout that it is all been one huge prank.

The funeral is a massive affair. There are six siblings to share the cost and no expense is spared to give her the right send off. In South London there's only one man to sort the funeral - Alf Smith. There'd actually been a line of Alf Smiths dating back to Victorian times. The original was a hatbox maker who lost one of his 22 kids and thought he could do a better job than the local undertaker. His sons, Alf and Henry, survived him in the business and were followed by their sons, also Alf and Henry. They built the business across South London and became noted for their Dutch-bred Friesian horses, appropriately jet black from head to hoof. When all funerals were horse-drawn, 40-odd stallions and geldings were stabled at the firm's yard in Kennington. Nan would always follow the horses with a bucket and spade to collect manure for the garden even though she rarely grew anything.

Nanny Jane is carried in a motorised hearse adorned with wreaths arranged in the letters Nan, and Mum. The cortège - 13 limos - blocks Camberwell Road for half an hour. Alf is a showman, clad head to toe in black, imperiously strutting at the head of the procession looking like Frankenstein in top hat and tails and leather gloves with a hint of white powder on his face. I am deemed too young to go the funeral but I watch as the cortège pulls away from the house at snail's pace - Alf walking with a stick, nodding solemnly to pavement mourners who doff their caps in respect. They've gone about fifty yards when horror suddenly dawns on me. For several hours I will be Home Alone with no money for Pie and Mash. I chase after the cortège and catch up with the lead car. Mum is sobbing under her black veil. I bang on the window and tell her of my predicament. My uncles and aunts look at me aghast. Someone throws two half-crowns out of the window. Pie and Mash money. Now, like my Nan, I am at peace with the world.

Nan as a girl (far right) and just before she died

18

After Nan

Janie can't understand why the Lord has taken her dear Mum. And in such tragic circumstances too. She is about to get her answer. Because we are all convinced we're gonna die any day now - in a nuclear war.

Keeping abreast with the news - via the kiosk and Dad's endless radio bulletins - is part of my daily routine. I'm aware there's something called a Cold War going on between the United States and the USSR. Eighteen months ago I'd marvelled at the bravery of Soviet astronaut Yuri Gagarin who became the first man in space when he orbited the earth in a rocket and landed back in a parachute. The next month an American piloted a rocket 116 miles into space. These could have been heroic adventures in the Eagle and Hotspur comics - but they were real. Now suddenly the rivalry between the Superpowers is extending beyond a mere space race.

Two months ago, the Soviets had erected a wall of barbed wire and concrete between East and West Germany. And now there's a far more sinister and frightening conflict that threatens to escalate into a full-scale nuclear war. The Americans have deployed nuclear missiles in Italy and Turkey and trained a paramilitary force of Cuban exiles to invade Cuba and overthrow the Communist dictator Fidel Castro. To protect their ally, the Soviets have begun building nuclear launch-pads on the island which is only 90 miles from the US coastline. President Kennedy has ordered a naval blockade to prevent further missiles reaching Cuba. He also insists that nuclear weapons already there be dismantled and returned to the USSR. The Soviet leader Khrushchev is having none of it.

The TV news reports every development and is full of images snapped by US spy planes of secret ballistic missile facilities on Cuba, and American and Soviet warships steaming towards each other. Archive footage of mushroom clouds do not help ease our anxiety. World War Three is imminent. And nuclear missiles stationed in East Germany can reach Britain. Everyone is terrified. I come home from school. ITV News has a headline over aerial footage of US war ships saying 'K Warns K'. Mum and Dad refuse to even discuss the crisis. But you can sense their concern. The world holds its breath for two weeks. Then, at last a diplomatic solution. The Soviets will stop their Cuba missile construction and America will quietly withdraw its weapons in Italy and Turkey. Sorted.

***

Battersea Fun Fair is becoming a frequent destination during school holidays. We go on the bus and walk to Battersea Park. You can see the John Collins Big Dipper in the distance towering above the trees. Our walk takes us past the famous Battersea Dogs Home and the constant yapping of the strays. We spend most of the day inside the fair, on the rides, the attractions and in the amusement arcades, being seduced by the aroma of freshly-made toffee apples and doughnuts.

I go on The Rotor, a giant cylinder which spins so fast it sucks you to the wall... and then the floor drops away leaving you stuck and stranded ten feet above the ground. The force is such that you can't control the dribble rushing from your mouth and it sticks to your face. Some of the females make schoolgirl errors going on in skirts which sail above their heads flashing their knickers for all to see.

We've perfected the Horserace Derby where you roll wooden balls up the ramp aiming for the central hole that makes your horse travel further and faster than the rest. Rather than rely on luck, we lean over and place the balls in when the operator isn't looking and earn a prize. Another attraction is to try to knock the lady out of bed. You throw three wooden balls at a plate. If you hit the middle button a loud bell rings. Everyone stops because they know that in the next moment or two a scantily-clad woman will be sprung into the air from her slumber.

But the main draws are the white-knuckle rides - the Big Dipper and the Water Chute. Johnny always finds a way around long queues with me a few strides behind. A favourite ruse is to pretend we've been to the toilet and that our parents are further up. We time our arrival just as revellers are jostling for the best position at the front of the train. At the end of a ride instead of getting off and heading for the exit we simply nip into another carriage for a free go and keep going until we get sussed.

As we shriek and laugh, how can we possibly tell that we will be the last generation to enjoy the fun of this fair? A decade later five children will die when a train on the roller coaster comes off its tracks. The rope hauling the ride to the top of the wooden structure will snap and because of a faulty brake, the carriages will hurtle backwards out of control. They will jump the tracks and crash through a barrier. One girl will escape - only to plunge to her death through a rotting wooden staircase.

A report will find 51 faults on the ride. The manager and engineer will be tried and acquitted of manslaughter. The fair will close a year later. And, as I write this fifty years on, the survivors will still be campaigning for a permanent memorial to the incident.

***

Nan's passing has left a huge hole in the running of the household. In addition to losing a loving and supportive mother, Mum has lost a companion, cleaner, babysitter and cook. Sadly, Nanny Jane hasn't passed on her culinary skills to her daughter. It hurts me to say this, but Mum is possibly the worst cook in the world. Meat is cooked to a dry frazzle and the vegetables all taste the same - the result of being boiled into a mush together in single one pot. Her 'signature' dish is meat pudding, made up of acres of suet tied to a bowl with string. I only eat the meat and gravy. To give her some credit she cooks a mean apple pie, served with Bird's custard and Wall's ice cream, but littered with black cloves which we don't really understand the purpose of, and which we pick out and move to the edge of the bowl.

Circumstances force us to eat out a lot. Fish and chips, pie and chips and Wimpy and chips are my favourite, in addition to our beloved pie and mash. Along Camberwell Road there's a café owned by a Greek guy called Michael. It's called The Savoy Grill. Any resemblance to the esteemed establishment in The Strand is merely co-incidental. It's very busy and the waitress doesn't bother writing down the order. She just screams across from the tables to Michael in the kitchen.

'Michael, I want egg on toast twice, three coffees and a meat pie and chips.'

Michael loves Dad, and occasionally treats him to drinks and bacon sandwiches. They do the most delicious sultana and custard puddings which I enjoy two or three times a week. I spend a lot of time on the pinball machine there and have become quite an expert. It hardly costs me sixpence. Someone has helpfully burned through the plastic fascia where the replay dial is. We go in armed with a needle so if we do win a replay we check that Michael isn't watching then jam it into the burn hole so the dial can't move - and continues to show a replay in credit. I play for hours or until an older boy or a man wants a go. I ingratiate myself by 'donating' my replay and surreptitiously removing the needle.

One day two of the totters are sitting in the cafe studying the Sporting Life before racing. What they don't know is that they've been followed and secretly filmed... by a TV crew. Someone has set them up as stooges for a stunt show called Candid Camera. One of the pranksters, Jonathan Routh, has offered them a tenner to deliver a suitcase to an address just up the road near my house. It's heavy and needs a van. They duly agree and transport the case to the empty office. When they get back to the café, Routh turns up again. He's made a mistake with the address, he says, offering them another tenner to shift the case a few doors along. They duly agree. Meanwhile, the programme crew have altered the room dimensions, narrowing the door so that it is impossible to get the case out. There is much effing and jeffing from the totters as they sweat over an impossible task. When the 'reveal' scene is filmed the two explode with rage. The air goes blue and they refuse to sign the consent forms. So that's one prank that backfires.

***

It's Sunday and I'm bored. Johnny is down East Lane with Dad and Mum's in the kiosk. I invent my own 'Smartie Derby' to determine which colour is the most prevalent. I empty fifty or so Smarties tubes onto the kitchen table to form a massive mound of sweets. Hundreds, in eight colours - red, orange. blue, green, yellow, pink, violet and brown. But what colour will win? I sort them into rows. Surprise, surprise, the mix is roughly equal. I declare it a draw. I know I will get into trouble so before anyone comes I frantically funnel them back into the tubes. Many roll over the kitchen floor. I rescue as many as I can, but it's panicky and haphazard. I clip the plastic lids back on and return the sweets to the racks in my room. No-one will be any the wiser... until a few weeks later when a lady complains that the Smarties she'd bought were all brown. Mum assures her she'll mention it to the Rowntree rep - a load of old baloney because there isn't one, at least not for our little enterprise.

19

Robbie Arrives

Mum often feels starved of love and attention. And she's about to go further down the pecking order. Dad turns up with a cuddly companion - a puppy purchased from a farm in Ashtead in Surrey. He's a black and tan Airedale terrier and comes complete with pedigree papers, a printed care plan, vet advice and certificates. We look at each other in astonishment as he arrives cradling this poor little orphan fresh from its mother's teat. Dad christens him Robbie. He creates a comfy quarter for him under the kitchen table, a blanket and basket. The room is already overcrowded and now we have to squeeze another in, and feed another mouth. At meal times I have to sit with my legs on my chair in case I accidentally tread on the dog.

My relationship with 'man's best friend' is already at rock bottom following the Leysdown Jack Russell incident so I try to get off on a peaceful footing. I crawl under the table to stroke him but he bares his teeth, snarls and barks at me. I flee terrified, banging my head on the table. Dad tells me off for invading Robbie's space and frightening him. As far as I am concerned that's it. The end of any potential reconciliation between boy and dog. It had been him or me. And he has won.

Dad smothers him with love and looks after all his needs. Traditional dog food products such as Winalot, Pal and Pedigree Chum aren't considered good enough. Robbie's daily meal is horse meat, purchased from a stall in Westmoreland Road, just outside the pie and mash shop, followed by shortbread biscuits. Dad always buys too much meat and keeps it in the fridge for days. It invariably goes off, causing us to recoil every time we open the fridge door. He boils it for ages, stinking the whole house out, then scrapes off the white scum before cutting it up into Robbie's bowl.

Meal times don't end there. During supper Dad slips another Peak Frean under the table, thinking no-one has seen him. Robbie responds by resting his head on Dad's thigh and looking up forlornly. I can see right through this tactic, but Dad responds with a reward - yet another biscuit. He's rarely taken for a walk and is becoming more and more obese. Unfortunately, the diet of protein and carbs play havoc with Robbie's stomach and breath. He passes the most vile-smelling wind, sometimes responding with a guilty look, but he does bark at the back door when he needs the toilet. It's another reason never to venture in the yard. Occasionally he gets the blame for us humans too.

Me aged 9

Without Nan's presence we have to step up to the plate to help out. Johnny does the paper round before school, whilst I become the errand boy, shopping for essentials, even paying the takings into the bank. It is only a five-minute walk along Walworth Road but I run everywhere - the Forrest Gump of Camberwell. The sight of a lad laden with bags of silver and copper and a wad of notes in his back pocket raises eyebrows among the staff and they reward me with sweets and mince pies at Christmas.

Mum gives me a list for the little supermarket on Westmoreland Road. One day it runs out of Heinz Salad Cream. But Ted Cutler nearby DOES have bottles on his stall outside the pie and mash shop. I try to buy a bottle but he embarrassingly calls me out in front of a load of customers, telling me to go and buy the salad cream wherever I bought the other goods. Mum gives him a roasting next time she sees him.

Another time she isn't best pleased with me either. On her list is 4 x ¼*lb* bags of PG Tips. This is of course four quarter-pound bags of tea. However, I interpret it as four and a quarter pound of tea, a total of… 17 bags. The lady in the shop says,

'That's an awful lot of tea.'

I reply that we are having visitors that weekend. She must have thought it was for a wedding or a funeral. After my clever arithmetic we don't have to buy tea for weeks! Mum thinks (wrongly I might add) that it was all a ruse by me to get the collectors' cards they give away in each packet.

I've developed a very sweet tooth. Growing up in a sweet shop means there's always a Mars Bar or a Crunchie within arm's reach. But you always want what you can't have. And it's sweets in a jar that I lust after. So, on the way home from my errands I spend any loose change in Walkley's on the corner of Albany Road which is stocked to the ceiling with glass containers. There are chocolate eclairs, flying saucers, jelly babies, gummy cola bottles, liquorice, caramel and, just invented, Fry Crème Eggs. Mum's always nagging me to eat fruit despite her own aversion to oranges. She makes sure the bowl is full of Cox's and Jaffas, although no-one eats them. I tell her not to worry… my fruit intake is sherbet lemons, foam bananas, pear drops, pineapple squares, and for pudding, boiled rhubarb and custard sweets!

***

I am about to be bloodied in the kiosk. Not by design, but by accident, or rather a call of nature. I've arrived home from school and Mum is hopping up and down behind the counter.

'I'm bursting - look after the counter for five minutes. If anyone wants anything tell them to wait 'til I get back,' she says, running up the path and into the house.

The News Box counter is high above the pavement and gives a splendid overview of the main road. It is a grey winter afternoon. Rush hour is about to begin. An estimated 40,000 vehicles arrive at Camberwell Green every day and a sizeable percentage pass our house. The Ford Prefects and Austin A30s already have their headlights on, and the London Routemasters beam like spaceships in the mist. A 196 bus going to somewhere called Tufnell Park is half full, a 68 on its way to Chalk Farm is packed. Where are those places?

'Twenny Woodbines, a Standard and a packet of Spangles.'

Almost out of nowhere a man in a donkey jacket and blue and white Millwall bobble-hat appears on the pavement below, shifting from foot to foot, and blowing warm breath into his cupped hands. He stares up at my paralysed frame. 'C'mon, son. I ain't got all day.'

I politely explain that Mum will be back any second; that I'm not allowed to serve anyone; don't know any of the prices; can hardly add up anyway, and am forbidden to touch the till. The customer is having none of it.

'… S'easy. Two bob the fags; tuppence the paper; and the sweets a penny. That's two and three. If I give you half a crown, you've gotta give me thruppence change.'

I'm in a pickle. If I don't serve him, he might never come back. But if I <u>do</u>, what will Mum say? I start with the paper. I look down at the display of mastheads. On top, are the two evenings - The News and The Standard.

Next, the fags. My eyes scan the display. Players, Senior Service, Capstan Full Strength. The packaging is works of art, ships, seagulls, weathered sailors. Packets of 20s, 10s, and 5s - some shops sell singles, even to kids, but Lights and Janie have always refused. And there, right at the end, the distinctive green and brown branding of Woodbines, the staple cigarette of the working classes.

The sweets are easy. Cadbury's Dairy Milk chocolate, golden honeycomb bars of Crunchies, Love Hearts with their daring messages, Opal Fruits that make your mouth water, and Mars Bars that help you work, rest and play. I reach for the Spangles and put them on the counter. He hands over a half crown and I rummage through the dirty wooden till for three pennies. The man picks them up, puts the fags and sweets in his pocket, folds the paper under his arm and disappears.

96

Janie arrives back looking suitably relieved. I get in first and explain the whole transaction, including how cross the bloke had got.

'Sounds like grumpy Gordon. He complains about everything - bus fares, the Government, the council... ' I show her the half crown. 'Hold out your hand,' she says. I wait, not knowing if I am in for a throttle or a hug. Instead she gives me the coin. 'It's yours. You've earned it.' I run indoors and find my cardboard shoe box under the bed. It's where I squirrel away any spare cash and other treasured possessions, such as the left-handed italic fountain pen Nan had bought me.

I've completed my first paid job - an acting temporary stand-in assistant - and I've served my first customer. And received my first pay. All at the grand old age of nine. Tomorrow I will go to the newsagents on the corner of Wyndham Road and put the money in my firework club account. Every October that corner shop is transformed into firework heaven with display cabinets full of rockets, bangers, Catherine wheels, squibs, roman candles, jumping jacks, crackers, fountains and sparklers. Some of the expensive high-end giant rockets are connected by detonator wire and hang on the wall. Every kid eyes them with envy.

Johnny has been out asking for a penny for the guy for the last fortnight, plotting down at the bus stop fifty yards from the house. He's commandeered Mum's pram and stuffed my old trousers with rolled up newspaper. He uses the same Guy Fawkes mask and hat from one year to the next. He's got quids in the firework club - but will only buy bangers. In their hundreds. These are rolled up like rounds of sniper bullets and held in place by elastic bands. There are too many to cram into his jacket and trouser pockets. Dad calls him a mug.

'You must have money to burn,' he says without realising the pun.

Mum is nervous. Last year a local lad David Cross suffered a badly burned foot when a banger landed in his welly. He had only seconds to get the boot off, hopping around like mad, but he didn't make it. BANG! Crossy ended up in Casualty, treated along with scores of other Camberwell burns victims on the most dangerous night of the year.

It's now Bonfire Night. And Mum comes up with an idea. Johnny must take me along with him. She finds an old shirt box. Johnny reluctantly puts his bundles of bangers in the box, which Mum secures with king-size elastic bands, crossed in each direction. I'm now the official Hurndall firework carrier and supplier, and walk around with the box under my arm.

There are no organised displays. Living where we do, surrounded by so many demolition sites, the adults try to outdo each other to see who can build the biggest bonfire mountain. Combustibles are stuffed between giant triangular prisms of wood. As we start our rounds, scores of fires light the autumn sky. Smoke and embers fill the air and there is the stench of gunpowder everywhere. I'm itching to light our supplies but Johnny says, 'Wait and watch the others first.'

So we flit from site to site enjoying the oohs and aahs and the booms and bangs.

Johnny's mates from the nearby Elmington Estate turn up. They've got rockets! One of their number has been grounded and they want to wind him up. We all traipse back to the flats behind Edwardes bike shop on Camberwell Road. I watch as they grab half a dozen milk bottles off random doorsteps and half bury them in the ground at an angle. The kid in question lives on the fifth floor of one of the blocks at the end of the row. His bedroom light is on but the curtains are drawn.

They light one rocket as a tester - but it zooms off dangerously across the estate reaching only head height before colliding with a garage-block wall and exploding with a whimper. They laugh at the excitement of it all. They then adjust the angle of the bottles and light the touchpaper of the other five. I duck behind a parked car. The rockets 'swoosh' in unison and sure enough explode in a blaze of colour ten yards or so from the lad's bedroom window 80 feet up. Curtains are pulled back and people come onto the balconies to investigate. We leg it in the darkness, adrenalin coursing through our veins. Thankfully, even with the box under my arm, I manage to keep up. Everyone's in fits of giggles.

But the drama doesn't end there. I hear a sizzling noise and look down to see smoke coming out of my box. I drop it on the pavement seconds before it bursts into flames and lets off a hundred bangs and whizzes. We leap back in horror as the biggest banger in Camberwell history goes off. In seconds the noise is over and the cardboard box reduced to ashes.

'What did you do?' screams Johnny.

'I didn't do nuffink,' I shout, holding back the inevitable tears. His mates are laughing like mad. We suspect foul play. And we agree not to tell Mum and Dad a single thing about our night of fun.

20

Taking Flight

I'm about to go on my first overseas adventure - if you can call the Channel Islands overseas. Uncle George has offered to take me and Mum on holiday with his family to Jersey. He's the comfortable one in the family, a surveyor with interests in a supermarket and a betting shop. He's already taken Johnny and our senior cousins on a camping trip around Europe and now it's my turn. He picks us up in his cobalt blue Ford Zephyr for the journey to London Airport. My cousin Peter and his sister Janice greet us with glee and excitement, bouncing up and down in their seats.

'Calm down, you lot,' says Aunt Dot. Uncle George is employed by the civil engineering firm Marples Ridgway, who've built the newly opened Chiswick Flyover en route to the airport. As we enter the elevated highway he can't help but boast.

'Beautiful, isn't it! My boss is Ernest Marples. He's the Minister for Transport so we're bound to get more contracts,' he says proudly. In fact Marples' reign would prove controversial, shutting down huge swathes of railways in favour of roads, several of which his company will construct. In time he would be made a Lord and eventually flee to Monaco at very short notice to avoid prosecution for tax fraud.

As we board the British European Airways plane to Jersey I'm full of beans but Mum is apprehensive. It's her first flight too. For some reason she doesn't like being strapped in and spends the whole of the short journey holding, but not fastening, the seatbelt. Emerging from the jet, Peter and I pretend we're the Beatles arriving to some rapturous reception, waving at the imaginary crowd screaming at us from the terminal roof.

Boarding our flight

Hello Jersey! Check out the braces!

It is the start of an idyllic fortnight. We stay on the north of the island at a tiny cove called Greve de Lecq, with its fine sandy beach, huge waves, caves, and views out to the island of Sark. Our guesthouse, the Prince of Wales, is the only holiday accommodation there and we all have rooms with a sea view. During the long summer evenings we have the beach to ourselves. However, on the first night we hear shouting from the car-park.

'GEORGIE, GEORGIE, GEORGIE…'

By a remarkable co-incidence Mum's cousin, 'the Brixton Kid', is staying here too with his partner and their son Danny Guest, whom I know from around Camberwell. They make all the right noises, but brother and sister are not jumping with joy.

'All the same if we wanted to be on our own,' says Georgie. But they're all leaving tomorrow. The grown-ups spend the evening in the bar, with us kids exploring the beach and daring each other to enter the dark caves. We will learn later that our cove is a drop-off point for smugglers and the caves a hiding place for contraband French whiskey. It's like something out of Enid Blyton. The Famous Four. All we're missing is Timmy the dog.

Jersey Boys – me and Peter

Out on the town

Our days are spent frolicking in the waves, blowing up lilos, playing beach football and head tennis, eating ice cream, and crashing out on deck chairs. It's scorching hot and no umbrellas. Luckily the deckchairs have shades which extend over our faces and we wrap towels around our legs and feet.

Brr…Mum and I leave the sea

George has hired a car and we explore the island - the magnificent St Brelade's Bay beach and the capital St Helier. On the road we stumble across an unusual attraction - a one-eyed lion. Simba is billed as the largest lion in Europe and Elizabeth Taylor's bodyguard in the film Cleopatra. Entrance is sixpence and we watch open-mouthed as its trainer enters the cage and feeds him with a cut of meat.

'Would you do that?' we ask each other. NO WAY!!!

Simba 'the largest lion in Europe'

Every August on Jersey they stage the Battle of The Flowers, an event which dates back to the turn of the century. The sun is blazing down and Mum buys us all straw hats for protection. Mine is canary yellow. We take our place in the stands with 50,000 others, cheering and clapping as the parade passes. Dozens of floats adorned with flower creations crawl along the seafront led by a marching band, street entertainers, dancers and majorettes. There's a giant snake and a ladder made from carnations and a cat and mouse of lilies. Shakespeare appears to be this year's theme - Romeo and Juliet toss roses into the crowd from the balcony. Behind them is The Bard himself, sitting aloft a huge display of flowers with the words All The World's A Stage. Finally, 'Miss Battle', the winner of the island's beauty queen competition, blows kisses to the crowd. The pageant ends with a naval helicopter dropping thousands of petals over the spectators. They cover us head to toe and we spit out bits of flowers. We arrive back burned and exhausted and singing Swinging On A Star.

The Pearly King and Queen: where did we get those hats?

On a normal vacation the Battle of The Flowers would have been the highlight, the one event we would remember for a long time. However, something is about to happen that will be talked about in family circles for years. Before leaving England, GEORGIE!!!, as we now refer to him since that opening encounter with his cousin, purchased a cine camera to record the holiday moments. He's terrified of losing it, dropping it, leaving it in a bar, or it being stolen. One day he takes the girls for coffee, leaving us boys on the beach.

'Look after the camera. Don't leave here until we get back,' is his final instruction to his 14-year-old son. At first Peter complies. We play 'keepie uppies' within a few feet of the camera and deckchairs. No-one can possibly steal it without us knowing. Two lads appear on the scene asking to play football. We agree and get involved in a competitive game of attack and defence, gradually moving further away from our base - and the camera. We eventually call time because it's too hot. Then we go to buy a cornet each. To give him his due, Peter hides the camera under a towel. But our timing is unfortunate to say the least. At precisely the moment we leave, the others arrive back to the deserted deckchairs with their drinks. Uncle George flies into a panic.

'Where's the effing camera?' Unaware of the drama, Peter and I nonchalantly stroll into the biggest bollocking either of us have ever suffered. George is ranting and raving that the camera's been nicked and it's all Peter's fault. Peter lifts the towel and there it is… exactly as he'd left it. The argument continues. Peter, who has quite a temper himself, hurls his ice cream at his dad. Unfortunately, his aim is spot on. The cone lands upside down in his dad's cup of coffee. PLOMP!!! George explodes. He chases his son along the beach screaming and shouting and threatening to kill him. It's like a scene out of Benny Hill. All we need is the music. The rest of us look at each other with stern faces. Then, in unison, burst out laughing.

Beep beep: all is forgiven

21

Taking the Michael

Like most kids, we live and breathe football. And our stadium is the local park off Addington Square, just a few hundred yards from my home. Burgess Park, as it's called, is the only bit of green for miles, but we play our games on the brown asphalt. The East Surrey Canal runs alongside the pitch, but the barge traffic has long dried up and the council are gradually draining the water and restoring the grounds. A family of swans lives on the bank. We eye each other suspiciously through the 10 feet high wire mesh fence. If the ball goes over and lands near them, that's it. The word among us lot is they can kill with a single swish of their wings. There are rumours too of a colony of king-size rats that get bigger at every sighting and are ready to bite anyone foolhardy enough to wade into the water to retrieve the ball.

The park is under the stewardship of the head keeper, Grumpy Old Tom. He patrols on his wibbly-wobbly bike, an overweight figure in a jungle bush hat, a brown uniform, hobnail boots, his trousers tucked into his woollen socks and held together with cycle clips. Between his rounds he retires to his cosy little hut, strips down to his braces and vest, and rests in front of the two-bar electric fire with a well-earned a mug of tea. There he sits for hours, peering through the top of the stable-type door, waiting for one of us to ruin his day. He keeps the gardens on Addington Square immaculate, creating circles of daffodils and tulips, but woe betide anyone who walks on the grass. An agonised roar will ring out from the hut.

Ours is a constant battle. We're barred from cycling in the park so we cheekily give him what for as he meanders by on his bike. There used to be two full-size goals on the ash but he had one taken down because it was 'noisy' and flying footballs were a danger to park keepers sitting in the hut! Remember this is a 10 feet high fence! To get back at him we play right in front of the hut, constantly kicking the ball against the fence, and shouting extravagantly at goals and near misses. It must drive him mad.

To him this isn't a workplace, it's his private fiefdom. And visitors, especially urchins like us, are definitely not welcome. God forbid that any of us actually want to *use* the facilities. The swing park, asphalt, and tennis courts are often 'locked' for repair. The only exception is during Wimbledon tennis fortnight when suddenly everyone wants to be the next Rod Laver and he takes two weeks off.

***

So, we're having a kickabout and into this arena steps this scruffy new kid on the block. A Connaught Ranger (stranger) on our territory! He asks if he can play, itself a brave and extraordinary thing to do. In a whispered huddle, we decide he can join the game but only if he goes in goal. Nobody ever wants to be goalie, particularly on asphalt where grazed knees are a certainty. If he wants to play he has to abide by the law of the street kids. The following day he turns up again - this time carrying a brand new Mitre size 5 leather football. Do we want to play with his ball instead? But only on condition he isn't in goal. He's played a blinder and won.

Michael Corbett has come into my life. We will become best mates. His sister will marry my brother. Our parents will become friends too. Throughout our teens we will get into all sorts of scrapes and adventures, selling stuff outside football grounds, bunking in sports venues, film premieres and major concerts. And eventually we'll achieve our boyhood dreams. He'll be a professional footballer, on the books of Charlton Athletic, and I will become a journalist. But one night we'll go out for a drink and then to a party. And only one of us will come home.

Addington Square in more modern times

22

Going to the Dogs

Mum has discovered Bingo. They've closed The Gaumont cinema in Peckham and converted it into a Top Rank Bingo Club. With cinema audiences waning, it's the first of scores of similar establishments all over Britain that will swop John Wayne for 'housey-housey'.

It's a drug. Four nights a week, four books a night, and a couple of Guinnesses to wash down her woes. After locking up, she gets the number 12 bus opposite our house which takes her to and from the Gaumont, as she still calls it. On the 20 bus - and in the breaks between games - she knits, following patterns given away free with My Weekly. She knits at speed, with the needles going like the clappers, drawing the wool up like a conveyor belt from her bag on the floor. Unfortunately the results don't always match the pictures on the patterns.

'Try it on,' she says, having completed yet another woolly jumper. The sleeves are adult extra large and the body would fit only a toddler. Maybe her mind is on the Bingo numbers instead.

It's costing a pretty penny but the prize money is good. And she is having some luck. If she wins, she wakes us up and we rush down in our pyjamas to witness the ritualistic emptying of the envelope onto the kitchen table. More often though it's a loser's lament - 'I only needed one number for a full house.' On the box is an American cop series called the Naked City, which always concludes with the narrator saying, 'There are eight million stories in the Naked City. This has been one of them.' Whenever Mum has a Bingo hard luck story Dad puts on an American accent and repeats that line to her.

'You won't be taking the piss when I win the jackpot,' she says.

She's met a whole new gang of mates. 'The Bingo Mob', Dad calls them - all women of a similar age, complaining about their other halves, celebrating their occasional wins and bemoaning their luckless losses. She's never been particularly happy with Dad's 'here today, gone tomorrow' philosophy. Putting money aside into a pension pot is the least of his priorities or concerns. Mum came home the other night and told him that one of her recently-bereaved friends had been left 'nice and comfortable' by her late husband. The message was obvious.

'Don't worry, darling. I've made plans to leave you nice and comfortable too,' he replied.

Wow. Does he really have a secret stash squirrelled away somewhere?

'How come?' she asked him.

'You'll have my pillows…'

***

One of the consequences of her Bingo craze is that I'm now Home Alone in an empty cold house. So Dad has begun taking me greyhound racing at New Cross Stadium. There's a song out at the moment by Joe Brown and the Bruvvers with the opening line *'Dad's gone down the dog-track, mother's playing Bingo... '* It could almost have been written about us…

He's lost his regular companion - his 15-year-old son - who's about to leave school and prefers the company of his mates. Johnny's schooling has been the subject of much strife in our household. He is forever hopping the wag, often with Dad's connivance and encouragement.

'You won't earn a living sitting in school,' he would say.

One teacher wrote in Johnny's report that he couldn't comment on his progress because he didn't know who he was. Once Mum was so fed up she took him to school in a taxi. When the cab pulled away Johnny got the bus home! Dad takes him to afternoon meetings at dog tracks like Walthamstow and Wimbledon where they swear blind he's 18 - then in the evening to New Cross, where under 13s are free, so he pretends he's an early-maturing 12-year-old.

It's Thursday night. Dog night. I arrive home from school with a spring in my step. Dad's greyhound gang are a gaggle of colourful local totters headed by Robbo who has a huge waist and weighs 20-odd stone. 'Peggy' Birchmore is another. He has a scrap metal yard beside the railway arches at the back of our house and gets his nickname because of his wooden leg. It is rumoured he once briefly lost it in the sea during a South London beano to the coast.

Then there's Nuckham, a loud gregarious character, with a voice like a foghorn. His real name is Billy Bungay. You always know what dog Nuckham is on from the cacophony of ear-piercing screeching at the final bend. According to his daughter Patti, he acquired the name Nuckham after losing his front teeth. He could no longer pronounce the 'F' word, telling people to 'Nuck off you Nucking bastards.' On another beano, Nuckham once chinned someone from a different coach for trying to nick their beer. The Camberwell bus was escorted out of town by the police.

Another regular, Terry, would be here tonight but he's doing six months. He's one of Dad's best mates. They've often walk home together 'potless'. 'Collars up, back to base,' they would say with a resigned smile, leaving the stadium for the trek though the backstreets of South East London. A few weeks ago Terry went skint and in a fit of desperation raided a bookie's 'hod' - the satchel where they keep the money. Lights had tried to talk him out of it, but he wouldn't listen. Terry waited until the race was halfway through then plunged his hands in the bag and legged it out the stadium. The bookie let out an almighty cry and mayhem ensued. He was caught by two cops in a Panda running along the Old Kent Road. Dad volunteered to break the news of his arrest to his missus - not an enviable task since she was very volatile and once emptied all her husband's washing, including his dirty smalls, on the floor of the saloon bar of The Castle on the corner of Wyndham Road.

'There you go. Maybe they'll do your washing in 'ere an all.' When he gets out he will forever be branded Terry The Hod.

***

Tonight Nuckham picks us up in his van. Dad sits in the front and I squeeze in the back sitting on the spare tyre. All around me is grime - the detritus of 15 years of rag and bone collection, scrap metal, bits of steel, bundles of copper wire, old tools, and mounds of rust. The first time I'd been in the van I ended up with an oil stain on my fawn overcoat that never came off. Mum gave it away to a charity shop and I saw the new owner down Westmoreland Road with the tell-tale black ring on his bottom. So now, I cover the wheel with an old bed sheet. Tonight, though, I have a fellow passenger in the back. His name is Yorkie, and he's possibly the lightest and smallest man I've ever met. Even jockeys look down on him.

We pick him up outside a pub on Southampton Way near the Samuel Jones 'Camberwell Beauty' factory. Yorkie enters via the rear doors and is surprised to see me. Nuckham turns around.

'Hope you two are nice and comfortable in the back there,' he laughs before screeching away from the grid like Stirling Moss. He's a no-nonsense driver. Speed limits are for wimps. Over every pothole the contents of the van leap in the air, we bang our heads on the roof, and hang on for dear life. Halfway down Southampton Way we turn into Commercial Way which leads to the Old Kent Road. From there the dog track is a few minutes away. We approach a humpback bridge over a canal. Nuckham accelerates over the brow, hits a bump in the road, and at 40 miles an hour suddenly the rear doors fly open, depositing Yorkie and a load of tools into the road.

'Oh shit,' says Nuckham, slamming on his brakes. I look back at Yorkie emerging from the debris. He's dazed and confused but miraculously unhurt. His light frame has saved him and he's getting to his feet wondering what on earth has just happened. Nuckham and Dad are now in fits of laughter.

'I didn't know you wanted to be dropped off early,' jokes Dad.

Nuckham chips in… 'Have you seen that film, Bridge On the River Kwai?'

Nuckham parks in roughly the same spot every meeting - in the tiny side streets. The ritual is the same. A kid will appear from the shadows and in a plaintive voice offer to look after the van. He's shivering even though it's summer. Dad is a sucker for any kid in distress and treats them generously. They instinctively know it's better to tap him before rather than after racing when the mood swing will have kicked in. I offer Dad some wisdom.

'You realise he doesn't watch the van, just comes out after the last race and pretends he's been there all night,' I say.

'Really? Thanks for the tip son,' he says, winking at the others.

New Cross is built on disused railway land. It's one of the smallest tracks in Britain. It started out as an athletic track and has since been used for speedway and greyhounds. It is spectator friendly, with a glass-fronted grandstand with bars and restaurants and covered standing in several areas.

A summer meeting at New Cross

The totters take the same position every meeting - halfway up the grandstand overlooking the winning line. They are very noisy and full of banter. Their gang include names like Sailor Harris, Swanny and Blacknob. Goodness knows how they acquired their nicknames but every totter has one. They're real characters. On his birthday, one even took his horse into a pub for a drink!

They all like to boast about their connections and there's always a whisper going around about a certainty. If it wins, there are hoots and cheers, and drinks at the bar. If it loses the excuses are plentiful. Missed its break. Got baulked. If their dog was in front but loses, they'll even accuse the race officials of deliberately slowing the mechanical hare to allow the other greyhounds to catch up. *It's effing crooked* is the lament. One time when his dog was tailed off a disgruntled punter - not one of Dad's entourage - threw a toy rabbit on the track creating mayhem, provoking a near riot and causing the race to be abandoned.

I have my own routine. To be polite, I watch the first race with the totters. Someone always buys me a Pepsi, the first of several on the night. Then, like going to the races, I do my rounds, enwrapped in the theatre of it all. The kennels are over the far side and for the second race I wait there for the dogs to emerge with their handlers. I follow them from the perimeter on their parade around the track. Behind the dogs is a bloke with a dustpan and brush whose job it is to scoop up any poo from the peat. I nickname him Poohey Pete. Bringing up the rear in tweed and a trilby is the starter - always the same guy, carrying a red and a green flag.

The jacket colours are the same every race - red on the inside, then blue, white, black, orange and stripes in Trap Six. You can tell which dogs are up for it. Some bounce along, others mope with their head down. I used to feed my observations to Dad, even telling him which animals had emptied their bowels.

'You mean Trap Four's had a shit!," he said, provoking merriment all around. I realised this was just theatre for his mates and he just wasn't bothered.

As the dogs enter the traps I wait and watch from a few feet away. The volume from the stands increases as the bookies frantically shout their odds, trying to squeeze one last pound from the punters. The huge Tote board goes into overdrive. The Tic Tac men, in their white gloves, frantically signal their last messages to the next ring. One by one the handlers push their dogs in the traps and close the hatch. They can't turn around. The only exit now is ahead. The starter signals to high in the stand. The stadium lights dim. The track lights glare. The mechanical hare starts its journey. The whirl gets louder and every dog instinctively crouches like an Olympic sprinter. From the middle of the track someone rings a bell like a fire engine. The greyhounds explode out in a cloud of dust. The 10,000 crowd roar. The ground staff have seconds to move the traps off the track until the dogs come round again. The winning line is a blaze of light. In 25 seconds the race is done and dusted. The hare disappears. A decoy one springs into the air and the greyhounds, breathless and foaming, scamper to get a bite. Their handlers - usually young men and women - chase after their breathless charges and make a fuss of them.

I follow the dogs back to the kennels. Bowls of water are laid out in the recovery area. Owners and trainers pat their dogs. Punters tear their tickets up and toss the shreds in the air. The lucky ones queue to be paid. The race is over. And the whole performance will be repeated in 15 minutes.

The journey home is often in contrast to the journey there. Hope and expectation have usually morphed into despair and resignation. Nuckham drops us off. If they've lost, that's it. If he's won, Dad will drag Mum and Nuckham into The Clyde in Bethwin Road. The 'old girls' will be delighted to see Lights. He'll stand them in stout for the rest of the evening.

All photos courtesy Greyhound Racing Times

23

Home Alone

Greyhounds is my Thursday fix but what about the rest of the week? I'm genuinely scared of being alone in the house, sometimes running the streets until either parent or Johnny surfaces. No-one has been upstairs since Nan died. Her room has remained an empty mausoleum. And last week in the kitchen I swear I heard the squeaking of mice in the corner behind the cooker. No-one has seen them but Mum did recently find droppings in the chip pan. The fear of rodents has forced me into using the front room more, so I begin playing the piano. Dad bought this expensive black shiny upright from Harrods but it hardly gets used except for parties and Christmas. And I realise quite quickly I have a talent for playing simple melodies... things like Beatles songs and the American National Anthem which is ingrained in my head following the recent Olympics. If a tune sticks in my brain I can usually play it within a few minutes.

The cinema is a regular hideout. For sixpence, I'm old enough to be allowed into Saturday morning pictures at the Regal at Camberwell Green, an important step on the road to independence for all kids. We scream the ABC minors song, sit on the upturned seats to appear taller and bang our feet in excitement on the underside as the show starts. I note how they 'hook' people into attending the following week. In the final reel the hero is always about to die - only to be miraculously rescued in the next episode. I soon feel it's all a big con, and much prefer the grown up cinema. I bunk in to see The Longest Day, a war epic about D Day, crammed with every film star you can think of. But it's not just the movie or the performances that will stay in the memory but the title page. 'Darryl F. Zaunck's The Longest Day.' How cool is that name?

My main refuge is the Church - or rather church organisations. I find actual churches creepy but the church halls provide somewhere to go. I have an unfortunate episode at The Cubs. I can't be doing with all the Dib Dib Dib Dobbing and promising Akela to do my best for God and The Queen but the activities and games are competitive and fun. Come Bob A Job Week I don't do a single job. Mum gives me five bob anyhow, to donate to the Scout Association coffers and I lie I've been helping out in the community.

'What did you do?' Akela asks. Thinking on my feet, I pretend that I'd cleaned cars and helped some old lady with her shopping.

'Oh, really, when was that?'

'Er, on Saturday,' I stutter.

Suddenly she is a female Poirot.

'Whereabouts? What were their names?'

By now I'm as red as a cowboy's bottom. She knows I'm telling porkies. And I know that she knows I'm flying by the seat of my grey shorts. Shamefully I even begin to wet myself. I can never go back there. I go home and toss my uniform - the green cubs hat, jumper, yellow scarf, and toggle - into the bin.

After that episode I join another Christian organisation, the Boys Brigade, primarily as a place to go after school, and to learn how to play the drums and the bugle. But I hate the street parades, fearing that someone might recognise me in my uniform. They hold meetings on Wyndham Road on the corner of Comber Grove. Long before Fireman Sam was born, one weekend they stage a revue about a hero fireman who attends local blazes. His name is Esau Sparks, adapted from the Bible. I think the sketch is hilarious.

'What's your name?'

'Esau Sparks.'

'Who did?'

'Quick, get the Fire Brigade.'

Soon the appeal of drums and trumpeting wears off. I leave knowing how to beat two threes and a seven whilst marching with a snare - and I possess a reasonably new bugle. I smuggle it into The Oval and give it a blast whenever Surrey score a four or take a wicket. On the way out, one of the spectators, an old colonel figure, grabs me angrily and says, 'Save that infernal thing for football matches.'

Fortunately, I can attend three youth clubs all within 600 yards from home and all born out of the area's historical depravity. The area is blessed with mission halls set up by churches, charities and wealthy colleges like Dulwich College. One example is The Holy Trinity Chapel in Cambridge who at the turn of the century began a mission to help Camberwell's poor. They rented premises in Albany Road and built a new mission building in New Church Road, a stone's throw from me. It flourished, providing day schools, a hospital for the poor, Bible classes, Sunday Schools, clubs for working men, soup kitchens and the like. Trinity's master, Montagu Butler, spoke of bringing the young men of Trinity 'face to face, heart to heart' with the poorer classes of London.

Image courtesy of Trinity College Chapel

Across the road from me is Cambridge House, formed in 1889 to provide social services to the urban poor. Indeed, it had been at the heart of the setting up of the welfare state. The Liberal MP and writer Charles Masterman lived a few doors along in Addington Square and worked hand in hand with Cambridge House. The crushing poverty he witnessed in Camberwell inspired him to write about his observations and foster the 1911 National Insurance Act through Parliament.

But those days of destitution have long gone. Few families are wealthy but few are down and out. This is the era of full employment, strong trade unions, cheap council housing and the welfare state where, if you do lose your job, you can go on the *jam roll* (dole). Kids are clean and well presented. Why, many families can afford a fortnight at Butlins. However, the legacy of giving remains… and who are we to look a gift horse in the mouth?

Cambridge House has a hall which is used for Polling Day, jumble sales and indoor fairs. The singer and actress Anita Harris comes one day to open a fete and kisses me on the cheek. Where else can you pop over the road for a snog with a Carry On star? It also runs a youth club which I attend every Monday. We play five a side in the hall and cards in the canteen. The supervision is quite lax. I'm only ten but they turn a blind eye to smoking and gambling. I have my first puff there - and promptly cough and splutter. I vow it will be the first and the last!

One day the youth leader takes us scrumping in the minibus to Dulwich, pretending we are thieves in the night, but not telling us that the orchards actually belong to the club's benefactors, Dulwich College. We think we're nicking apples from someone's gardens when in actual fact we are being used as cheap labour!

The secretary of Crystal Palace Football Club, a small bow-legged guy called Chris Hassell, gives up his time to take football sessions. The goals are upturned gym benches. But his attempts to recruit fans to Palace is a mission too far. This is Millwall territory. He will later go on to become Chief Executive of Yorkshire County Cricket Club.

24

The blagger in a dog collar

It's Tuesday 9th April 1963 and I can hardly contain my excitement. I'm about to brush shoulders with royalty - a real live Princess. Her Royal Highness Princess Alexandra of Kent is about to enter our gym. And to watch me box!

Johnny and I are members of Clubland, a youth club with a difference. While Hollington and Cambridge House indulge our fags and 3-card brag, at Clubland it's debating and board games. Both of us learned to play chess there. The club is mixed, strict and structured. And we love it! We have house competitions and a hierarchy of officers who supervise activities not often found in the inner-city such as photography and theatre. We pay subs of course but by far the biggest source of income is the founder's obsessional fund raising. He's simply a genius at persuading the great and the good to empty their wallets. Camberwell has its share of street blaggers. But this man doesn't hide behind a mask or brandish a shotgun. He dons a trilby. Smokes a pipe. And wears a dog-collar.

The Reverend James Butterworth
Photos by kind permission of Isobel Durrant

Clubland was devised by one of the most remarkable people Camberwell has seen. The Reverend James Butterworth was born into poverty on the edge of the Lancashire moors. He was the eldest of five children and after his dad committed suicide he was the breadwinner at the age of 12, forced by circumstances to work in a factory. He saw early service on the Western Front, but religion was his calling and in particular the Wesleyan Methodist Church and its belief in the Holy Trinity - one true God, united in three persons, the Father, Son and Holy Spirit.

In the 1920s he was appointed to Camberwell where, inspired by his own hardship as a youngster, he transformed a decaying Victorian chapel into a youth club. Within a half mile radius lived 85,000 people, many of them of course children. He believed that for all their bravado, kids enjoyed and responded to structure and devised a programme of activities founded on accountability and self-discipline. He started off with Friday night bible classes for six boys in his study. This was the beginning of a youth empire, with modern buildings to include carpentry, chess and board games, football, cycling, athletics, rambling societies, film clubs, music and drama, even a parliament. His mantra was that anyone could achieve anything.

JB, as he was known, was a diminutive figure, almost midget like, but he possessed a dynamism that betrayed his frame. Even his family regarded him as a rebel, a magician, a showman, a clown and a miracle worker all rolled into one. He opened the wallets of film stars, politicians, business people, and sportsmen for hundreds of thousands of pounds. One of his favourite ruses was to slip inside the boardrooms of London's football clubs and make contacts at the bar. No one was going to ask a man of the cloth for credentials! Clubland became a nursery to painters and politicians, actors, journalists and musicians. Superstar Sir Michael Caine, who lived around the corner from us, was one. 'I owe my personality, my life and my career to this man, the most important person I ever met,' he wrote in the foreword to a Butterworth biography *The Temple of Youth*.

Clubland member Maurice Micklewhite aka Michael Caine

Maurice Micklewhite was born in Urlwin Street, 200 yards from my house. The Micklewhites were like hundreds of local families - poor and living in cramped conditions. His mum was a charlady and dad a fish porter at Billingsgate Market. He was a gambling addict and heavy drinker, spending most evenings propping up the bar of the Fountain on Camberwell Green.

'I was 12 years old, and on my way to becoming a juvenile delinquent when a very pretty girl who I liked said she had joined a youth club and would I like to come along. It was a joyous place with loads of things to do. I wound up doing basketball but found that none of the boys would join the drama class because it was too sissy. They said they had no boys in the class so I joined and that is how I became an actor.'

His first role was a robot in an obscure intellectual play. He had one line which he didn't understand. But he did understand the sarcasm of the 'bastard' reviewer. Clubland Magazine noted the handful of words were delivered to perfection with a 'dull, mechanical, monotonous voice' - a review which Caine joked in his own autobiography *The Elephant to Hollywood* laid the ground for a lifelong dislike of critics. His breakout role of Alfie was based on a fellow Clubland member called Jimmy Buckley who loved and left most girls in the club (literally not metaphorically!). Much later in life, a journalist friend of mine discovered that Caine had an 'illegitimate' half-brother he never knew about. David, who was brain-damaged, was living in a garden shed in Surrey. My friend Bob had the delicate task of breaking the news to the superstar who was forever grateful for the information and paid for his brother's care for the rest of his life.

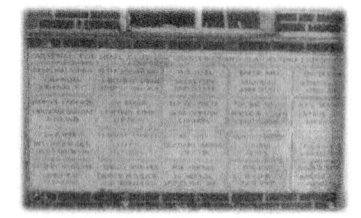

Donators' names were set in stone in the courtyard, among them Sir Laurence Olivier, Gracie Fields, and the great American director Cecil B. DeMille

With The Beatles: who's that little old man?

Jimmy Butterworth's own breakthrough idea was to get on the boat to America to tap up Hollywood. On the journey he slipped into first class and began building connections. Fellow passengers were left wondering who the little man with such a benevolent smile actually was. Literally he was a man on a mission. Among those he met was the British born comedian Bob Hope who promised to visit the next time he came to the UK. Sure enough, nine months later, he starred at the London Palladium and visited the club, attracting huge crowds, and donating a chunk of the show's proceeds.

With Bing Crosby and Bob Hope

But Butterworth's biggest coup was persuading the Queen of England to give his work the royal stamp of approval. Queen Mary dedicated new buildings in 1939 - much of it only to be subsequently damaged in the Blitz, requiring more rounds of money raising. It became the best youth club in Britain - and was just a couple of hundred yards from my house. Lucky again!

Alfred Hitchcock and Carey Grant

Before one Sunday sermon he was photographed at East Lane Market rattling a collection tin asking shoppers if they could spare a few pennies. Our local paper, The South London Press, whilst supporting the club and everything it stood for, hurtfully accused the good reverend of shamelessly begging. My old man held a similar view. Whenever Johnny or me arrived home with an envelope requesting yet more donations he smiled, shook his head and lamented, 'Here he goes again... that bloke's always on the tap.'

Pleading for pennies in East Lane market

Butterworth needed the thickest of skins. He endured more than his fair share of humiliation and brush-offs. Often on trips to The States he was cold-shouldered and left sitting alone in waiting rooms for hours on end. He became depressed by the American experience and after five excursions called it a day. On his first Sunday service after returning home it was standing room only at the Walworth chapel where he preached. He told the congregation, 'I have placed my trust in film stars, financiers and fund-raising tours but in peace and confidence I now trust in the purposes of God for my life and this place called Clubland.'

Cartoon on the US experience by Andy Burton in the Clubland Review

***

But big trouble lay ahead. Our manor, particularly Walworth, the Elephant and Castle and Camberwell Green, was the breeding ground of a new violent youth cult that would sweep Britain - Teddy Boys. Disaffected teenagers hung around on street corners with knuckledusters and coshes, jeering at passers-by and wolf-whistling at girls. Indeed, as a kid you learned to avoid The Elephant or The Green at night in case you got beaten up. After the showing of *Rock Around The Clock,* the Teds smashed up The Trocadero picture house on New Kent Road and many cinemas and dance halls subsequently banned them.

Gangs infiltrated the club, leading to fighting and vandalism. Once they went on the rampage with knives and razors, slashing furniture and smashing fittings, slitting the expensive curtains and flooding the building by bursting the pipes. The story reached the national Press who reported that 'mad dogs' had wrecked Britain's finest youth club. For a while, local Bobbies had to patrol the entrance. Members were attacked, intimidated and threatened and began to stay away, leading to a drain on funds.

JB was in a dilemma. He refused to report the culprits to police, believing the hooliganism reflected the way that society was changing rather than the fault of the club or its members. He believed there was a general lack of discipline among British working-class youth. So he decided to close the club for a while and introduce a junior section which, luckily for me, paved the way for ten-year-olds to join. Naïve or not, he felt it was a way of preventing us being groomed by razor gangs and becoming cosh boys. Hundreds of boys and girls joined and discipline was strict. We weren't allowed to run in the corridors and were required to attend Church on Sundays (although I never actually did). For a while, even jiving was banned at the Clubland senior dances. But on the whole we liked the law and order and the chance to experience a range of activities.

**

I race the buses along Camberwell Road and I'm there in minutes. The doors open at six with queues spilling onto Grosvenor Terrace waiting to be registered and to pay our subs. The first half an hour is usually free time and small games with our customary comically fast walk to the limited number of table tennis tables in the games room. Formal activities run from 6.30 to 7.30 with a changeover bell at 7pm for house competitions. Then it's usually queuing in the canteen for Coca Cola and bread pudding followed by Popeye cartoons.

However, tonight is different. Security is tight. There are men outside talking into their lapels and I have to show my membership card twice before being allowed in. Staff are on edge. The word is Princess Alexandra has left her London palace and is due in half an hour. We're briefed on Royal protocol - only speak when spoken to - then told to go to our normal Tuesday clubs. Keen as mustard on sporting matters, I'm trying boxing for the first time even though the thought of a punch on the nose fills me with dread. Elsewhere, the usual activities are in full swing. On the roof, which they've converted into a football pitch with high fencing and floodlights, they're playing seven-a-side. In the art studio youngsters are drawing pencil sketches of crockery stacked on the side of a sink.

We start our gym session with warm ups, then hitting punchbags and then Ted Cutler, the gym teacher, starts the first actual bout. Except we don't have a ring. So he 'seconds' four of us to hold the ropes around our backs, one in each corner. It's my turn to box and within 30 seconds I'm hit hard on the nose which feels like I've run into a lorry. I even see stars. A smattering of blood appears and Cutler stands me down, saying I can't be dripping claret all over the Princess. I now take my place in the corner as a human stanchion. Suddenly there is movement at the door. The Princess, looking gracious and smiling, enters the gym accompanied by the Rev

James and a load of suits who must be Palace officials and church elders. She makes a beeline to me straightaway.

'And what's your job?'

'Ringholder, Ma'am.'

'Jolly good. Keep up the sterling work,' she says and moves on to the others. And that is it. My brief encounter with royalty. Gone in a jiffy.

The Princess chats to us lads

***

Nothing lasts forever and sadly this was true of Clubland. Much to the relief of Dad's pocket, along with scores of other juniors, I didn't progress into senior membership. We found other interests. And whilst as ten-year-olds we thrived on the special form of discipline provided by the club, by the time we became teenagers it felt restrictive and too much like school.

As for JB, he was reluctant to change with the times and, gripped by ill-health and depression, the poor man had to be dragged kicking and screaming into forced retirement by the Methodist Church who owned the buildings. He moved with his wife Anna to a cottage in East Sussex. He died a year later, a few days after his 80th birthday. And alas, Clubland as we knew it passed with him. RIP both.

Reading the Methodist Recorder

Pictures from The Temple of Youth, JB Club Press and Southwark Local History Library

25

'The Train'

Ayton House

Later in that summer of 1963, in a maisonette in Ayton House on the Elmington Estate, two sisters are indoors playing. One is nine, the other aged seven. They are called Marilyn and Lorraine and they are my cousins, the daughters of my Mum's youngest sister Rene. They're only a five-minute walk away through Addington Square, and quite often we play together, although as with all dogs now, I'm frightened to death of their snappy little black poodle Perry. They kindly lock him away when I call, which I'm sure only adds to his animosity towards me. And I will feel sad in the years to come when I learn that he's choked on a chicken bone.

Rene pays me five bob to clean her car, filling up a bucket with tepid water and suds which I carry in the lift down to the pavement. She has a little red and black Austin A40 and after sponging it down I make several visits back up to the third floor for rinsing water. Rene has a soft spot for me. Maybe I'm the son she doesn't have, although our relationship had been strained last Christmas when me and my cousin Peter ate all her festive tangerines in one afternoon. Mum went mad when Rene told her, but I blamed Peter, who is four years my senior, for leading me on.

Lorraine and Marilyn

121

Their game today is hide and seek. The cupboard under the stairs is just about the only option in the cramped flat. The girls move some blankets and... several bottle-green balaclavas pop out. They put them on to scare each other; only their eyes and mouths show through the slits. Their mother has a hissy fit. She thinks she's hidden them out of sight of any prying eyes. Rene is an accomplished seamstress and these are part of an order placed by her husband for 16 adult balaclavas to be ready for the August Bank Holiday Weekend.

Rene hadn't asked the obvious question. Why would anyone want a woollen balaclava in the height of summer? But deep down she knows these are for business not pleasure. Her old man - my uncle Tommy Wisbey - is a professional thief.

Tommy and Rene

They met as teenagers at a dance. He was full of fun, generous and could handle himself on the rough streets of SE5. They held their wedding reception at her home, 104, in what would eventually become my bedroom.

Tommy as a kid

Tommy's life of crime began when he was 8. Near our house is the R. Whites lemonade factory on Albany Road. As the delivery trucks stopped at the gates, Tommy and his mates would climb on board and steal bottles of pop. Sadly, it ended in tragedy when one of the lads fell off and into the path of a car, killing him instantly. Tommy graduated from stealing lorries at the London docks to become part of a team nicknamed by police as the South Coast Raiders, half-inching moneybags from the guards vans on trains. Now he is lining up a major heist - one, unbelievably, that will make headlines across the world and one that The New York Herald Tribune will call *History's Greatest Robbery*.

Tommy plans to rob a train

It's 18.50 on Wednesday 7th August and a travelling post office sets off from Glasgow Central station en-route to London. It's due to arrive at Euston Station at 4am tomorrow morning. The train consists of 12 carriages and 72 Post Office staff who will sort mail as it thunders through the night.

The second carriage, behind the engine, is known as the HVP coach (high-value packages) which carries large quantities of cash and registered mail for sorting. Usually, the value of the shipment is in the region of £300,000 but because the previous weekend has been a Bank Holiday the loot is considerably larger.

It's a routine run until the train reaches the Buckinghamshire countryside, forty odd miles from London. The driver, 58-year-old Jack Mills, is suddenly confronted by a red light, highly unusual in the skeleton overnight timetable of British Rail. What he can't possibly have suspected is that a gang of robbers have put a glove over the green light and connected up a red battery lamp instead. Mills applies the brakes and the train grinds to a halt at a place called Sears Crossing, between Leighton Buzzard and Cheddington. Mills instructs his deputy, David Whitby, to climb down onto the track and call the signal box to find the reason for the delay. Whitby reaches the trackside phone to discover the wires have been cut. He's then overpowered by one of the robbers hiding in the darkness. At the same time, a gang, wearing my aunt's homemade balaclavas, enter the engine cabin from both sides. Mills grapples with one robber but is struck from behind with a cosh.

Meanwhile other members frantically uncouple the first two carriages from the rest of the train. The plan is to drive the HVP coach 800 metres further up the track to Bridego Bridge where a Loadster truck and two Army-style Land Rovers are parked ready to ferry the loot away. They've even brought their own driver, a retired British Rail employee, to take over the controls. However, he's unable to operate the newer type of locomotive. They then 'persuade' Mills to move the train instead, roughing him up in the process.

Inside the HVP coach, the staff carry on sorting and counting, unaware of the drama outside and no doubt relieved that the stationary train is at last setting off again. But a few moments later it grinds to a halt again. They are about to encounter the biggest shock of their lives. An 'assault force' attacks the carriage, ordering them to lie face down on the floor. One or two offer resistance but are hit with coshes.

The high-value HVP coach

With military precision, the robbers form a human chain and remove all but eight of the 128 sacks of new and used bank notes. Within 30 minutes the whole operation is complete. Under the cover of darkness, the gang motor along minor roads to their isolated hideout, Leatherslade Farm, about 40 minutes away where they proceed to divide their spoils into 16 equal shares.

The hideout – Leatherslade Farm

Meanwhile, back at the scene, the shocked staff begin to raise their heads. One is assigned to find a phone along the track. He phones the signalbox and says, 'We've been held up.'

'I know. You're very late. But we've no signal issues,' is the reply.
'YOU DON'T UNDERSTAND. WE'VE BEEN <u>HELD UP</u>!!!'

The gang intend to stay in the farmhouse for several days and then burn it down to destroy any evidence. But on their VHF police radio they hear officers order a dragnet of all rural farm buildings within a 30-mile radius of the robbery. After dividing the spoils they flee and go their separate ways. However, the man they assign to set fire to the property bottles it, leaving a treasure trove of clues for police to discover.

No doubt delighted by his night's work, Tommy slips into his flat at Ayton House and whispers to Rene he will be laying low for a while. The girls are asleep. He kisses them and disappears into the night. That is the last he will ever see them together as a free man. A few days later he arranges a secret rendezvous with Rene at my late Nan's chalet at Leysdown. They've always agreed that she will never ask about the details of his work and today's no exception. He gifts her a packet of fags. Inside, instead of cigarettes, there's £500 in neatly folded notes.

'Blimey,' she says. 'After that I need a cigarette!' They decide he should scarper until the heat had dies down.

The Great Train Robbery, as the media calls it, takes the country by storm. The banks and insurance companies offer huge rewards. Politicians condemn the robbers but the Man-In-The-Street holds a sneaking admiration for the planning and audacity.

The first of several rewards

***

I'm getting ready for school when news of the robbery breaks to a startled nation. Dad is shaving at the kitchen sink listening to the radio. He likes to think he's the oracle of the South London underworld.

'That's the northern mob,' he utters, foaming his face with a shaving brush. He can't be more wrong. The robbery has been planned right on his manor by his own relative and, he'll soon discover, carried out by some of his acquaintances!

Meanwhile Uncle Tom has fled to Spain with a group of mates unconnected to the robbery. Perhaps he should have taken them into his confidence. To impress a group of girls at the bar, one of his pals jokes they can be generous because they carried out the train robbery. Everyone laughs… except Uncle Tom!

Every day the estimated haul rockets. '£100,000 train robbery'; 'Robbers' haul £500,000'; 'Great Train Robbery amount tops one million'. When the dust finally settles the actual proceeds will be £2.6m - the equivalent of nearly half a billion pounds today. Each robber has walked away with around £150,000 in cash. Today's valuation? £2.6m each!

I don't know exactly when or how my parents first become aware of Tommy's involvement. He's certainly gone missing from family circles and one day my Mum sees Rene across the road carrying shopping bags from West End stores including Harrods and Selfridges. Her usual shop is via catalogues and East Street market! Instead of coming up to the kiosk to say hello she grins from the other side of the street like a cat lapping up cream!

Somewhere in some underworld rendezvous, someone hands police a list of names… of virtually every member of the gang. At the abandoned farmhouse they find Tommy's fingerprints on a Monopoly set and palm prints on a bath rail. He will forever deny playing the board game or entering that bathroom.

Scotland Yard raid their flat but Rene swears blind that she's split from her husband who has run off with another woman. The detective looks on the mantlepiece. On full view is a postcard from Calafell saying how much he's missing her and the kids… rather destroying her story that they're living apart. There's no extradition treaty with Spain, so all police can do is wait for him to come home. Which he eventually does. He's convinced they've nothing on him and goes to Scotland Yard to front it out. He volunteers his dabs. And is arrested.

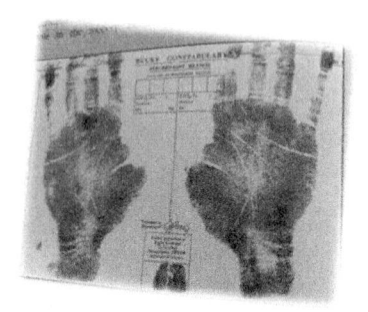

Fingerprints are the only evidence

Tommy is arrested

Unaware of his involvement, my poor cousin Marilyn goes into Tatnells, her local sweetshop, for some Sherbet Dabs and sees her dad's mug shot splashed all over the London Evening News. Tommy is placed on remand, but the police fail to find his share of the proceeds. They search the homes of all his known associates and even some of his relatives. I come home from school to find six police cadets digging up our front garden. Mum pretends to customers that the young coppers sweating away with spades, forks and shovels are from a local gardening firm! Needless to say, nothing is found. Mum is ashamed, but Dad jokes about the whole incident, saying the police have saved him from paying his usual down-and-out to dig over the overgrown grass!

In later years Marilyn will write a book called Gangster's Moll in which she says the money was hidden for a while in wall panels in her grandad's home. The police made several searches but failed to find it. But it was deemed too hot to handle and eventually moved around by trusted faces.

Marilyn's book Gangster's Moll

I shall never know for sure if Dad was involved in transporting or hiding the money, but he was certainly trusted and respected in South London. He starts taking me to various sports events virtually every night, always paying cash on the bus, train, or taxi, buying me food and drink at the beverage stalls, all the time paying with grubby fivers to get change. We even get a taxi miles across South London to a Tooting and Mitcham lower league match on a Thursday night! It's certainly ideal cover - an innocent ten-year-old boy unwittingly laundering money from the train robbery.

Rene and Tommy before 'the train'

Rene, Lorraine, Marilyn – and Perry

26

The Sentence

Five months after the robbery most of the gang stand trial at Aylesbury Assizes in Buckingham. It lasts 51 days and includes 613 exhibits and 240 witnesses. The hearing is reported daily in every newspaper, on television and radio. I secretly follow its progress every day. Mum loses weight with the worry and shame of it all. It's impossible to ignore the coverage. It's there before her eyes in large headlines for over seven weeks. She goes as white as a sheet when the Guilty verdicts are announced, feeling shame and sadness in equal measure.

If the crime itself was a sensation, the sentences send shockwaves throughout the country. The judge, describing the robbery as a crime of sordid violence inspired by vast greed, gives seven members, including Uncle Tom, 30 years. At first Rene thinks they've got a result, assuming that 30 years is the accumulative sentence for the whole gang. Then a friend says, 'No, it's 30 years EACH!' She faints.

There's widescale public sympathy over the length of the terms. Others feel it was an outrageous crime against the establishment and it is right that they be made an example of. All the family hold a soft spot for Tommy and now have huge sympathy for Rene and the kids. Like all her brothers and sisters Mum will stand by her youngest sibling who faces the prospect of many years without her husband. Marilyn will write in her book saying how supportive my dad was, remembering him visiting her dad in jail, and how she and Lorraine used to climb on his ulcerated leg on their journeys to prisons all over the country.

Mum insists that the crime never be mentioned indoors and we should hide that our relative was a train robber. No chance! Suddenly at school I've become a lot cooler. But like most of my cousins it will be many years before I want to discuss or admit to this shameful chapter in our family history. But his antics become part of the family folklore. When Dad wants to use the toilet he says, 'Quick, I need to let Tommy out of jail'. Charming.

Fifty four years later
Feb 1st 2017

We gather under a pallid sky, huddled in small groups in the cold wintry air, shielded from the rain and sleet under black golf umbrellas. The mourners have come from all over, but most have their roots in South London.

We've come to Camberwell New Cemetery to say farewell to Thomas William Wisbey - Tommy, Uncle Tom, or simply TW as he was sometimes referred to in our household. There are hundreds of us, a mix of family, friends and associates, many from the criminal fraternity where 86-year-old Tommy was held in the highest respect.

It's like a scene from The Sopranos. Men in dark cashmere, with lived-in faces, share a joke or two, remember old times, swap 'war' stories about fellow lags and regale with opportunities won and lost. There's Eddie Richardson, half of the notorious Camberwell Richardson twins, and Freddie Foreman, a former associate of the Kray twins, a convicted murderer, now making a living from his reputation as the self-styled 'godfather' of British criminals, and who held his wedding reception at our house. Freddie is a real godfather too - to Tommy's daughter Marilyn. Another South London lad, 'Mad' Frankie Frazer, would have been mourning too had he not passed away a few years back. He was Tommy's friend, lived for a while with Marilyn and was cremated here.

A handwritten sign pinned to the chapel door informs everyone of the wake, a karaoke at The Rising Sun in Newington. I sit in the pews with my cousin Christine. Apart from her mum Freda, all of our aunts and uncles are now gone, including Tommy's wife Rene, who was cremated at this same cemetery. The cortege enters. Marilyn is supported by her son, Tommy's grandson Jonathan, who reads a tribute, a poem about a man who robbed a train. A life now defined by crime.

Tommy's book published just before he died

Love, laughter and tears is the theme. The funeral brochure is adorned with his happy face, is full of family snaps and shows Tommy as a young scallywag growing up in Walworth. There's also a picture of him with Rene behind the bar of the pub they owned in Islington. They play music from the Premier League of entertainers - Ella, Frank, Aretha and Bobby Darin.

I sit and stare at the coffin. I reflect how 'the train' has cursed the lives of so many people, not least the robbers themselves. Buster Edwards, found hanging in his lock-up; Charlie Wilson shot and killed by a hitman in Spain; Roy James, jailed again for shooting his wife's father; Bob Welch left crippled after an operation on his leg went wrong; the gang's crooked solicitor Brian Field who died in a motorway crash; and poor Lorraine also killed after a road accident.

Suddenly, halfway through the ceremony, there is a skirmish in the row immediately behind. I turn around. It is Foreman and Richardson slagging each other off in the crudest of terms. Two of Britain's most notorious criminals almost coming to blows in a sacred building with Tommy's coffin just a few feet away. One is mopping blood from his face, although no-one exactly knows how this happened. They are in their eighties, but old feuds, it seems, never die. It appears that Richardson is upset about remarks in Foreman's autobiography that he'd once put a gun up Eddie's nostrils. The confrontation will make the national press the following day, provoking Eddie Richardson to put out a statement.

"Forman (sic) run (sic) away ten minutes before the end of the service and I couldn't get out of the row because of the people in front of me, but he knew I would be on him if he stayed. He said on TV that he once held a gun at my head which is a complete load of fucking lies. He knows I'm not too old to see off a wanker like him. After the funeral everyone went back to the pub where there was lovely food laid on and live music. I stayed there for over four hours but there was sign of Forman (sic) who was putting his nappies on at home."

I think about the last time I saw Tommy Wisbey - at a family gathering at my house. He was late arriving. The train had been held up... but not by him, he joked. I showed some old cine of family Christmas parties recovered from my uncle's loft after he died by my cousin Janice, who herself died of Motor Neurone disease. The footage was shot in the years when Tommy was serving time - Marilyn and Lorraine and Rene singing, all dancing joyously. Tears formed in his eyes.

'I missed all that, didn't I?'

'I guess so, Tom,' I replied.

We hugged. Our last words. Uncle Tom. Gone. Denigrated by society but loved by everyone who knew him.

27

Loner

Anyway, back to a ten-year-old Alan. Dad is in prison. Pentonville. Six months. I'm not told why or how. Things haven't been going too well of late and stealing is usually a desperate resort. Apparently, it was an opportunistic theft in the West End that went wrong. He couldn't see the cops. But they sure saw him. This time even one of Mum's famous pleading court letters couldn't save him from another spell inside. And we won't be seeing him until after Christmas.

Mum's naturally furious with him. She threatens to put Robbie in a kennel as punishment. In a letter from the *'shovel and pick'* (nick) as he calls it, he knocks that idea on the head. 'You go in the effing kennel,' he writes back.

I'm terrified at the prospect of visiting him and make my feelings clear that I won't be going to jail. But Johnny, now 16, steps up and makes the journey to the 'Ville' in Caledonian Road when Mum can't make it because of kiosk commitments. He's now working as a porter in Covent Garden, rising at the crack at dawn to catch the Night Bus to take him over the water, and we both relieve Mum in the kiosk for a few hours in the afternoon.

Serving behind the counter on a regular basis I'm getting to know the customers and the characters. All human life is here - and I'm growing up fast. My 'people skills' are developing, and I'm becoming more and more comfortable and confident in conversation with adults of any age of gender, even throwing in the odd quip. I'm learning an awful lot about people and how to deal with their various idiosyncrasies - the customers who in the mornings are all rush, rush, rush to get to work, but who in the evenings stand chatting for ages because for some reason they don't want to go home. I learn instinctively to weigh people up, whom I can trust, whom I should be wary of, whom I can joke with and those to whom I need to be more formal and polite. I'm serving an apprenticeship in human management.

It's certainly an interesting mix. Funny, shocking - even sad. One customer Billy Grant, who lives in the flats on the Goschen Estate, has a reputation as a dog whisperer. So much so that at closing time in The Clyde one night all the customers were locked in - not by the guv'nor, but by a mad dog. The beast was outside the doors barking and snarling at everyone who tried to go home. No-one had the guts to take him on. The landlord phoned Billy to come down and help. Apparently, he was already in his pyjamas but ventured out to take on the aggressive canine. Billy approached cautiously speaking to the dog in a hushed voice. At the appropriate time he produced some biscuits from his raincoat and within seconds the dog was literally eating out of his hands and the regulars could slide past.

The word was that Billy was taken on by the Krays in one of their Soho clubs to impose his charm on unruly customers. It came about after one of the South London chaps opened a club at The Elephant and Castle and employed him to man the door. Reggie Kray arrived with an entourage of villains but Billy refused to let him in because he wasn't wearing a tie.

'Don't you know who that is?' someone said.

'I don't give a fuck… no-one gets in without a tie.'

The twins were impressed rather than offended and later offered him a job!

Another occasional customer is the 'White Lady of Camberwell'. She was born black but is obsessed with the colour white - leggings, gloves, hat, bandages, even painting her face and her hair with paint and calamine lotion. She's polite with a high tinkling voice as she purchases cigarettes. It isn't just us kids who stare at her, but adults too. Strolling gracefully along the streets of Camberwell she stops the traffic. There are rumours she was raped as a kid by a white man, even that she is mentally ill. But no-one knows for certain.

The White Lady of Camberwell

In the many idle moments I read all the papers and analyse their styles, not realising I'm gradually assimilating the art of writing in a direct, snappy newspaper style myself. It serves me well in school essays. Weirdly, I love the precis exercises where you have to boil down a piece of writing into the most salient facts.

I'm also becoming consumed by the human-interest stories in the weekly tabloid magazines, such as Titbits and Reveille, and even have a sneak a read of the agony aunt columns in Woman, Woman's Own and My Weekly. Very revealing!

Titbits - human-interest stories

On Saturday evenings, the kiosk even becomes exciting! There's a real buzz as the newspaper vans race each other along Camberwell Road to be first with their Classified sport edition. Television news is in its infancy and people get sports results from newspapers. Football results, match reports and league tables are put together at break-neck speed. Until a few years ago London had three evening papers, The Star, News and Standard, selling hundreds of thousands of copies every night. *"STARNOOS 'N STANDOOOOORD"* was heard on every corner. Now it has two - The Evening News and The Evening Standard.

Like most of the English newspaper industry, they're produced and printed in and around Fleet Street, three miles from our kiosk. For the delivery drivers it's a Grand Prix - ducking and diving through the London traffic, horns blaring, lights flashing, over Blackfriars Bridge, around the Elephant and Castle, along Walworth Road to the News Box. It's a frantic, cut-throat business, with lads in the back of the vans bundling up the papers with string as they speed through the roads. The papers are literally hot off the press. There's not much between them editorially or in price. As long as they carry the racing and football results no-one's bothered which title they buy. People take the first one that arrives.

The drivers never bother to stop. As they approach the kiosk the van's doors spring open and the bundles of rolled-up newspapers are tossed into the air, the waiting customers catching them with the aplomb of Rugby international full backs. It all helps to create a frenzy of want among the customers.

'Now, who's first?' Janie says. When the rival van arrives the crowd are gone, resulting in a mound of unsold papers which have to be returned the next day. It's an early lesson in being First With The News. And, unwittingly, I'm being sucked into a love of journalism.

I will later appreciate just how cleverly crafted these match reports are. There's an on-the-whistle intro, then a set-up section about the significance of the fixture, the weather, state of the pitch and important team news, almost certainly written in advance, then a blow-by-blow account of the game itself - phoned over from the stadium to a copytaker in the newspaper building. With football fixtures ending around 4.40-4.50 it's quite a feat to have the Classified editions printed and ready for delivery half an hour or so later.

***

I'm being forced to grow up very quickly, and, hiding the shame that Dad is inside, I'm becoming more and more of a loner. I make the most of my freedom, staying out late, going to youth clubs and to football on Saturdays and midweek. My independence means I can go virtually anywhere I want - the West End, cinemas, sporting events. London is my new playground. I travel alone, easier that way to jib fares and bunk into places. I know every bus route and their destinations. The Routemasters go by the house every minute on their way to central London.

The numbers 12, 35, 42, 68, 171, 176, 184, 196, to as far away as Park Royal, Hackney Downs, Aldgate, and Camden.

The tube map is ingrained in my brain. I even know the best carriage to be nearest the exit, crucial when beating the rush at football matches. At the Elephant and Castle Underground there are two entrances and exits, each side of the huge roundabout, both served by lifts and both manned at street level by ticket inspectors. But when I'm jibbing, I work out that by waiting a few minutes for a trainload of passengers to clear, I can nip up or down the stairs when the barrier staff are safely back in their office.

During one school holiday I jump the tube to see the Bertram Mills Circus which is resident in Olympia. The shows are in the evenings, but I'm there for midday. There's a queue at the ticket office but there's no-one on the entrance gate and I wait patiently for the opportunity to walk through unchallenged. As usual, the theatre behind the scenes is as exciting as the event itself. No-one bats an eyelid at this solitary schoolboy watching from the sidelines. They probably assume I'm related to one of the troupe. Backstage the whole place reeks of animal manure. I watch the elephants be washed and watered, filling their huge trunks with liquid which they spray over the staff; the horses being groomed; and the tigers being fed strips of raw meat in their cages. They look fearsome and angry but snap into line at the crack of a whip. Staff are checking the trapeze equipment and inspecting the safety net. Beneath them the clowns rehearse in the ring without their costumes and make-up. I watch them practise the bucket routine when they chase each other around the perimeter pretending it's full of water and throw it over the audience. The water has magically transformed into shreds of paper.

Bertram Mills Circus courtesy V and A

Come the show itself, there's a problem. All the seats are taken and I'm forced to move on several times as people arrive. I have to melt into the shadows and watch the show standing at the back. The ring has been transformed from earlier. The band strikes up, spotlights pick out the Ringmaster dressed in red velvet and a top hat, whilst Coco The Clown in his tartan outfit, oversized boots and ginger wig that stands on end, thrills the kids. Acrobats somersault on horseback and the elephants are now adorned with star-studded headgear as they perform their tricks for an appreciative audience. I've noted some suspicious looks from staff so rather than have my cover blown, I leave early to meet Mum off the bus from Bingo, thus missing the big finale.

**

Our school is near a teaching training college and one Monday morning a group of 18-year-old women enter our classroom accompanied by a flushed headmaster Mr Godden. It's been deemed that we are a 'deprived' community and we are about to get one-to-one tutoring from students for one afternoon a week. They'll scratch our backs with personal schooling and we'll scratch theirs, affording them valuable experience coping with often unruly inner-city kids.

A special timetable has been drawn up to cover subjects outside our normal curriculum - art and crafts, music, pottery, and, one that catches my eye, Exploring London. We have to write down which group we want to join. I'm assuming that everyone will plump for Exploring London, a carte blanche to disappear from school for the afternoon to roam the capital. If it's oversubscribed, I know that our male-hating teacher Miss Jones will favour the girls and dump me into basket weaving lessons or some such. Surprisingly this proves not to be the case and I'm in - or rather I'm out!

There are roughly 20 students. All are female, some attractive, some not so. The lads are at the beginning of puberty now and we giggle quietly who will end up with a 'dog rough' one. Sexism rules OK for boys in their last year of primary school! To my horror I get the one we've decided none of us would want. She is tall, plump, no make-up with dark curly hair. As I sulk forward to be introduced, the other boys heckle, snigger and make raspberry noises behind their hands. She holds out her hand and introduces herself as Linda from Blackburn.

'And what's your name then?' I can barely reply in case I cry. I'm behaving like a spoilt brat.

We sit down at the back, an excruciating one-to-one.

'So, where would you like to go?' she asks. My intention is to make impossible demands so that I don't have to be seen in public with her. Bloodied by the Spurs European triumph, I'd become a regular at White Hart Lane. They are due to play Manchester United in the first round of the UEFA Cup Winners' Cup the following week.

'Spurs,' I say, knowing full well she can't possibly deliver. She thinks for a second or two and replies in her funny northern accent, 'OK... I love footy. I'm a Blackburn fan myself.'

I play my trump card.

'It's a night match. We won't be able to go,' I say.

But no... 'Leave it with me. I'm sure I can sort it.'

I'm startled. And conflicted. Do I really want to go to a match with a girl? On the other hand…

On the day of the fixture she arranges to meet me in the classroom after school. She'll take me home and we'll go to the match together. We walk through Crown Street with me trying to distance myself from her in case we're seen by anyone I know. I'm worried too that she'll ask questions about my family. Does she know that Dad's in prison? That my uncle is a train robber?

We arrive at the kiosk. Mum welcomes her warmly, thanks her, and instructs me to take Linda inside the house and make her a cup of tea. At the front door Robbie, who hasn't seen a soul for most of the day, bounds towards us and immediately puts his nose up her skirt. A real ice breaker. I don't know whether to giggle or die with shame.

'I'll get changed,' I say, running upstairs and leaving her in the hall still grappling with this randy Airedale.

It's a relief to travel 'legit', and she's surprised how much I know about the transport system. She'd researched the route herself - bus to the Elephant then on the Tube. But I tell her my way is quicker. We take a 35 bus to Liverpool Street, then a British Rail train to Bruce Grove to avoid the crush at White Hart Lane station. From there it's a ten-minute walk to the ground. Our conversation is muted. She delicately pumps me for information about myself and my family but I'm non-committal.

It's a cold, misty night. We are at the head of the queue. She dips into her purse to pay. We are handed ticket stubs and we scramble to my favourite position - high up in the East Stand in the front row of what they call 'The Shelf'. She's as excited as me. It's a full house, more than 60,000 spectators full of anticipation at seeing the two biggest names in English football. The match has special needle because United have beaten Spurs 4-1 only two days ago with a hat-trick from Denis Law. The teams come out to a rapturous reception. The Lillywhites and the Reds. They've got Charlton, Law and midfield dynamo Paddy Crerand. We've got Jimmy Greaves, one of the game's greatest goal scorers. A new starlet called George Best has burst onto the United scene but he's not playing tonight. In fact, no one is…

As the captains toss up, a blanket of fog descends upon the stadium. In just a few minutes all the players disappear from view. From high up in the stands we can't even see the pitch. The public announcer says the referee has taken the players off the field in the hope that the fog will clear. I immediately think what will happen if the match is abandoned? Surely our ticket stubs will be valid? I then have a brainwave. I go ticket hunting on the terraces, a ten-year old crawling under the feet of men, with a grown-up girl in hot pursuit wondering what an earth I'm up to. I find three and we work our way back to our perch. After half an hour, the inevitable happens. The game is called off. And the PA urges fans to hang onto their ticket stubs because they'll be valid for the re-arranged fixture.

There's an immediate scramble as fans desperately search the terraces for their discarded tickets. I'm disappointed at the weather, but delighted to be sitting on a few quid from the ticket stubs in my pocket. And I sell my three for half-price! Linda seems enthusiastically surprised by my Cockney entrepreneurial skills. She offers me to be her guest at the next home match. I'm beginning to warm to her.

She takes me to my first ever stage show, The Sound of Music in the West End, sparking a lifelong love of musical theatre. At the close of the first act, the emotional Climb Every Mountain brings me to tears and I pretend there's something in my eye.

During her assignment we'll go to the Kensington Museums, Trafalgar Square and to Buckingham Palace for the Changing of The Guard. But no sooner has it started than our affair is over. The term is finished, her time is up, and I will never see her again. But I'll always remember her kindness and generosity. And feel guilty how appallingly offhand I treated her. In later life I will think of her and sincerely hope she had a fulfilling and successful career.

28

It's My Round

Johnny is about to join the list of Hurndalls who've fallen foul of the police. He goes with a group of mates including Joey Abrahams, Alan Kirton, Brian Vernon and Pete Busby, to Box Hill in Dorking, Surrey for a lads weekend. They've told their parents they've booked a youth hostel and intend enjoying a couple of days hiking. No such booking has been made. And not much walking envisaged either. These are inner-city kids, full of bravado and derring-do. They plan to live rough and take on whatever the countryside throws up. Fortunately, they find a deserted old caravan which provides shelter, a dry place to light up, play cards and to kip.

Come Sunday morning, they're ready to go home and at dawn start their hike to the railway station. On the route is a small dairy. And outside, in the road, are several crates of orange juice waiting to be collected by the local milkman. Thirsty, cold and tired, they help themselves. The dairy manager, watching from a window, calls the police. Within minutes eight or nine Old Bill arrive on the scene… a response worthy of the Great Train Robbery. Johnny is the first to be rounded up and is put in the back of a police car. One by one the Great Dairy Robbers are tracked down, Johnny famously shouting in jest though the car window, 'Don't run, lads. We've got you surrounded.' The group are taken to police cells, charged and bailed to appear before Dorking Magistrates on the following Tuesday. As you can imagine, the parents are not best pleased about the theft and being lied to.

Come court day, Derek, the Hollington Youth Club leader, drives them in the club minibus thirty-odd miles to the Juvenile Court where they plead guilty to stealing the said bottles of juice. The magistrate raises his eyebrows at the fuss over a relative triviality. Derek speaks on their behalf saying they are good lads who have never been in trouble with the law. They were tired and thirsty and had no intention to permanently deprive the dairy of their goods. In fact, they'd have been happy to pay if only given the chance. The Bench gives them all a conditional discharge and they walk free.

Back home there is relief. There's a celebration in The Clyde in Bethwin Road and then Mum invites the parents round for more drink. Several of the mums are decent pianists and instead of the expected tears, the day, which started in a courtroom, ends in a singsong and knees-up.

***

Johnny's job means the end of his role as paperboy and I'm told that if I want to continue my gallivanting about town, I'll have to take over and earn my pocket money. The whole thing is ghastly. Up at 6.30am, Mum running in from the kiosk to yank me out of bed. She arranges a 'handover' day for him to show me the ropes.

We walk the streets together in the dark. He insists I carry the bag 'to get used to the weight'.

In Bethwin Road, next to the pre-fabs, there are two tall tenement blocks earmarked for demolition but still housing a few tenants. And on the top floor of one, Cadogan Mansions, I have to deliver a Daily Mirror. Inside, the staircase is dark and dingy. It smells of Sunday's roast dinner. There's no lift and I start the climb to Number Ten - 18 staircases in all, getting darker and darker after each flight. Suddenly out of the blackness I hear the terrifying roar of a dog barking furiously from behind a cage seemingly inches from my face. I drop the paper and gallop down the stairs like lightning. Back in the street, Johnny is in fits.

'Oh, I forgot to tell you there's a dog at the top.'

The round takes half an hour. I start in Addington Square, where there are two dentists. The first smells of gas, the other smells of fear. It's the Richardson scrap metal business where (allegedly) they used to pull rivals' teeth out with pliers.

It's the smells I'll always remember - the stench of cooking fat from the chippy and stale ale from The Clarence on New Church Road. In the flats you can always tell what they had for supper the previous evening, usually involving fried onions, cabbage or curry, which makes me retch but will one day be my favourite dish. The tower block lifts are a nightmare. They stink of urine and are often out of order which means I have to scale a dozen floors.

I'm press-ganged into selling the evening papers outside the local factory. Hilger and Watts, makers of specialist scientific instruments, are based just across the road near Addington Square. Every weeknight, I take 50 or so papers to service employees after they finish at five. I'm not allowed inside and have to stand at the gate in all weathers. It is here I learn the art of playing the sympathy card. The Head of Security is a kind old fella who'd obviously suffered a stroke at some point. His left side seems paralysed and his arm is protected by plastic casing from his elbow to the end of his fingers. Tonight it's raining and I pile on the agony. As he peers at me through the factory window I begin to shiver extravagantly.

'Come inside, you'll catch a death of cold,' he says.

From this day onwards I will sell from the warmth of the hut where the workforce clock in and out. It's productive too. Mum is pleased because I sell more papers there rather than trying to stop cars at the factory gates.

***

The Alan Hurndall luck is about to manifest again, earning instant welcome relief from all my paperboy duties. A vicious winter storm is brewing over Scandinavia. And it's heading our way, bringing the coldest winter for 200 years and having a devastating effect on the country. A week before Christmas a high-pressure system moves to the north-west of the British Isles dragging bitterly cold winds across the country. On Christmas Day my mum's family all brave the cold to come

140

to 104 for the traditional party. My uncles and aunts and their offspring are invited too. There are of course two of the male fraternity missing - Dad in Pentonville and Uncle Tom in Parkhurst High Security prison.

Prepping the Christmas Party

There's singing, dancing and Santa handing out gifts to the 15 cousins. The aunts have all chipped in making food - sarnies, puddings, snacks etc: the music is provided by Aunt Nell on the piano and the record player which belts out the Beatles hits and Rockin' Around The Christmas Tree by Brenda Lee. After party games of musical chairs and statues, my uncle Tommy Shaw takes over as compère and announces 'cabaret time' when everyone, including the kids, have to perform a turn.

My family are fine singers and each has their own song they perform year upon year. My female cousins are excellent dancers and singers and have rehearsed for weeks, but, racked with embarrassment, I can only usually manage to play air guitar to The Shadows with a tennis racket. This year however I've got a second-hand drum kit and I'm Ringo. After a joyous day, everyone gets home just in time. Tomorrow morning the first flecks of snow will fall and will continue for several days. The Big Freeze will begin.

Snowdrifts of up to 20 feet deep are reported; roads and railways are blocked; phone and power lines are brought down and villages are cut off for several days. There are pictures in the papers of kids ice-skating on the Thames and at Herne Bay on the south coast even the sea freezes! Farmers can't reach their livestock and many animals starve to death. Virtually all outdoor sport is crippled. And this weather will continue until March!

School's out, snow's in

For us kids it's sheer joy. School is closed for days. The council are in the middle of demolishing whole streets of 'slum' terrace houses to build high-rise flats. However, building work has ground to a halt. Diggers and equipment are abandoned in a frozen wasteland. Huge mounds of earth and rubble are now covered in several feet of snow. It's a perfect winter playground. We 'borrow' oven trays from home to use as sledges, climb on tractors, jump from half-demolished upper floors onto snow mounds, hiding and sliding and generally having a whale of a time. Forget St Moritz. We have our own alpine holiday retreat! It's the source of fun but very dangerous. One of the girls in my class, Marilyn Caterer, slides down and cuts her bum on a protruding piece of metal requiring stitches in a delicate place.

***

Slowly our winter wonderland begins to thaw, and life gets back to normal and school is reopened. The teachers at Comber Grove have been there for years and all seem on the brink of retirement. The head is Mr Godden, short and bald, who sports a moustache, a three-piece suit, and who must have been the model for Captain Mainwaring in Dads' Army which will arrive on our TV screens in a few years time.

His deputy is Mr Page, skinny and tall, with a chin as long as his beloved violin; the matronly Miss Adams, in her long skirts, always surrounded by the girls who all love her, and who sometimes brings her Afghan hound into school; and the perpetually young and petite Miss Boyce, whose Barbara Windsor figure is the source of much scrutiny and fantasy among the boys.

Then there's Miss Jones, who unfortunately I have had the displeasure of being saddled with for the last two years. A tiny stooping figure, she is the first 'woman' I've met with whiskers. She accompanies Mr Page on the piano at Christmas concerts, her tongue poking out of the corner of her mouth in deep concentration. As I said earlier, she simply hates us boys, favouring the girls at every opportunity, ignoring us when we have our hands up.

She once took delivery of a glockenspiel from London County Council. Everything stopped in the classroom as she excitedly unwrapped the keys and arranged them in note order. For a few moments she lost herself in her new toy, hammering out tunes with the little mallets. She must have felt slightly guilty because she looked up and asked the class if anyone wanted a turn. Virtually everyone put their hand up.

'Right,' she said. 'I'm going to play a tune and the first person to play it correctly can play the instrument in school assembly.'

A few hands went down, but mine stayed up. She then proceeded to play what I now know to be the Triumphal March from Verdi's opera Aida. One by one the girls went up and played and one by one they made mistakes. Even though I'd never heard the tune before, I was confident I could play it, through a mix of memorising the notes she'd struck and the melody still whirling around in my head. I was bursting to have a go, virtually out of the chair touching the ceiling for attention. When all the girls had finished she ignored the boys.

'Ok, that's it. We'd better get on with some schoolwork.'

A couple of us complained.

'That's not fair, Miss. We haven't had a go.' Even some of the girls thought it unjust. She reluctantly relented. Whereas she'd been patient with the girls, she shook her head as each lad got it wrong, as if it were a male thing. I was last to try. My big moment. I managed to get it note perfect. The class applauded but she said nothing and started to pack the instrument away. And I never did get to play in Assembly, a trivial injustice that I'll remember forever.

The previous year I'd come top of the class and was looking forward to Prize Day, when it's tradition for the top scholar to get a gift, usually a book, or a fountain pen, in front of visiting dignitaries and parents. However, as each pupil went up to receive their prize, I had an uneasy feeling that I'd been cold-shouldered. Sure enough, at the end of the ceremony, I was empty-handed.

A few of the girls took pity. The lads, particularly those who'd won a prize, took the mickey. Mum was livid. She went up the school to have it out with Miss Jones who told her I was the class clown and a troublemaker and didn't deserve a prize.

This wasn't a description everyone recognised. I wasn't an angel, liked a laugh, yes, and certainly had a sense of humour. But I wasn't a mischief maker. OK, I know that I left salmon sandwiches in my desk during the school holidays, creating a rotting fish smell that permeated the whole school, but come on! That was an accident!

On one occasion a whole group of our class were caned for hopping off school and going to Kennington Park for the day. But during my whole time at Primary School I was never slippered or caned, as many pupils were, even the girls. One girl, Joyce Abrahams, was even dumped into a wicker basket for being naughty.

***

They say revenge is a dish best served cold. And it's about to come in the wake of this terrible winter. Miss Jones travels to school in a Morris Traveller. One afternoon we plan to ambush her with snow and ice.

She leaves at the same time every evening, turning left out onto Comber Grove, then left again at Wyndham Road. The snow mounds, or should I now say ice mounds, overlook a zebra crossing. We plan a military-style operation. On the hill we'll stockpile dozens of snow and ice balls. Then, as her green and brown estate car approaches, one of our gang will amble across the crossing forcing her to stop. As she pulls away, three of us will bombard her car with missiles.

As it turns out, several miss, but enough hit the car to force her to pull up and get out to inspect the damage. By then we are sliding away down the ice hidden from view and in fits of uncontrollable laugher, the adrenalin rush to be remembered forever.

We turn up at school next day all pure and innocent. She probably knows it's the usual suspects, but without proof she has to swallow her anger. I boast to Mum about the incident. She shakes her head but probably loves that Miss Jones has at last got her comeuppance.

***

Our final year at Comber Grove - and Miss Jones is nowhere to be seen. We've a new teacher. Suddenly this Mr Pickwick character arrives in polished brogues, and dressed in a smart three-piece suit with a pocket watch and chain hanging from his waistcoat. His name is Mr Wotton, strict and experienced, and obviously now at the back end of his career. He demands instant order. It's clear this guy means business.

The first thing he does is stand in front of the blackboard and asks the class to recite any number between 11 and 99. There's a buzz of interest. *What's happening here?* Each time someone calls out a number he transposes it on the board. So 39 becomes 93, 81 becomes 18 and so on. *I'll show him.* I put my hand up and call out the number 44. This is what he was waiting for - the class clever Dick. He asks my name and then replies, 'You will do well, young man.'

He rules with a rod of iron - or rather a three-foot cane. And the class responds to his no-nonsense approach. I'm not much of a book reader except for Enid Blyton's Famous Five novels, but his end-of-day story-telling captures our imagination. His first book is White Fang by Jack London, set in the Klondike Gold Rush, about a wild wolf cub and his fight to stay alive at the hands of abusive owners. With our own savage winter fresh in our minds, we sit mesmerised as Wooton brings the snowy wastelands alive with gripping reading...

'Dark spruce forest frowned on either side of the frozen waterway. The trees had been stripped by a recent wind of their white covering of frost, and they seemed to lean towards each other, black

and ominous, in the fading light. A vast silence reigned over the land. The land itself was a desolation, lifeless, without movement, so lone and cold that the spirit of it was not even that of sadness.

But there was life, abroad in the land and defiant. Down the frozen waterway toiled a string of wolfish dogs, their bristly fur was rimmed with frost. Their breath froze in the air as it left mouths, spouting forth in spumes of vapour that settled upon the hair of their bodies and formed crystals of frost...'

Wotton's story-telling inspires me to join the library. I call in to borrow books at the building near Camberwell Green Swimming Baths. They want parents to sign the form but I forge mum's signature without her knowledge. Wotton had recommended a book called The Grapes of Wrath, a Pulitzer Prize-winning novel by John Steinbeck. Set in the Great Depression, it opens my mind to the evils of discrimination, injustice and exploitation.

My last school photo

29

A Merry Go Round

It's Spring. And love is in the air. I have my first crush. Her name is Susan and like me, the offspring of shopkeepers. She is good-looking, athletic and speaks in a sexy husky voice. I watch her every day across the classroom and stalk her when she's playing with her friends at breaktime. She's excellent at hand stands, tucking her dress inside her navy knickers and bringing the boys to a standstill to gawp in admiration. She has a twin sister, Pat, but they are so different in personality and looks. I haven't the guts to ask Susan out but devise a cunning plan. Three of us lads nonchalantly invite the twins to the funfair at Peckham Rye.

The invitation is full of risks. The main one of course is rejection. I could never hold my head up in class again. The second is the location itself. Like the animal kingdom, we've learnt that in the concrete jungle you simply never stray outside your territory. Who knows what dangers lurk there? And Peckham Rye is two bus rides and three miles away. The third peril is that she might fancy one of the other lads instead of me!

The girls are up for it and the five of us set off after tea. The proviso is that they have to be back by 8.30pm - enough time surely for me to woo her and make my move. On the bus I crack jokes and nervously show off, trying to make Susan laugh and notice me. Someone is going to be playing gooseberry tonight and I don't want it to be me.

It's a decent enough travelling fair, but not a patch of course on the permanent one in Battersea Park with its white-knuckle rides. Tonight, there's the usual lower-grade attractions that make up a travelling fair. We treat the girls to candy floss and toffee apples and a turn at trying to hook yellow plastic ducks. We go on the Dodgems. We bump them playfully. There's much laughter. At the shy, I try to win them a coconut but fail miserably.

Next, the Big Wheel. I grab Susan and ask her if she'll come on with me. She says YES! My heart thumps. We all queue for our turn. The wheel stops and I race to the seat and jump in with Susan hot on my heels... only to find that her sister Pat has overtaken her. One of the other lads has hijacked Susan. The wheel moves up in stages to allow more riders on. Stranded for a few seconds at the top, Pat pulls me to her and plants a smacker full on. Fear-stricken, my lips are clasped together and do not move. It's as if they're stuck together by Superglue. My first kiss... looking out over the dark South London sky. And I've got the wrong twin! The next five minutes are purgatory, me pointing at the views, trying to distract her from attempting any repeat. For the rest of the evening I avoid all physical contact with her and sulk as my mate walks arm in arm with my one true lust.

***

I've found a new love to ease the pain - Chelsea Football Club. They are my third team in as many years and I've become a football whore.

This affair came about by accident. On the way to see Spurs play Burnley one day with my cousin Peter, there's a sign at Liverpool Street Station saying the match has been called off because of a waterlogged pitch. So instead, we divert to Fulham Broadway where Chelsea were taking the Second Division by storm. Their manager, a fiery Scot called Tommy Docherty, 'The Doc', has moulded a group of youngsters into an exciting team playing attacking football. People like Tambling up front, Venables in midfield, Bonetti in goal.

At half term I go to Stamford Bridge with my autograph book. I'm hoping to see the players training but none are there. Outside the ivy-covered main office, I see Docherty chatting to staff inside. He's apparently got a fearsome temper but when he emerges I risk asking for his signature. I give him a sob story about making a long journey for nothing and he takes pity.

'Wait here,' he says and goes back into the office block. A minute later he comes out carrying a pile of press photos - absolute gold dust to any autograph hunter. Usually we cut pictures out of newspapers, but these are glossy and on proper photographic paper. One is of top scorer Bobby Tambling celebrating after netting a goal.

'Bobby's having treatment inside. If you wait, I'll get him to sign it for you,' he says. 'What's your name?

'Alan,' I say. Sure enough, five minutes later he appears with the photo duly signed '*to Alan, from Bobby*'. I'm made up.

My cousin and I become regulars and watch them win promotion. Years later I will work with Tommy's son in TV - Tom Doch Junior - and tell him that story about how his dad had given me a special childhood memory. Unfortunately, by then will have fallen out with his dad and will merely shrug his shoulders.

***

It's our final term and Wotton is prepping us for what he says is the most important exam in our lives, one that will determine our futures. It's the 11 Plus. The choice is pretty stark. Pass, and you've a chance of getting into Wilson's Grammar School near Camberwell Green. It's either that or the local Secondary Modern called St Michael's in Wyndham Road. Further afield in Dulwich is London's biggest comprehensive, William Penn, a mish-mash of 11-Plus failures and academic also-rans. We have several practice tests. They are written in language we don't understand. *A train leaves London at 11.30am and arrives at Bristol at 1.30pm, after stopping from 12.10pm to 12.20pm at Reading which is 36 miles from London. It travelled both parts of the journey at the same rate. Find the distance from London to Bristol.*

Wotton does his best but it's clear few of us, if any, will pass the exam proper. And any that do probably won't get into grammar school anyhow. It is heavily oversubscribed and boys all over South London have been cramming for years to secure a place. However, there are rumblings afoot to change things. A teacher in Hampshire complains to his MP and writes to his local paper…

'It's 11-Plus day tomorrow, a bleak day for me their teacher. I see Ian going off with his two sharpened pencils and his name card neatly printed, aged 10 years 9 months. He is not sure whether he wants to be a doctor or a poet. He will not be going to grammar school.

Can you describe an avocet and draw one accurately? Stephen can. He will be called a failure tomorrow. And how do I tell Patricia's mother without sounding crude and patronising that her daughter is a gifted mixer and is friends with everyone? Socially she heads any list, but the 11-plus will call her a failure.

Nervous children foredoomed to failure will sit tense in their seats tomorrow, their visions obscured by the glimpses of promised bicycles, train sets and even ponies, dripping slowly away in the torture of irrelevant questions.

They are certain failures, because the grammar school will only take four at the most from my class and I have known who they will be for two years. The unfairness lies not in the competition; some children are always better or worse than others in all ways. The unfairness lies in the fact that parents believe that all children have a chance and that there enough places for those that merit it. They are therefore disappointed when Jane and Roy and Alan and Mary, and Sue and Peter, all above average children, fail. I try to ignore it while doing what I can to change it. In the meantime my class will be branded as failures before they are 12 years old.'

We get our results. As far as I can tell no one has passed and therefore no one will get to grammar school. We must make our way in the world at a disadvantage. I shall follow in Johnny's footsteps and go to William Penn. Wotton hands me an end of year prize. Surprisingly it's for Maths - a subject I'm indifferent about. It's called The Coral Island by R.M. Ballantyne and will remain unread in my bookcase for at least 60 years. One day, sir, one day…

A prize at last – in my last year at school

I shall remember Comber Grove with affection - the place where I traded Brooke Bond tea cards, penny book matches, fag cards, stamps, autographs, played conkers, failed to master the Hula Hoop, failed the 11-Plus and failed to get a girlfriend.

And as we say our goodbyes on the last day, it's unbelievable to think that I'll never see any of those kids again. But it will prove to be the case.

I'll never know their fate, except for the tragic few. Classmates like Keith Killingback, killed in a car crash a few years later; Jacqueline Heathfield, the girl always in plaits, brutally raped and murdered by a psychopath who'd been released from a psychiatric hospital. She was found by her father in the well of their tower block near the school. Pat, my first kiss, who died young from sickness.

And the school itself. In the autumn of 2023 the council announced the impending closure of Comber Grove, ending a 200-year-old history of schooling. It survived disease, deprivation, explosions and bombs; the likes of Zeppelins, Doodlebugs, and the Luftwaffe; and, more recently, an epidemic.

But not, sadly, not falling numbers and council cuts. RIP.

30

Billy Biro

William Penn School is almost three miles from my house. Almost is the key word here because kids who travel three miles or more are entitled to a free bus pass. It means that boys who get on the bus just a few hundred yards before me not only get a complimentary ride but also the pick of the seats. There's no point appealing. Dad has already been through all this with Johnny but since he hardly went to school it didn't really matter. The old man tried all sorts of measurements, tricks and alternative routes to show that we are in fact more than three miles away, but the education authorities got their slide rules out and measured how the crow flies. And their word was final.

So early September 1964, shortly after 8am, I traipse over the road to the bus stop to get the 68 to North Dulwich - a scenario I will repeat for the next five years. I have a briefcase and wear the compulsory school uniform - a new blazer, long grey trousers, a dazzling-white Bri-nylon shirt fresh out of the box from Marks and Spencer, the oversized collar squeezed into my neck by my tie. Bri-nylon - basically plastic spun into threads to make women's stockings, shirts and even bed sheets and blankets - is supposedly the best thing since sliced Sunblest. But it will prove cheap and nasty, like wearing a bin liner. Sweat has nowhere to go and the shirt slimes all over the upper body and sticks to the skin. It creates static too. Many a time after playing football in the playground I'll go back to the classroom dripping in perspiration with my hair standing on end like Stan Laurel. I will be bawled out and ordered to the toilets to wash, a pointless exercise since although I'll become clean and dry, my shirt will still be smelly and sodden. It will take a year to persuade Mum that old-fashioned cotton is the way forward. And years before Bri-nylon is finally branded a fire risk.

Mercifully, we've been given the day to ourselves to integrate us into our new environment before the older pupils descend tomorrow to make us their slaves for the rest of the year. We assemble in the main hall and are welcomed by the genial headmaster George Dennis, who greets us as if we've just arrived at Butlin's. But a holiday camp this won't be. The head is accompanied by a teacher on the piano playing the school hymn which we will be expected to learn by heart.

We bear the name of William Penn who valued freedom more
than rank or title wealth and ease
Who braved the peril of the Seas
To found a Christian Commonwealth
Upon a distant shore.

It turns out that old Billy Biro, as we now call him, was a Quaker who founded Pennsylvania in English North America, although what his name's doing above the door of a South London School is anyone's guess. He was friendly with the Indian natives but also an old fool who was gifted a huge chunk of America but yet died penniless after spells in debtors' prisons from being duped out of his money by opportunist staff and dodgy friends. Apparently, the genial geezer on the Quaker Oats packet is modelled on our man! Rather apt, because being ruled at this school by no-nonsense, cane-wielding authority figures will often feel like doing porridge.

The Quaker Oats logo and William Penn

There are nine public schools in leafy Dulwich where the privileged send their charges: all proud bastions of learning with a rich cultural heritage, elegant listed buildings and rolling sports fields. William Penn isn't one of them.

There's Dulwich College for example, nearly 400 years old and boasting famous pupils such as Sir Ernest Shackleton, Raymond Chandler, PG Woodhouse and an opinionated young upstart called Nigel Farage who riled teachers by singing pro-Nazi songs. We are literally the other side of the railway track and will breed the likes of Wesley Dick, one of three armed robbers who'll be involved in the infamous Spaghetti House siege when nine waiters will be held hostage for five days in a Kensington restaurant. Dick, bright and articulate, became a black activist who changed his name to Shujaa Moshesh. He became the scourge of the prison establishment, leading a number of civil rights protests while serving time in jails.

William Penn is London's biggest comprehensive, with well over a thousand pupils, all boys. We are split into six houses, named after inventors, scientists and scholars - Bessemer, Goldsmith, Paxton, Ruskin, Faraday and Wilson. In our year there are nine classes, each with more than 30 kids, making around 300 newbies all trying to find their feet. What none of us know is that we are guinea pigs in a massive experiment. We're starting our secondary education in a comprehensive, a new type of schooling that doesn't select its intake on the basis of academic achievement, but is open to kids of all abilities. Nobody will be allowed to feel a failure, they promise. The hope is that the learning ambitions of the brighter pupils will rub off on the dimmer souls. The problem is, academically-challenged boys often cause disruption and need more of the teachers' precious time and attention, and might thus hold back the aspirations of the brainier ones.

At William Penn they're seeking the best of both worlds. We are not a pure comp, more a hybrid. Kids are streamed… according to their 11-plus results. I'm in Form 1G1 - the higher of two grammar stream classes. I must have come quite close to passing. Indeed, there are boys in our class who DID pass, but were cruelly squeezed out of grammar school by the numbers game. In addition to the G stream, there are four 'L' classes and three 'N' classes. We don't know what those letters stand for, although we patronisingly joke it's for Losers and Nutters.

After being sorted into our forms we're handed timetables which look on the face of it an exciting menu of subjects - English, maths, chemistry, history, geography, French, religious education, art, music, woodwork, technical drawing, PE and games. Sadly, any initial enthusiasm will not last long. We will soon find the teaching here is more about keeping control than inspiring pupils.

***

After the head's hello, we scramble to find the right floor and classroom. Teachers are on patrol yelling out the highway code as we stumble up and down staircases bumping into each other. The school is the size of a small village with five playgrounds each assigned to a year. It consists of five modern blocks - classrooms, gyms, chemistry labs, wood and metalwork rooms, an assembly hall, admin offices, concert stage, and 'house' quarters which double as dining rooms.

A modern site

In our class every kid is a stranger and I warily find a desk. I'm in luck. I've randomly sat next to Roy Slack, from a hardcore family in Peckham, whom we'll all soon discover will be the best fighter in the class. Roy and I will pal up for the rest of the term and become close friends. He's bright and doesn't have to try an inch, coming top in most subjects without doing a stroke of revision. More importantly, he has an older brother Billy - a ringer for Bill Sikes, the fictitious criminal gang leader in Oliver. Reputations travel fast. He's in the 4th year and probably the best fighter in the school - essential protection for both of us.

The register is taken in alphabetical order - Avery, Baines, Drake, Frankling, Groves, Harris, Hurndall... The teacher stops in his tracks.

'Who's Hurndall?'

'Me sir.'

'Are you OK?'

'Yes sir!'

'Do you have a brother, John Hurndall?'

Ah, so this is what it's about, I surmise. 'Yes sir.'

'But you can speak okay, yes?'

He's obviously trying to make some pathetic joke about Johnny never being at school. I smile nervously and he moves on with the register. I think nothing of it until the next class when exactly the same thing happens. Again, the master stops at Hurndall and quizzes me. Do I have a brother? Er, yes. I'm thinking that Johnny must have made more of an impact than anyone realised.

The real reason for their interest in the name Hurndall will materialise the following day. In my tutor group is a boy called... John Hurndall. It's an unusual name and an amazing co-incidence. But I soon realise there's more to this Johnny than meets the eye. He doesn't speak. Ever. Not a word. He's extremely shy too and acknowledges my hello with an embarrassed smile. But the extraordinary encounter doesn't end there. It turns out that this John Hurndall is my cousin! - the son of my Dad's brother. None of my family knew of his existence or that he was a pupil at William Penn! Sadly he suffers from mutism - a complex childhood anxiety disorder characterised by his inability to speak and communicate in social settings. He's in his last year at school and although I will smile at him each day in tutor group we will never have a conversation.

***

The teachers prove to be an odd bunch. All male. Their ambition appears to be to plough through the syllabus as a tick-box exercise without any thought or ambition to try to capture the imagination of pupils. It's learning by numbers - or should I say lists. Maths is a list of equations, history a list of dates, French a list of verbs, chemistry is more about learning the periodic table than firing up the Bunsen burners. This failure to stimulate is foodstuff for this pack of baying hyenas waiting to pounce at the first sign of weakness.

The school badge: bullies used to fill pockets with WP - Waste Paper

Their answer is corporal punishment. Davey, the gym teacher, and Hoskins in the science labs have fearsome reputations as one-man execution squads. Several teachers have the cane or slipper permanently on their desk as a warning against bad behaviour. Eardley, the geography teacher, even has a custom-made weapon of choice - a size 12 piece of compressed rubber shaped like a shoe - which he will wield on everyone's bottom in that first term. Shockingly, he will ask the class whom he hasn't 'rubbered' and boys who'd literally not put a foot wrong all year will be lined up before the class and assaulted. He thinks it funny and maybe he secretly derives pleasure from it. But many victims are in tears at the humiliation and injustice of it all.

Those masters that don't resort to physical retribution become sitting ducks. There's Shildrick, the history teacher, who's nearly seven feet tall and possibly the tallest man in Dulwich. A First at Cambridge, no doubt, but he has zero communication skills, merely leaning beside the blackboard, staring at the ceiling and reciting dates. Within minutes his class becomes a noisy rabble that often attracts passing teachers who embarrassingly have to intervene on his behalf. I'll give him something though, he's the smartest giant in town. His made-to-measure three-piece suit must have cost him a fortune.

The same with poor 'Kenny' Kingston, the RI teacher. He's a fresh-faced, neatly-parted part-time vicar who turns the subject into a glorified Bible Class of Loaves, Fishes and Good Samaritans. When you think of the influence of religion on much of the world and the wars and conflict it's caused! And yet I will leave after five years not knowing a jot about Islam, Hinduism, Buddhism or indeed any religion outside the Christian faith. He simply can't cope when we inevitably lose interest and start messing about.

Also, unfortunately for him, his classroom overlooks the James Allen girls school playing field and there's always a rush for window seats. The blackboard, Kenny and poor Jesus don't stand a chance against the attraction of scores of nubile young women in their navy knickers playing hockey outside the window. We all get cricked necks. They install plastic blinds supposedly to protect us from the heat of the sun but we think it's more to prevent us watching the girls and our raging hormones from boiling over. Our answer is to bend the slats just wide enough to ensure our fantasy peepshow can continue.

Not that we're supposed to even *think* about girls. The 'Chemistry Caner,' Clarke, doubles as the master of sex education. His message is plain and simple. DON'T!!! Five minutes of him is the greatest contraceptive ever. If a girl gives you the come on, remember you're almost certainly not the first she's been with. She'll almost certainly have pubic lice or another venereal disease which could send you blind and require the hospital to put a needle up the hole in your willy. The imagery is effective. It's like a horror movie. At least two kids faint at the thought.

Kohli, the maths teacher, is a likeable Indian but very difficult to understand. *You must do your mathematics. Velly, velly important.* He tells me that my brother was a fine mathematician but didn't try. He's right. Johnny didn't have to learn about algebra and trigonometry when he could already work out a bet - a knowledge that will one day help him become one of the country's top bookies and gambler.

As for Elliott, the woodwork teacher, we get off on a very poor footing. My DIY skills will become the source of much hilarity amongst family and friends. And this is the start. We're making a shoe-box. Unfortunately, I've chosen the wrong size bit and it gets stuck in the wood which then revolves round and round on the electric drill. I try to free it by speeding up the drill, only for the wood to spin across the room like a boomerang. Both teacher and classmates think I've done it on purpose - but only the boys are laughing. Elliott retrieves the wood and throws it at me, hitting me on the shoulder. I go down like John Wayne shot by a rival gunslinger. I sense he regrets his outburst. And it's enough leverage for me to negotiate doing PE with another class instead of woodwork and I'll never have to set foot in there again.

***

All of us wet new recruits are trying to make our mark in this frightening new world. At playtime on the fourth day this tall, elegant man wearing a tweed jacket, red tie and horn-rimmed glasses strides across our territory with his hands in his pockets, no doubt on his way to the staffroom for a cup of tea. He's as bald as a coot and already has acquired the nickname 'Peanut Head' among us first years. I happen to be holding a tennis ball.

It's time to show off, become Jack The Lad, and display just how fearless I am. I boast to the lads that I can hit this teacher's head with the ball.

'Oi, Baldy,' I shout, and throw the ball at him as he walks away in the distance. He's at least twenty yards away. It needs a miracle, like hitting a coconut at the fairground blindfolded. And this, remember, is a moving target. There's absolutely no chance of the ball getting anywhere near him or his head. It's pure bravado. Now, I'm not too bad at sport, particularly football and cricket. I can catch okay, but have always been a lousy thrower. The ball sails into the autumn sky. Surely it will sink harmlessly down to earth. Then comes a moment of abject horror - a realisation among myself and the watching throng that the ball has transformed into a guided missile with a mind of its own, and is indeed heading straight for its intended target.

SPLAT!!!

A direct hit straight to the back of his head. He spins around to see who the culprit is. But in that split second us streetwise urchins have all melted in the chaos of hundreds of boys playing football, running in different directions, chasing balls, larking about. I'm in a state of shock and suppressing nervous laughter, relieved that I'd got away with it.

Until…

Someone taps me on the shoulder. It's another teacher - unseen by me, and on playground duty.

'Go and apologise to Mr Dalton,' he says before adding sternly, 'and remember… I'll be watching you all the way.' Suddenly my swagger disappears. The other kids look at me, wondering what I will do. At a stroke the whole playground has frozen into a silent still frame waiting for the outcome. I nervously pace up behind him. Even from behind I can see his face smouldering with suppressed rage. He's embarrassed and angry. Not a good combo for a teacher/pupil encounter.

'*Sooorrrryyy sir,*' I stutter a few feet behind him.

He can't even look back at this pathetic perpetrator, and ups his pace to make me jog to keep up. I'm interrogated on the move. We swap details - name, form, etc - as if our worlds have collided, which indeed they have. He orders that I report to the Head of Year's office at 4pm that very day. Even though I've only been at school only a few days, I know what that means - the room where they mete out corporal punishment - either the slipper or, God forbid, the cane.

During the rest of that day I sweat like an onion on a low heat. After much anguish and internal deliberation, I decide on the right and proper course of action - to bottle it and go straight home. Hopefully he will forget. And if he does pursue me, I will simply say that the meeting had slipped my mind and apologise for being so forgetful. But at 3.30pm - half an hour before our allotted meeting - Dalton comes into our classroom and whispers in the teacher's ear. He leaves without even a glance. He wouldn't have spotted me anyhow. I am cowering behind the lad in front. Our teacher picks me out with his eyes, and with a knowing glare says, 'Mr Dalton says he hopes you haven't forgotten your appointment with him after school.'

As if!

Roy Slack looks at me and grins. We both know I'm doomed.

At the appointed hour I edge towards the discipline office. The other kids wait behind to goad me… 'You're gonna get it Hurndall. I bet that cane <u>really</u> hurts.' Dalton is already there, with a no-nonsense look, sitting behind the desk, screwing the top back on his fountain pen having already filled in the punishment book. The ink is still wet, my name glistening under the harsh fluorescent light. On the desk, tilted at an angle, is the dreaded cane.

'Can you tell me why I shouldn't give you six of the best?' he says.

My chin wobbles, which is genuine, but I turn on the tears with the aplomb of a Hollywood actor. I splutter my apologies, gulping for air like a toddler in a tantrum.

'I didn't mean it, Sir, not in a million years. You just happened to be in the way. I promise I'll never do it again,' thus stupidly betraying the notion that the whole thing was an unfortunate accident. There follows what seems a lifetime of silence. He milks my discomfort to the maximum, allowing the fear and regret of the moment to sink into my very soul. Suddenly he closes the punishment book with a thud.

'Go away. You're a very lucky boy,' he says.

Phew!

***

Tuesday afternoons are scheduled for 'games,' a distinction from PE which is just one lesson a week and is more about gymnastics than outdoor sport. The destination is a place called Ewell. None of us have a Scooby Doo where it is or how to spell it. We think it's called 'Yall.' It turns out that the Priest Hill Playing Fields, as they are called, form part of a huge chunk of land near Epsom. It was once owned by a rich aristocrat family called the Glyns and rented out to a tenant farmer. Following the death of Sir Arthur Glyn the site was put up for sale. Some hapless education officials thought it would be the answer to schools' recreation needs and it was purchased by the London County Council who converted 200 acres into playing fields complete with changing pavilions. There are football, hockey and rugby facilities and rather rough cricket pitches in summer.

At 2pm we assemble at the top gate ready to board the bus or coach. That first afternoon, as we eagerly embark with our kitbags, we are excited at the thought of a trip to the countryside and getting away from the concrete jungle. The novelty will soon wear off. What no-one had taken into account was the huge cost financially and environmentally in bussing thousands of kids from inner-London to Surrey every week. And also what a complete waste of time the whole exercise would be. Priest Hill is 13 miles from our school and can take up to an hour to get to through the busy South Circular and the congested arterial roads linking Streatham, Mitcham, Morden, Sutton and Ewell. What's galling is that our journey takes us past the wonderful facilities of the various Dulwich public schools, with their rugger and plush cricket grounds right on our doorstep.

Our teachers today are two familiar faces - footballers earning an extra bob or two outside the basement of the Football League. They are Harry Cripps and John Gilchrist, two Millwall defenders. Off the field they are completely the opposite from their football personas. Cripps is a hard, roly-poly left back and a fearless tackler. But in real life he's a teddy bear, friendly and polite, always smiling and sharing a joke. On the other hand John 'Skidmore' Gilchrist, a former Scottish soldier, is a quiet unassuming fullback, yet treats us like Army recruits, screaming and shouting, 'GET IN TWOS, GET IN TWOs... ' Anyone who moons out of the window will be caned, he lectures from the front of the bus.

157

At 2.45pm - 45 minutes after setting off - we arrive at 'Yall'. Gilchrist makes us run to the changing room, yelling we have two minutes to get changed. Shortly before three, we set off for a cross country run. I'm good at running and come in the first three with hardly any effort. It lasts 20 minutes or so and we are instructed to run through the shower without stopping and be back on the bus in the prescribed two minutes or else they will go without us. Not having a bathroom at home, it is my first ever shower - and it lasts less than five seconds.

On the way home, as we crawl through the early rush hour, I muse that we could just have easily run around the local park. We arrive back at school ten minutes after home time. For the rest of my school days the pattern will be the same. On one famous occasion a teacher will blow the final whistle after just three minutes, before most kids have even had a kick of the ball. Another time I will be given out in cricket because I hit the ball too far. The 'umpire' said retrieving the ball was too time consuming and called the next boy in to bat. I bet that doesn't happen on the playing fields of Eton.

***

It's Friday. And the end of a long first week. To avoid the nightly scramble and guarantee a seat on the bus, I walk to the preceding No 68 stop further along Herne Hill. There, I'm about to commit a classic schoolboy error. When I board, the bus is virtually empty and calamitously I decide to go on the upper deck at the front so I can look out of the window. I might have a great view but I'm out of sight of the conductor - they tend to turn blind eyes to unruly behaviour and under-age smoking up top.

As the bus approaches the main stop at Red Post Hill, there must be up to 100 kids pushing and shoving to board. Three or four fourth formers come upstairs and demand my front seat. I should have read the signals and moved but I merely shift towards the window to make more room. That's when the bullying starts.

I've developed the habit of untying my tie after school but leaving it draped loosely around my neck like a garland. The main bully grabs it and proceeds to tie me to the seat rail. I instinctively pull away to make him stop but he threatens to hit me if I do it again. All the other boys look on in silence, thankful it isn't them being picked on. The conductor is nowhere to be seen. The bully carries on knotting the tie and again I try to break free. He then headbutts me in the face. My nose takes the brunt of the impact and it starts bleeding. I also start crying. For ten minutes or so I'm stuck to the front seat with blood running into my mouth and dripping down my shirt.

We sail past my stop and the perpetrators get off in Walworth laughing and joking at my predicament. By now all the William Penn pupils have left... except for me, trying desperately to undo six or seven knots. Eventually the conductor arrives. I ask him to stop the bus until I'm freed. He refuses and tells me it's my fault for messing about! An adult passenger steps forward and unties me but by now we're halfway along Waterloo Road approaching the station! In addition to my bruises, blood and tears I now have to pay the fare back to Camberwell.

In just five days I've literally been bloodied to life at secondary school. I've escaped a caning by the skin of my teeth, discovered a mystery cousin, and been bullied in a most upsetting and humiliating fashion. From now on I will always travel downstairs on the bus. A valuable lesson for life at William Penn.

**

Each afternoon at precisely 3.45pm the comforting voice of the headmaster echoes on the Tannoy with announcements and to wish everyone a safe journey home. He also calls out a list of pupils he wants to see in his study after school. This can only mean one thing - six of the best, and it's often the same names. If there's been a bundle in the playground the combatants will be called to face the music. Fighting is against school rules, even in the park opposite the main gate where many differences are settled. In the playground I overstep the mark with one kid - Joseph Ramadan - who offers me out to a fight.

'After school. Top gate,' I say.

The problem is that word of a scrap spreads like wildfire ensuring a bigger crowd than they get at Manor Place baths for boxing. Kids come up wishing me luck. Also, I'm warned that Joe is a very tasty fighter who knows how to handle himself. Discretion is definitely the better part of valour and come 4pm, with crowds gathering at the top gate, I bottle it and nip out of the bottom gate, through the Sunray Gardens, and take the back route to the bus stop.

'Where were you?' he says the following day.

'More like where were _you_?,' I say. 'I waited by the bottom gate but you didn't turn up.'

'No, you said top gate,' he says.

'All right. You win,' I sigh. Honour is satisfied. And that is that.

**

In these first few weeks there's only one Tannoy message I want to hear - details of the trials for the First Year football team. Much to my huge disappointment, during my years Comber Grove School never had school teams in any sport and now I'd gladly volunteer to do the Paper Round for the rest of my life or even walk to school if it meant getting into the school team.

I've now moved into my Nan's old quarters, going from a cramped Aladdin's Cave of sweets to a bedroom the size of a squash court. I've inherited her furniture too and there are numerous hidey holes to hoard the detritus of a schoolboy's pocket - conkers, fag cards, marbles, coins, peashooters, penny book matches, and catapults. Mum has bought me my own electric blanket and I live under the covers listening to big fights on my new tranny. I'm on the first floor and no-one cares or dares to go up here. Most important of all, it means I can practise ball skills and diving headers on the bed, and fantasise about being hailed as a hero after scoring the winning goal for the school.

At last, the announcement I've been waiting for. *'Good afternoon. This is your headmaster speaking. Will all boys interested in playing for the First Year football team report to the gym block immediately after school tomorrow.'* I can hardly contain my excitement.

I've worked out the odds of being selected. They are huge. Of the 300 kids, well over half fancy themselves as the next Pele. Sure enough, come 4pm the next day, we turn up in our droves.

The 'manager' is a teacher called Dawson who arrives with a clipboard and pencil with a rubber on the end. I can see he's already run off a blank sheet of paper showing a 2-3-5 formation ready to fill in the names of the successful triallists. In later years the comedian Harry Enfield will invent a character called Tim Nice But Dim. I'm sure he must have met Dawson. He's an Upper Class Twit with an *'OK Ya'* accent. He knows little about football and has clearly been press-ganged into this extracurricular activity. How will he choose the lucky few? He asks us to form a line. This stretches virtually the length of the playground. We are about to engage in a Spartacus moment.

'Step forward if you played for the District at Primary School.'

A couple of lads oblige, including my mate Roy Slack who was the South London Schools goalie.

'Now step forward if you played for your school football team.'

Scores of boys step forward. The writing is on the wall here. Despite the fact that our school never had a team, I join them. A voice down the line is about to burst my dreams. 'Hurndall. We didn't have a school team, remember?'

It's the only other boy from my school to go to William Penn. And he's destroyed any hope of either of us being selected. I call him an idiot. Dawson tells me to step back in line despite my pleas that we DID have a school team, it's just that we didn't actually play any matches. He then disappears to the top playground with 50 or so kids who did represent their school, leaving us no-hopers to play amongst ourselves. *What's the point, if there's no one here to watch us!* I'm in the depths of gloom, and sit sulking on a bench plotting revenge on the kid who dobbed me in. And then a miracle happens.

I see my cousin Peter (remember him from Jersey?) emerging from the main teaching block. I call out to him. It turns out he's just had detention and is on the way home. He asks what I'm doing and I tell him about the frustrating trial process.

'Leave it to me,' he says, disappearing to the top playground where the action is and where Dawson is making his choices. After ten minutes or so Peter comes running back breathless. He's been watching proceedings and noticed just one position blank on Dawson's sheet - that of left half.

'He's coming back. If he asks, say that you're a specialist left half,' he urges.

I spring into life and start playing. I'm everywhere. Dribbling, chasing every ball, making every tackle, playing out of my skin. Dawson arrives looking pleased with himself. Peter sidles up to him and whispers, 'Blimey, that kid's a good player. I've been watching him for ages and he's different class to the rest.'

Dawson falls for it and comes up to me. 'What's your name?'

'Hurndall sir.'

'What position do you play.'

'Left half sir. It's where I play for my youth club.' Porky pie alert!

'Well I never. That's just the position I'm looking for!'

Dawson is so pleased with himself and tells me that I'm playing on Saturday. At 'Yall'. And I will not care how long it will take to get there!

I run home to tell my parents the news. 'I'm playing for the school. Out first match is Saturday,' I say excitedly.

'How much they paying you?' Dad asks.

'Nothing. It's for the honour,' I say.

'A boy of your age should be out working,' he commands.

I am all of 11 years old.

31

Down The Lane

Part of our weekend ritual is going to East Street on Sunday mornings. It may show East Street on the map, but everyone calls it The Lane. It's one of London's oldest markets and just a half a mile away. On the way, we listen to new releases in the booths of A1 Records on Walworth Road. Afterwards we wander down the Lane and are entertained without spending a sixpence. There's the Sally Army tambourines, a man and his monkey takes pictures of kids, sailors in uniform singing on their accordion, and we watch the stallholders and fly-pitchers with their amusing sales patter alluding to the dubious source of their produce.

'Don't ask me where I got these from, ladies. Let's just say the owner was looking the other way. Ask no questions and I'll tell you no lies. My tongue may be fast but my feet are even quicker. And if a policeman comes one way, I'll be running the jolly well other...'

At the junction of King and Queen Street there's always a guy selling stuff literally from the back of a lorry. He's a master of his art and we watch him for ages one week cutting bananas from the vine or, another week, unloading boxes of bottled sherry, port and muscadet which he sells in triple packs. He throws the fruit and bottles in the air with great theatre and his staff are like Rugby fullbacks catching them before they smash on the pavement.

Customers on the whole are quite shy and never want to be the first to buy. So, among the onlookers are the 'ricks' who, at the end of the sales spiel, step forward and loudly proclaim their interest and make that crucial first 'purchase.' This allows genuine punters the freedom to follow suit without feeling they are alone in taking a risk. This is not only great showmanship but a lesson in sales psychology which Johnny in particular studies and takes on board.

I am more fascinated by the 'Find The Lady' three-card tricksters. They hate me spying on them and often order me to run along. But it's easy for a lad like me to sneak to the back of the crowd. I watch every move and become an expert at spotting their sleight of hand. What the casual gambler doesn't know is that every one of the operatives are in cahoots trying to befriend them and to persuade them place a bet on which one of the three cards is the queen. The dealer pretends to cough and turns his back to the table. In this split second, one of his men turns over the queen, quickly places it face down again, and then persuades a shopper to place a tenner on it with him. The gang create a commotion whereby unseen by the gallery, the queen is switched. When the cards are revealed the poor punter has been relieved of his hard-earned. Rinse and repeat for an hour or so.

Down the bottom of the Lane are the eel and sarsaparilla stalls where we finish our morning with a traditional Cockney snack of jellied eels and a drink - warm in winter and cold in summer. Back home we swear blind we've not had any, but

Mum's no fool. When we leave food on the side of the plate she blames it on us having filled up on eels.

***

Johnny, now seventeen, is fed up with the early starts at Covent Garden, and wants to embark on a career as a suitcase salesman. His disdain for dawn starts isn't helped by his penchant for gambling with Dad all night at the kitchen table. I once came down to breakfast to go to school and they were still playing cards from the night before! Dad wouldn't let Johnny go to bed because he was losing!

Dad knows most of the wholesale jewellery merchants in the East End and takes him over to the Petticoat Lane area to buy various bracelets, necklaces and the like. All legit and with a receipt. My brother employs me to be his lookout at East Street and my cousin Janice as his 'rick.' Given he's selling jewellery it's better to have a female. He's been practising his sales patter in the kitchen all week and he nervously sets up at the junction of King and Queen Street near the banana man. He's 'borrowed' three milk crates from somewhere - one for him to sit on, another to rest his open case on, and the third for me to stand on next to him. My instructions are to look out for coppers and to shout *'Up, Up, Up'* if I spot a helmet snaking towards us in the crowd. If I miss, and he is nicked, he'll be taken to Carter Street for the rest of the day and probably charged with obstructing the highway. There'll be a court appearance too and a fine which will wipe out all his gains.

'Gather round ladies. I've some real bargains here today, straight out of the backdoor of HM Samuels...'

After a few minutes or so he comes to the 'bat' - the climax of his sales pitch, the moment he reveals the price. Step forward Janice, suitably made up to look much older than her 14 years....

'Can I have two please?' she says confidently. I have to say, he's a pretty good salesman, quickly learning the routine of rapping and wrapping the jewellery and taking the money all at the same time. A natural instinct is to snatch a buyer's hand off. However, if a punter is holding out a pound note Johnny instinctively delays taking it or giving change so as to hold the 'hedge' of customers for as long as possible. He knows that people are always curious when there's a crowd around a salesman but melt away when there's nothing to see.

Now at this point I'd like to make a confession. I have a butterfly brain, constantly needing more stimulation. And staring at the same spot for minutes on end is... well, boring. So my mind drifts. I look at the shoppers. What they've bought. Their clothes. The stallholders. Their wares. I look at the sky, the clouds, the sun. And I fail to spot the navy Met helmet with its silver badge floating on the sea of heads. He's on to Johnny in a flash.

'Come on, sunshine, you're nicked.'

My brother looks at me with daggers.

163

'Much obliged,' he says, slamming his case shut and accompanying the constable to Carter Street nearby. Del Boy and his plonker bruv! There's nothing much I can do except gather up his crates and stack them on the side of the road. Janice and I go our separate ways. She'll be paid later and so will I - after a deduction for incompetency and a Big Brother bollocking. And, like a failed football manager, I'll be sacked in the morning.

***

My teenage years are split between school, playing football, the cinema and making money on the side.

At William Penn I have the honour of wearing a special tie to mark my achievement at sport. There are six houses and everyone has to wear a tie in their house colour. Everyone that is, except me. If you represent the school at three sports you are presented with a commemorative claret and blue tie which I proudly wear as a badge of honour. I am now captain of the school football and basketball teams and open the batting for the cricket team. I am also selected to attend trials for the district soccer and cricket teams and am a fringe member of both squads. But after 12 months I stop wearing the tie. They've changed the rules so that boys who are in just two teams now qualify. This 'special' tie is now commonplace and in a display of immature petulance I dump mine in my bedroom drawer and revert to my Paxton House purple one.

Basketball team: that's me! Back Row, No.8.

***

The Grand Cinema at Camberwell Green is a rite of passage for all teenagers. It's the proverbial 'flea pit', the sort of place where men of dodgy disposition lurk in the darkness and the same person sells you a ticket, operates the projector, and comes round with the ice creams in the interval. It's in its death throes as a picture house and they don't seem to care who they allow in or about any age restrictions. It's well-known you can see adult films without any age proof and we spend many an hour watching Hammer Horror movies - mostly Peter Cushing and the horror icon, Dulwich born Boris Karloff - which as young teenagers we aren't supposed to do. Leaving the cinema is scarier than any Frankenstein and Mummy Monsters. You exit at the rear into a dark alley, a haven for dirty old men and Teddy Boys. We sprint like the wind back to the main road.

The Odeon further up from Camberwell Green and the nearby Regal are regular haunts, often jibbing-in via the push-bar exit doors as people are leaving after an earlier performance. I once spent the whole day in The Odeon watching the same film over and over: Shenandoah, starring James Stewart as a proud God-fearing widower left to bring up his six sons on his Virginian farm whilst trying to resist the implications of the Civil War which crept ever closer to his land. For some reason it struck a chord and I even memorised the opening lines.

As the distant guns grow ever louder, one son says, 'They seem to be gettin' closer every day, Pa.'

To which the James Stewart character replies, 'Are they on our land yet?'

'No sir.'

'Then it ain't none of our business.'

Funds for such ventures come from unlikely sources. One of my schoolmates has a cousin who owns a number of night clubs and who pays us to hand out flyers outside Underground stations. He picks us up at the school gates in his Jag - much kudos there - and drives us to the West End to intercept office girls on their way home from work. Only girls, is the instruction. And preferably pretty ones! It's my introduction to accosting girls on the street!

I'm about to betray my entrepreneurial roots and realise once and for all that selling in the street isn't for me. Dad has a mate called Bill Smith who is looking for kids to sell posters at football matches. For two shillings fans can buy a giant-sized photograph of their favourite team. The customers are usually dads with their lads. Me, Michael Corbett and my cousin Peter decide to go into business selling the posters outside London football grounds. It's proving quite lucrative if hard graft, and boring. When Manchester United are in town we sell scores of black and white Man U team line-ups and top up with coloured portraits of George Best. At first we attend matches as a threesome, standing at different gates. But we soon realise that doubling up is a waste of resources when there are other games going on in the capital. So, for weeks we lug the photos on the tube to West Ham, Chelsea, Spurs and Arsenal and meet up afterwards at Bill's office in West London to divide up the takings. It's a gruelling day, getting to the ground early in the morning and not getting home until the evening.

All good things come to an end. Millwall, languishing in the lower divisions, are playing first division Fulham in the Cup. It's decided that I'll go to the Den and the others will work other games in the capital where Man Utd are also playing. Millwall proves to be a disaster for me. There's chaos outside the ground which is not used to dealing with such a big crowd. I deem it too risky to plot down at the main gate and try to sell pictures further away. I hardly sell one. At 3pm, my previous affiliation for The Lions skewers my judgement and I go in to watch the match rather than rendezvous with the others. I arrive late and exhausted from my travels. They've had a good day but I've taken less than a pound. They are naturally upset and accuse me of not trying hard enough. We split the profits and I announce I'm leaving and don't want to sell pictures any more.

***

Michael's and my own relatives work in the bars at the races. They're brilliant barmaids, flirting with punters, encouraging groups of men to buy drinks and snacks etc. What the bosses don't know is that the women smuggle in their own bottles of spirits which of course they sell at racecourse prices. One school holiday Michael and I travel with them on the company coach to Brighton Races. We set off bright and early because they've to set up the bars. We kill time by walking around the racecourse. On the far side of the circuit we're approached by two men doing track maintenance. They ask if we know anything. We immediately cotton on that they think we're stable lads. And we go along for the ride, so to speak. Our Cockney instinct tells us there's money to be made. I happen to have studied form on the bus and know one or two of the afternoon runners.

'We do, but it's inside information. We risk the sack by even talking to you.' They offer a pound each for any tips and hand over two quid.

'Back a horse called Eze in the third race,' I say. We walk off giggling to ourselves at our unexpected windfall. But the story doesn't end there. The horse actually wins at 6-1! You don't need to tell us what to do tomorrow! Sure enough we walk the course at the same time. We're approached again - this time by four men. They'd all backed our tip the day before and are willing to pay handsomely for more inside information. We make about £20 on two horses. Sadly they lose, but we are the real winners.

Vouchers are the source of more pocket money. Michael has a relative who works in the headquarters of Kensitas cigarettes. Manufacturers put vouchers in the packets to entice smokers to buy their brand. People trade them for goods. He somehow acquires hundreds of these vouchers and we are paid to go to the store in the West End and redeem them. There's also a black market throughout South London of Green Shield stamps and most homes and kitchen contain items like toasters and ash trays courtesy of their gift catalogues.

The £21 million Elephant and Castle Shopping Centre opens in a blaze of publicity. Billed as South London's 'Piccadilly Circus', it's next to one of London's busiest roundabouts. The arcade is one of the most modern in Europe and supposedly the continent's first covered shopping mall. It covers three storeys and boasts an underground car-park, a retractable glass roof and a bronze statue of an elephant. But the take-up is poor. Only a quarter of the 120 outlets are occupied. The centre is forced to react and mounts a massive promotion campaign which includes 'money-off' vouchers.

One of our lads - I shall call him Jimmy- is quite a tea leaf, and is always laden with fags and other shoplifting booty. Somehow he's acquired dozens of new voucher booklets which are as good as cash. He shows us. They're like raffle ticket books, literally hundreds of vouchers, each worth five bob and redeemable in any shop. He's been using them every day in the Wimpy Bar on the bottom of the complex and invites a few of us Cambridge House Boys for a free meal.

I'm sceptical but the owner greets him like an old friend. We aren't going to look a gift horse in the mouth so we steam in ordering double cheeseburgers and chips and Knickerbocker Glories - oozing ice cream, fruit and meringue served in a tall conical glass and eaten with a long spoon.

For a fortnight we dine out in style. Until one day a security officer from the centre approaches and asks us where we got the vouchers from. Did we know they'd been stolen? We all look to Jimbo. He says he found them on the pavement. The guy allows us to pay with vouchers this time but we must hand over all the rest and never return to the shopping centre again. Much to the relief of our waistlines, this is the end of our freebie dining club. The centre will not last either. It will be razed to the ground in 2020, another disappearing chapter of my childhood history.

32

No-Pay TV

There's much excitement around our way. We've been selected to take part in a ground-breaking experiment which might change the face of television forever. Our TV is rented from the cable company British Relay. Every month Mum goes into their little shop on Walworth Road and pays the rental fee. But last month she came home with a glossy leaflet asking if we want to be part of an experimental pay TV channel called, er, Pay TV.

The flyer explains it'll be the first time viewers can pay directly for what they watch. We're unique. There's only a handful of streets been selected in Southwark and Westminster, a couple of thousand subscribers in all.

The Government are backing the scheme to test the viability of pay per view on a much wider scale. British Relay will dish up a collection of premium films and events, including ballet and theatre, all priced accordingly. It'll be transmitted for 50 hours a week from 7pm weekdays and an all-day service at weekends. No more expensive cinema tickets or trudging in the rain to sports events. We'll have a ringside seat and popcorn in our own home.

We'll be sent a monthly menu, and given a little grey box that rests on top of the screen where we'll slot in our two-bob pieces. For six bob a pop, we'll be able watch films that we might have missed at the cinema a few years back.

***

We're only days into the experiment and someone has already found a loophole. They 'accidentally' knocked the operating box off the telly and it fell to the floor, thus snapping the mechanism inside. The result? Free films. News of the unfortunate mishap spreads like wildfire and now half the subscribers are dropping the boxes on the floor and realising they'll be permanently switched on for free!

Ours too has 'fallen' off and we are revelling in movies like the Cold War spy thriller The Ipcress File, the gritty comedy Billy Liar and the Peter Sellers laugh-a-minute A Shot in the Dark. Dad's enjoying the free live horse racing from meetings that are not on terrestrial TV, and I'm even tasting the delights of American wrestling.

The man from British Relay comes round to empty the box and collect the money. He doesn't need a security guard. He says somewhat sarcastically how strange it is that so many people have broken boxes and how his bosses have been scratching their heads wondering why the income in Southwark contrasts so poorly with Westminster even taking into account the economic disparity of the two communities. Never mind, he says. Soon they'll be bringing out a new generation of boxes which are much sturdier and resistant to Camberwell's 'knockout drops'.

***

It's May 1966 and we are about to witness one of the great sporting attractions ever. In our front room! British Heavyweight champion and fellow South Londoner Henry Cooper is taking on the greatest fighter ever - Muhammad Ali. It's a rematch of their clash three years ago when 'Our 'Enry' famously knocked down Cassius Clay as he was known then. Only a cruel cut eye prevented Cooper from going on to claim a famous victory.

South London loves its boxing heroes. It boasts several boxing clubs and the Thomas a Becket pub on the corner of Albany Road and the Old Kent Road has an upstairs ring where many of our fighting stars train.

A year previously, local world champion Freddie Mills, in his day one of the best-loved figures in British sport, famed for his bravery and aggression, had been found shot dead in his car in an alleyway behind the Soho nightclub he owned. He had lived in 'Jogging Villa' near Ruskin Park on Denmark Hill which I passed on the bus on the way to school every day, hoping to catch a glimpse of him on his drive. I had seen him occasionally in the Walworth Road laughing and joking with shoppers who tended to surround him and demand autographs.

The funeral service took place at St Giles Parish Church at Camberwell Green, where my parents were married. Shocked mourners turned out in their thousands. The entertainer Bruce Forsyth was a pall bearer and gave the funeral address.

Mills was heavily in debt and had borrowed a shotgun from a friend who ran a rifle range at Battersea Fun Fair. The weapon was resting between his knees when he was found. The Coroner ruled it was suicide, a verdict disputed by the family. In the weeks after his death, rumours surfaced that he was in fact murdered. Rival gangsters - the Chinese and American Mafias and the Kray Twins - were names in the frame. But the most extraordinary allegation was that he took his life because he feared being exposed as a serial killer. Jimmy Tippet, a reformed gangster and son of a boxing champion, claimed in a book that Mills was responsible for the deaths of at least eight prostitutes whose naked bodies were found in and around the River Thames in the early sixties. The so-called 'Jack The Stripper' murders stopped after he died and the killer was never found.

Mills is buried in Camberwell New Cemetery near my uncles and cousins. His grave has a marble boxing glove on it and an urn containing one of his gloves. But the real circumstances of his death were buried with him and will be forever shrouded in mystery.

***

Following Mills' sad demise, Henry Cooper is our new boxing idol. Tonight's fight is being staged in the open air at Highbury, the home of Arsenal Football Club before 46,000 spectators, the largest live audience ever at a British boxing event. It's also being shown in 16 Odeon cinemas across the country and, exclusively, on Pay TV. Our family and friends are green with envy that we can watch the fight live while they'll have to wait with the rest of the nation for the delayed broadcast on BBC later in the week.

Suddenly, everyone wants to be my friend. *Can we come over and watch?* Sadly, Dad has already promised half of Camberwell and there is no room for Alan's teenage mates. Our front room is packed with bodies and crates of light ale. People are sitting on the floor, even on the stairs, just to hear the commentary and feel part of the action. I'm appointed treasurer and chief operating officer for the evening, squatting down below the telly which we've elevated onto our 'cocktail' bar. The fight via the newer robust boxes costs four quid. Even though Dad wouldn't dream of asking anyone for money everyone is chipping in with two-bob coins which I stack like King Midas ready to slot into the machine.

The action starts with a roar you can hear down Camberwell Road. We are all screaming at the screen for Cooper to land another of his famed left hooks and send the cocky Ali to the canvas again. Unfortunately, Ali's a quick learner and doesn't allow himself to be exposed again, holding his opponent tight inside. Each time the Ref yells 'break' Ali makes sure he pushes Cooper back. Ali stays away for three rounds as Cooper continues to stalk him. In the next two rounds Ali allows Cooper to come closer, but counters with a succession of blows. A heavy punch opens up Henry's eyes again, the blood spouting in the air. Game over in six rounds.

Neither Henry nor Pay TV will last long. He will retire in five years time following a controversial loss to Joe Bugner. Unlike Mills, he'll be the only British boxer to be knighted and a plaque will be erected on the Bellingham Estate in Lewisham where he spent his early life.

Pay TV will close in two years despite expanding into Sheffield. The Government will be unwilling to remove caps on subscriber numbers and it will become unprofitable. But extraordinary to think I am literally on the ground floor of what years later will be commonplace.

Freddie Mills: murder or suicide? Right: Our 'Enry battered by Ali.

33

How the World Cup was lost - and won!

Camberwell has had more than its share of scandals and scoundrels over the years committing crimes that made headlines. Remember the Great Train Robbery? And the Richardson Torture Gang? And the shooting in an East End pub of Camberwell gangster George Cornell by one of the Kray twins? Well, we're about to be the centre of a theft so notorious it will be talked about across the globe for years.

It's 1966 - World Cup year. And England are the hosts. Everyone is anticipating a feast of football, particularly yours truly who's simply soccer mad. The Football Association has invented the first ever mascot for such an event - World Cup Willie, a cartoon lion decorated in a Union Jack, whose cheeky smile adorns everything from bars to bedrooms - badges, beer mats, even bedspreads and bras. The tournament even has a song - World Cup Willie, sung by the skiffle Scotsman Lonnie Donegan with lyrics rooting for England.

World Cup Willie - the first mascot

The trophy itself - an eight-inch high solid-silver figurine covered in gold plate - has arrived in the country under strict security. In pure metal terms it's not worth that much. But its symbolism, named after the father of the World Cup Jules Rimet, makes it priceless. It was made in 1930 and of course held by the country that last won it. During the Second World War, the Italian Football President hid it in a shoebox under his bed to protect it from bomb damage or theft by marauding Mussolini troops.

The famous Jules Rimet Trophy

The English FA has locked it in its safe at its headquarters in Lancaster Gate. But they've been approached by a stamp company for permission to include the statuette in their 'Stampex' exhibition at the Methodist Central Hall in Westminster. Money has no doubt changed hands because the man from the ruling body FIFA says 'yes'. Its English President, Sir Stanley Rous, insists on a number of conditions. These include transportation by a reputable security company; it being placed in a locked glass case; be guarded day and night; and be insured for £30,000. The stamps on display are valued at £3m so Rous thinks that being on show amongst far more valuable exhibits the trophy will be relatively safe from any sticky fingers. There's the added comfort too that the venue is nestled nicely between Scotland Yard, the Home Office and the Houses of Parliament. Nearby, at the Whitehall Theatre, Brian Rix is starring in the latest of his long-running farces. What can possibly go wrong?

Step forward two of Camberwell's finest tea-leaves. Sid and Reg Cugullere are brothers grim. Known as the 'Cooeyies', they were brought up near East Street market off the Walworth Road and learned their trade when kids stealing from kiosks and stalls. Reg's son will later recall how acting as a pair, one would pinch something under the nose of the stallholder who would chase after him. While he was gone, the other would help himself.

The brothers graduated into more serious crime such as safe-breaking and stealing mail bags. Sid Cugullere, who served time with another local lad, "Mad" Frankie Fraser, once cheekily dressed up as a Securicor guard and arrived at a bank in uniform, crash helmet and with a crackling personal radio on his lapel. The staff thought he was legit and helpfully loaded bundles of cash into his swag bag. But there is an element of Dumb and Dumber about these two. They once buried a quantity of cash in their garden but the containers weren't watertight. Reg's son remembers walking into the house wondering what the terrible smell was. Upstairs were washing lines pegged with bundles of notes hanging out to dry.

It is March 20th. The World Cup is four months away. It's a Sunday. There's a church service on and the exhibition is closed. But two of the 200 congregation in the building have screwdrivers and a bolt cutter hidden under their coats and are here not to worship the Lord, but to pray for lax security around the valuable stamp collection, if you get my drift.

The golden goddess of victory stands gleaming in a display cabinet in the deserted first floor exhibition room. Shortly after midday, a security guard returns from a tea break and rubs his eyes in disbelief. Someone's nicked the World Cup! So much for round-the-clock protection! Later inspection reveals the thieves have entered the hall from the street by unscrewing the mounts holding a bar across the rear exit doors and then cutting the padlock at the back of the display case.

Reg's son Gary will one day reveal to the Daily Mirror that his father knew nothing of the theft and that his uncle Sid stole the trophy 'for the honour' and not for financial gain. They'd been intending to nick stamps but on the street outside, Sid lifted his jacket and said, 'Ere you are, Reg, take a look at this.'

Reg replied, 'F***ing hell, Sid. What the f*** do you think we're gonna do with that?'

The World Cup's a gonner guv!

The loss of the sport's premier trophy is an acute embarrassment for FIFA, the FA, politicians, the police and the country as a whole. We've become a laughing stock across the globe. International football authorities condemn the English stating how foolish we are. The Brazilian reaction is typical.

'Even Brazilian thieves love football and would never commit this sacrilege,' says their football president. (Rather unfortunate in that the trophy will later be stolen again - from under the noses of the football authorities in Brazil!)

The FA put out a statement. 'We deeply regret this unfortunate incident. It inevitably brings discredit to both the FA and the country.' It quietly commissions a silversmith in Fenchurch Street to make a replica in case the original doesn't turn up.

With a General Election imminent, the Prime Minister Harold Wilson, who has just a single seat majority, worries it could even cause him reputational damage. His aides secretly order the Yard to stop at nothing to retrieve the trophy and even to do deals with the thieves if required. Just get it back!

Meanwhile the brothers hide their hot property in their father's coal bunker in Camberwell while they work out how to monetise their opportunism. They phone their mate, a local villain called Teddy Betchley, a car dealer who lives round the back of me on the Brandon Estate in Walworth and who pops by for the occasional newspaper. For a cut of the proceeds, Betchley offers to act as a go-between. He rings the FA and Chelsea chairman Joe Mears calling himself 'Jackson'.

In a scene straight from a crime caper movie of the 50s, he nervously whispers down the receiver…

'There'll be a parcel at Chelsea Football Club tomorrow. If you want the trophy back, follow the instructions inside.' Sure enough, the parcel arrives containing felt ripped from the bottom of the trophy and a typed ransom note composed by the brothers. *'Dear Joe. Kno (sic) doubt you view with very much concern the loss of the World Cup… to me it's only so much scrap gold. If I don't hear from you by Thursday or Friday at the latest, I assume it's one for the pot.'*

Coincidentally, One For The Pot is the title of a comedy of errors starring Brian Rix about to be televised on BBC about grown men making fools of themselves using deceit to try to get their hands on a ten grand reward.

Betchley, still calling himself Jackson, then phones Mears again and demands £15,000 for the cup to arrive safely back in a cab. Payments must be in £5 and £10 notes. If the FA are willing to do business, they must place a notice in the Personal Column of the Evening News saying 'Willing to do business. Joe.' If not, or if the police or Press are told, the trophy will be melted down.

Mears has no choice but to call in the Yard and they send Detective Inspector Charles Buggy of the Flying Squad to take control. Buggy instructs that the ad be placed in Thursday's edition of the paper. He also arranges for bundles of scrap paper to be arranged as 'cash' with real notes only placed at each end.

The next day, Buggy and two other colleagues wait at Mears' home in Fulham Road for Jackson's promised phone call. The officers are chosen because they look more like football officials than police officers! The operation hits a snag as Mears has an angina attack due to the stress of it all. His wife takes the call from Jackson and hands over the phone to her ailing husband's 'assistant' Mr. McPhee, who is in fact DI Buggy. Jackson is uneasy at the sudden change of arrangements but Buggy talks him round. They agree to swap the trophy for the agreed amount. A rendezvous is arranged in Battersea Park. Buggy drives Mears' car to the park followed by various unmarked Flying Squad vehicles.

Just inside the gates Betchley, pretending to be Jackson, approaches the car to meet Buggy, who is pretending to be McPhee, and is shown the suitcase full of pretend money. Parked nearby are cops pretending to be ordinary motorists, including two pretending to be a courting couple.

Betchley asks to see the readies but is only allowed a glimpse. Buggy insists he won't hand the money over until he's seen the trophy. Betchley says it's just ten minutes away and gets in the car. He directs them around in circles, constantly checking the rear to see if they're being followed. He orders the car to stop because a 'funny old van' is tailing them. Buggy allows the van to pass and Betchley says he recognises the vehicle from its distinctive barred windows at the rear, saying he knows for a fact it's a type used by the Flying Squad. Buggy dismisses it as a coincidence but a few minutes later the same van is behind them again.

On the edge of Kennington Park, Betchley orders Buggy to stop and wait while he retrieves the cup from a location nearby. Farcically for an undercover operation, and reminiscent of the Keystone Cops, the 'funny old van' pursues him along the pavement. A rattled Betchley spots it and runs back to the car. They travel a few hundred yards, he sees they're still being followed, then jumps out the moving vehicle and legs it without the cash. He is chased around the Brandon Estate and is eventually cornered and taken to Kennington nick.

Edward 'Teddy' Betchley

Under questioning, 'Jackson's' true identity is revealed. His name in police files is Edward Betchley, 47-year-old dealer of fancy goods, with a conviction for theft and receiving dodgy corned beef for which he'd served a six month prison sentence. He is charged with intent to steal and demanding money with menaces and will be sentenced to two years. He denies anything to do with the theft and claims he'd been offered £500 by some mysterious Pole to act as an intermediary. But he refuses to grass the Polish gentleman, or anyone else for that matter.

It's been a week since the audacious theft. The handover has been botched and the trophy still at large, who knows where? Now, the whole episode is about to take the most extraordinary twist of all. After the arrest of their associate, the Cooeyies brothers' dad is freaking out fearing that the dear old Nike goddess has become too hot to handle. He demands their sons get rid. He doesn't care where - just not on his premises or in the coal shed.

Around 9pm that evening a young Thames lighterman called David Corbett leaves his house on Beulah Hill in South Norwood to make a phone call. He decides to take his dog Pickles, a one-year-old black and white crossbreed collie, with him for exercise. In the road outside, he tries to put his lead on but Pickles is distracted by something under the hedge and starts sniffing. Corbett pulls him away, but the dog is yapping and persistent. His owner discovers his pet is obsessed by a parcel tightly wrapped in old newspaper and securely tied with string. He tears the wrapping open to reveal a gold-coloured trophy. He doesn't recognise it until he sees the wording... 'Brazil 1962' inscribed on the plaque.

'Blimey, Pickles. You've found the World Cup!'

He takes the trophy to Gypsy Hill police station and hands it in. The police themselves are unsure if it's genuine or some prank and transport it to Cannon Row nick where the publicity officer for the FA's World Cup Organising Committee is dragged out of bed to formally identify it.

The recovery is revealed at a news conference the following morning. The football world, including the prime minister, breathes a sigh of relief. Dad immediately suspects that Pickles' involvement is a shaggy dog story - and so at first do the police. Corbett is the prime suspect and is questioned until 2.30am. But he has a clear alibi for the time of the theft the previous Sunday.

Corbett with Pickles the World Cup hero - credit Press Association

Corbett claims that as the finder, Pickles is entitled to the reward money. The dog turns into a cash cow, appearing on TV, opening supermarkets, starring in adverts, and even in a film with Eric Sykes and June Whitfield called The Spy With a Cold Nose. He's awarded the silver medal of the National Canine Defence League and given free food for life by the pet food manufacturers Spillers. Sadly, that life isn't to last for long. Next year he will be strangled by his own lead which catches on a tree branch whilst he chases a cat and Pickles will be buried with his medal in the garden of the house his master bought with the royalties and rewards. The South London crossbreed collie will enter sporting folklore and be toasted by the family for years with a summer glass of Chardonnay.

And what of the other players in this drama? Pickles proves a pet from heaven for Harold Wilson who basks in the new feelgood factor and romps home in the General Election a few days later. Betchley will serve his time in Pentonville Prison but his accomplices will go to their graves masked men. The only hint of the brothers' involvement will be on the order of service and wreaths at Reg's funeral - images of the World Cup trophy that posthumously brings them fame…if not fortune.

A wreath and order of service at Reg's funeral - credit Daily Mirror

***

It's been three weeks since the World Cup trophy saga and now matters on the field take my attention. My team Chelsea have made it through to the FA Cup Semi-final against Sheffield Wednesday at Villa Park. On the way they've beaten the likes of Liverpool and Leeds and are also destined to play Barcelona in the semi-final of the Fairs Cup, claiming the scalps of Roma, Milan and 1860 Munich. With luck, they could win two cups in a matter of days.

The club has certainly bounced back from the Blackpool scandal the previous year. Then, challenging for the League title, they faced the Seasiders with just two games to go. Unfortunately, a few days before the match, eight of the players broke the manager's curfew and went out clubbing until three in the morning. The boss Tommy Docherty will later reveal that he went into one of the hotel rooms and there was midfielder John Hollins pretending to be asleep. He pulled the cover back and his player was still in his jacket and tie. Docherty publicly humiliated them by sending them back on the train to London, thus missing the match. With a weakened team they lost to Blackpool and threw away any chance of the title.

But now hopes are high of cup success. The club announce that tickets for the FA Cup semi are going on sale at the ground on Sunday morning. I get up early to join the queue. At least that is the intention. Arriving a few hours before the sale, it's already back as far as Fulham Broadway Underground station. I decide to by-pass the six-deep line of fans six and head to the front. There, alone, I 'blend' into the queue. Getting a ticket is such a thrill and I zip it up in my coat in case the unthinkable happens and I lose it. Walking back to get the Underground home, the line of fans now stretches beyond the station as far as the eye can see. My match ticket tucked away, I go to Euston and buy a return seat on one of the many British Rail special trains.

I decide to make a flag for the occasion. I purchase a pole and a roll of iron-on tape and scour East Lane market for the right colour blue material without success. However, I notice that one of Mum's kitchen aprons is a perfect match. I figure she won't miss it if I... well, cut it up. I start ironing for the first time in my life, cutting strips of white sticky tape into letters saying 'Chelsea For The Cup', not the most original flag in history. The message goes across two lines and looks great although the letters are very square! I nail the apron to the pole and roll the flag up so that Mum can't see what I've done to her M and S essential. I now have my own unique flag to take up North.

I arrive at Euston mid-morning. The atmosphere is electric. There are four or five trains waiting to ferry the fans to Birmingham. Chelsea songs echo around the rafters. The club has a reputation for hooliganism and I sit alone, well away from any likely trouble-makers. As we approach Aston station, I pull down the window and wave my flag to make the locals aware that the mighty Blue Army has arrived. When I retrieve it, my carefully arranged slogan has all but disappeared - blown off in the turbulence. All that's left is three letters - L, A and a very droopy C. The rest are somewhere down the track. The carriage is in hoots of laughter and, red-faced, I snap the pole in half and deposit the bits in the station bin.

To make matters worse it starts to pour with rain and I've no coat. I walk to the ground wishing I'd not been so hasty discarding the flag remnants which I could have draped around my head and shoulders. Inside the ground there are 60,000 fans but I'm horrified that there's no cover at our end. The bone-dry Sheffield Wednesday supporters taunt us from their covered stand while we risk pneumonia from the Spring showers. Worse, the muddy pitch conditions don't suit our fancy style of football and we are literally muscled out of the cup 2-0. A miserable day all round.

On the train home I ponder if and what to tell mum about her apron. The tattered flag is a metaphor for the whole day. And I decide to let sleeping dogs lie.

***

That summer of 1966 will be remembered by every sports fanatic for years to come. England are hosting the World Cup for the first time. Johnny is making a name for himself as an ace street trader selling at markets across the South and supplementing his income buying and selling tickets at football matches. He has a reputation among his mates as the best money-earner they know, able to turn a profit out of any situation.

England has made it through to the quarter finals and like every kid in the country I want to be there. I ask him what the chances are of getting a ticket. None, is the reply. But he says if I want to take a chance and go to Wembley you never know...

Sure enough, on a hot sunny day I get the Underground to Wembley Park ticketless but full of hope of somehow seeing England versus Argentina. Who in their right mind would turn up ticketless when the match is live on the telly anyway? Me! Ticket touting is one of the most fluid of markets. It literally is supply versus demand. And early prices are through the roof. But as kick off nears it's apparent the market is flooded with spare tickets, sending prices crashing. As the band plays God Save The Queen the touts literally cannot give tickets away. Johnny comes up and offers me a choice of seats! All for free! I choose the centre, just below the Royal Box. Maybe it was foolhardy of me to contemplate going to Wembley that day but I'm now the luckiest 13-year-old in London.

The match itself is riddled with controversy. Argentina play hard and dirty, fouling and arguing with the referee at every turn. The England manager Alf Ramsey will later describe them as 'animals'. Their captain Antonio Rattin becomes the first player to be sent off in an international at Wembley. But he refuses to leave the field and has to be persuaded to exit by two London policemen! With 12 minutes to go and Argentina down to ten men, Geoff Hurst heads England through to the semi-finals. Everyone goes wild. While England perform a lap of honour, Argentina slump on the pitch, distraught in the heat. They will forever call it *'el robo del siglo,'* - the robbery of the century.

To reach the final, England must now overcome Portugal who possess one of the game's all-time greats, Eusebio. It's a midweek game under floodlights. Having gambled attending the quarter-final without a ticket and won, I do the same again, rushing home from school, changing and making the 45-minute trip to Wembley scared I might miss the most important game in England's football history. It's a repeat scenario. Ticket prices an hour before kick-off are sky-high. I've no chance. But I wait, and wait, and wait. And again at kick-off, the touts are running around with bundles of spares, and again Johnny gives me a ticket for free. How fortunate I am to have such an enterprising brother!

This time I'm behind the goal. England win 2-0. Bobby Charlton overshadows Eusebio and scores both - the second right in front of where I'm standing. I can see the ball heading into the net long before it crosses the line - an image that will never leave me.

The final against West Germany is a different matter. Do I want to risk going ticketless for a third time? I can't possibly miss the biggest game ever and I bottle it, deciding to stay at home and watch it with the rest of the nation on the telly. The rest, as they say, will be history...

34

Hard Core Pawn

Barrett the pawnbroker in 1967: right - the same site 2024 (c. Google Earth)

A hundred yards along from my home, on the corner of Albany Road and Camberwell Road, is the most important shop in my parents existence - J.J. Barrett & Sons, jewellers and pawnbrokers. The fortunes of a gambling household have many ups and downs and Barretts feature prominently on both counts. After a win Dad will often buy Mum a diamond ring or a necklace from their glittering displays, but that same jewellery will inevitably find its way back into the shop - this time via the pawnbroker counter.

The way it works is that the broker will lend you cash against the value of the item. When you can afford to repay the money, you get the item back, minus of course his commission. The shop owner knows Mum and Dad personally and makes a fair profit from their helter-skelter lifestyle, indeed from the ups and downs of many folk living in the inner-city.

So, approaching my 14th birthday, Mum tells him she wants to buy me a decent watch and asks him to look out for something suitable. Sure enough, someone has pawned a Rolex and failed to reclaim it. He offers it to Mum at a knockdown price. Come February 4th, I open the nicely wrapped parcel and discover a silver Oyster Royal all nicely polished and looking like a new timepiece.

At first, I'm only allowed to wear it on special occasions but soon its preciousness wears off and it's on my wrist at school, youth club, even playing football.

We go on a school trip to Spain and naturally I take it with me. We stay in a resort called Callela and spend an enjoyable few days lounging on the vast beach, swimming in the sea, going to a bullfight and visiting the Camp Nou stadium, home of Barcelona Football Club. One of the lads smuggles a football inside and we have a kickabout in the goalmouth. I don't think I've seen anyone more angry than the groundsman who comes racing across the pitch having a apoplectic fit. We are asked to leave.

But worse is to follow. Some of our party go 'shopping' around the tourist quarter and help themselves to a glittering array of tat including fake-jewelled bracelets, shiny rings and knives, even a 'diamond'-studded silver sword. The shopkeeper remembers that one of the thieves was black - a rarity in the resort. It doesn't take long to trace the young black male back to our hotel - indeed to my room. He's my roommate and our cupboards and drawers are crammed with contraband. We are raided by Spanish cops in their smart navy uniforms and highly-polished boots. Our teacher looks on concerned and acts as interpreter. They ask me where I got my watch from. I tell them it's my own - a gift from my mother. It's clear they don't believe me. I explain that I've never been to the store in question and that indeed I was with our teacher elsewhere at the time of the thefts. They are about to confiscate it when the storekeeper appears up the stairs breathless. The police show him the Rolex. There's a conversation in Spanish which ends in the man shaking his head and the policeman handing the watch back to me.

However, it appears that at least a dozen pupils were involved in the thieving spree. No charges are made but the whole school party are ordered out of town by the police, much to the embarrassment of the teachers. We arrive home early with our heads hanging in shame - the first school trip from William Penn ever to be cancelled.

That watch will remain a precious memento for almost thirty years. It'll be proudly adorning my wrist throughout my teens, at work, rest and play, at my wedding, celebrating the birth of my children, and at the funerals of Mum and Dad. Indeed, after Mum dies, it will cling to my wrist as a precious personal reminder of her memory and her generosity, and be worth hundreds of pounds as a collector's piece.

Several years after her funeral, one day the watch will suddenly stop. It just so happens that my route to work will take me past the factory in Kent where they repair Rolex watches and I will take it in for a service. Ten days on it will arrive in the post and will I open the packaging ready to unite it with my wrist once again. Instead there'll be note from Rolex. Unfortunately, it will say, 'we must put this little fellow to sleep', the spares needed to repair it being no longer available. Saddened, I will put it in my bedside drawer to remember Mum each time I open it.

A few months later, our home will be burgled - four houses in our road broken into and ransacked. The watch, along with other jewellery, will be stolen and never recovered. Someone, somewhere will have a silver Oyster Royal: broken, worthless but of huge sentimental value to its previous owner. My only consolation is that I shall claim £1,000 on the insurance. Thanks Mum!

***

The Sixties will always be known as the 'Swinging Sixties'. And I'm growing up with one of the drivers of that label, the Beatles, who've already become the most influential band of all time. They formed in Liverpool when I was seven and most of my generation are fanatical passengers as they progress through skiffle, beat, rock 'n' roll, traditional pop, classical music, Indian music, psychedelia and hard rock.

It is May 1967 and I'm about to have the most fulfilling school lesson any pupil can wish for. We have double French. Our master is a Yorkshireman called Malcolm Laycock, who in addition to being a teacher, has a keen interest in music and will even host a weekend jazz hour on Radio London and BBC Radio Two.

We are assembled in the classroom waiting for Laycock to arrive. It's noisy from the usual idle chat and schoolboy banter. Suddenly the door opens and Laycock bursts in excitedly pushing a trolley stacked with a record player and speakers. He also has a brown paper bag in the shape of an LP record. We obviously think we're gonna spend the next 90 minutes listening to some woman going shopping at a French market for *oeufs, pain et lait. Parfait!* (non monsieur).

However, he practically tears open the bag and reveals an intriguing record cover that will soon become the most elaborate and most expensive ever. It's The Beatles! They're are dressed in neon colour British officers' uniforms - pink, blue, orange and yellow - inspired by the military bands of the First World War. They are standing behind a marching drum inscribed in bold lettering, 'Sgt Pepper's Lonely Hearts Club Band'. Behind them are cardboard cut outs of scores of famous faces from the arts, science, sport and politics. Figures include Mae West, Lenny Bruce, the German composer Stockhausen, WC Fields, Edgar Allan Poe, Fred Astaire, Bob Dylan, Aldous Huxley, Dylan Thomas, Marilyn Monroe, Laurel and Hardy, Karl Marx, Sonny Liston, Lewis Carroll, Shirley Temple and Albert Einstein.

'This is the new Beatles album!' he boastfully proclaims.

We gasp in disbelief.

Beatles releases are big events and most of us know the album isn't out for another three weeks. Yet here it is in front of our eyes, thanks to his contacts in the record industry.

'You mean, the actual record or just the cover?' we ask.

'Let's find out, shall we…?'

With that, he carefully takes out one of the two shining vinyls and puts in on the turntable.

He seems to know all about the album content. He explains it's a concept album based on a mythical band. We are about to go on a musical journey through vaudeville, circus, music hall, avant-garde, and Western and Indian classical music with ground-breaking sound effects and tape manipulation. And, a real bonus for us, the lyrics are printed on the back of the cover so before each track Laycock explains what the song is about and any hidden meanings. For example, he convinces us that Lucy In The Sky With Diamonds is about an LSD trip with *'cellophane flowers of yellow and green'*. (Lennon will reveal later that the drug reference was just a coincidence.) We marvel at the skill of the compositions and the sheer variety of music. Track after track. Different sounds, different genres. We discuss and pick apart each one. I'm Fixing A Hole *(where the rain gets in)* is surely about getting off heroin. Is A Day In The Life about a drugs trip on a bus? Does With A Little Help From My Friends have a double meaning? Do they get by with help from mates or pills? The lesson flies by. There's even a round of applause at the end from us usually cynical kids. Before it's even hit the shops, we'll boast to disbelieving mates that we've already heard the latest Beatles album.

Laycock has ignored double French but given us a double treat - an LP that will become one of the best-selling of all time. And he's given us lucky boys something to remember long after any regular and irregular verbs or masculine and feminine nouns have wandered in and out of our heads.

Thirty years or so from this day I will attend a production of the Stephen Sondheim's musical Follies in a West End theatre. Buying a drink during the interval I will hear a distinctive Yorkshire voice behind me. I will recognise it immediately. I will turn around and say hello to Laycock, now of course older and greyer and probably all of 64! I will introduce myself but I'll not be sure if he really remembers me. And then I'll mention the Sgt Pepper experience and his face will light up. Ah yes, of course, he will say. And I'll say, 'Thanks Sir for such a memorable day.'

He'll pass away years later aged 71 having worked in radio for more than four decades. His Radio Two Big Band Show ran for 14 years, he became a controller of Jazz FM and won a Sony Radio award for his programme Billie Holiday in Her Own Words. But his memory stays alive in my head.

The Beatles and Laycock - A Class Act

35

Crisis, what crisis?

We're about to endure the biggest financial crisis of our lives. For years, Dad has made money from his bookmaking activities (albeit immediately giving it back when backing horses himself). He has a regular clientèle of what he calls 'mug punters' who pick out multiple horses with a pin and put them into four, five, or sometimes six accumulators. For them it's only a small outlay - sometimes just a bob or two - but needing a minor miracle to get any return. Money for old rope.

Enter a bloke called Connie Mould who lives on the estate behind our house. He's a regular punter, always cheerfully handing over his coins wrapped in notepaper carrying his distinctive scrawl. One Saturday afternoon, Connie's first two selections win - at big prices. Dad's not unduly concerned. The bet is a five-horse accumulator - a five fold, as they say in the game - so three more of his selections have to win for him to qualify for a payout. However, the third horse romps home as well. From an outlay of just two bob, Connie notionally has nearly a hundred pounds going on the next leg.

Just in case, Dad has a score on Connie's next horse which is 3/1. If it loses, Dad loses £20 and Connie's bet folds. If it wins, he's got £60 towards any eventual pay out. Of course, if the last horse loses, Dad will have made money on the whole episode. However, the fourth leg of the "acca" wins. It means that Connie now has hundreds of pounds going on his last selection - a 4-1 chance. A win will ruin us.

Dad is bricking it. The air is blue and we hold our collective breath as he decides what to do. Even if we agree with him he tells us to mind our own business and to keep our mouths shut. Johnny urges the old man to wipe his mouth and put a hundred quid on Connie's horse. That way if the bet comes in Dad has acquired nearly £500 towards the mega payout. With the clock ticking down to the race, Dad frantically scours the phone book looking for Connie's phone number. He gets through with five minutes to spare. He asks him if he'll accept a negotiated settlement BEFORE the race.

'That way, you are guaranteed a win. If the horse loses, you get nothing at all,' says Dad. Amazingly, Connie says no… he feels it's his lucky day and wants to take his chance.

With the horses at the start, Dad decides not to lay the bet off. He's gonna ride his luck and pray that Connie's horse loses. It's a five-furlong sprint. In less than a minute we'll know the outcome. It's so tense, I'm ordered out of the kitchen where the race is being transmitted live on TV. I'm summoned to the kiosk so that Mum can come in the house and watch as well. Within a matter of seconds she is back to relieve me behind the counter. She doesn't have to say anything. Her face says it all.

'I should make yourself scarce if I were you,' she says and I go to the park looking for my mates.

Connie's winnings are nearly a thousand pounds - money that Dad just doesn't have. He pays him as much as he can and promises the rest in instalments over the coming weeks and months. Dad is determined to pay him in full as soon as possible. The last thing he wants to do is to welch. His name would be mud throughout the whole of South London.

Gamblers are at their most vulnerable when they are desperate. Trying to pay his debts as quickly as possible, Lights goes on a betting spree - backing on every race, sometimes betting two horses in the same event, even three! He virtually lives in the betting shop. It's a recipe for disaster and the family debts spiral out of control. Mum can't pay the cigarette and confectionary firms and they begin to stop deliveries. It's a vicious cycle - holes in the supply chain means customers start going elsewhere and takings tumble. Bills from the gas, phone and electric companies are now red. We don't allow the meter readers in the house. Worse, Mum, whose name is on all the accounts, is getting letters from suppliers threatening to take her to court and to call in the bailiffs.

We are on the brink of ruin. Dad wants to declare ourselves bankrupt and not pay the big firms who he says can afford such losses. But Mum tells him that they'll have the right to take all our possessions because as a sole trader, she doesn't have the protection of what she calls 'limited liability' like commercial companies do. They argue into the night and she has a permanent headache with the worry of it all.

Our debts are now over £1300, plus of course Connie Mould's arrears. Mum's only release from the pressure is Bingo. Every night she escapes from the worry of this impending catastrophic collapse and quietly prays for a miracle. Even winning a full house at the Peckham Top Rank club won't be enough.

It is Friday night and she gets the number 12 bus to Peckham as usual and buys her normal four books. Top Rank has clubs all over the country and one game per night serves as the national 'jackpot' game, where the winner who gets a 'full house' in the least number of balls across all the venues wins. Mum wins this house prize in 38 numbers - quite a feat considering there are 90 balls and 15 numbers on a bingo card. The house prize is a couple of hundred quid - handy considering our predicament. She buys her friends a Guinness at the bar. Strangers approach saying they think she's a good chance of scooping the national prize. She puts her hands together in mock prayer. The results of have to be collated by head office. Each club phones in the details of the jackpot game.

Suddenly a buzz goes around the Peckham hall. There are rumours that they've won the jackpot. Mum begins shaking but has to wait for official confirmation. The manager approaches her in the bar with a smile on his face. Can she follow him to the stage? There he announces to the whole hall that indeed Peckham has won the national prize. And that Janie here is £1500 richer! Spontaneous applause breaks out on all tiers of the former cinema. People are genuinely thrilled and come up to shake Mum's hand.

The cheque for the full jackpot will be presented in due course but she collects an envelope containing £258 in ready money to take home. They call her a cab. She rings home. Her voice is quivering, trying to keep calm. Can we all meet her at The Rochester Steak House at Camberwell Green? She's had a win, but is tantalisingly keeping the amount to herself. I've passed The Rochester many times on the way to Camberwell Swimming Baths but I've never been in. It's Camberwell's most elite restaurant.

Johnny and I get the bus to The Green while Dad says he'll follow later. He wants to go for a drink in the Clyde first.

When we arrive at the restaurant Mum is sitting alone beaming.

'I've won the jackpot,' she says. 'Fifteen hundred quid!' We all hug. The manager brings us drinks on the house.

The place is in full swing with families celebrating birthdays etc, courting couples enjoying romantic dinners, a group of lads on a night out. And I'm about to eat fillet steak for the first time in my life.

Word gets around the restaurant of Mum's win. The mood is celebratory. But that's all about to change. On the other side of the big front window I suddenly notice Dad on the pavement leaning against the glass trying to see inside with one hand shading his eyes from the glare. In his other hand is Robbie on a piece of rope who is scratching at the window and barking. They're getting strange looks from the diners. Some are laughing.

We all know what's about to happen but are powerless to stop it. Robbie barges the door open and runs excitedly at our table - a panting, foaming beast out of control, knocking over glasses and crockery. Girls scream, diners jump out of the way. Dad is half cut and says in a loud voice, 'Robbie wants a bit of steak.' He laughs hysterically. Robbie jumps up at our table trying to lick our faces and eat our food! It's chaos. In a few seconds the whole mood of the restaurant has changed.

Dad seems oblivious to the carnage but the three of us put our heads in our hands. It's probably the most embarrassing episode of our lives. Mum is livid and ushers her man and dog outside. There are obviously choice words on the pavement. We smile at the waiter and ask for the bill. A few minutes ago we were his guests of honour. Now he can't get rid of us quickly enough. Mum comes in shamefaced and settles the account.

The Lord has led the way. We are now solvent. But he does work in mysterious ways.

***

186

That Bingo Jackpot changes everything. The writing is on the wall for Dad's bookie business. After paying off all his debts to punters he packs up. And there are signs that they both intend to give up the kiosk. And get proper jobs!

Push comes to shove when our landlord John Bloomfield gives us notice that he intends to raze his whole row of grand Victorian houses to the ground and build a petrol station. Mum puts the word out amongst the customers that we're looking for a council flat - ground floor, with a little garden, not too far from the main Camberwell Road. Not asking too much, is she? However, we leap to the top of the housing list because of the impending demolition. And lucky old Mum - a customer hears that a widow living in a two-bed maisonette on the Goschen Estate, not half a mile from 104, is planning to move to live with her sons on the South Coast. Mum approaches the council who are yet to receive notice from the tenant and with everybody's co-operation the deal is done. We move into a delightful little maisonette at No 2 Boundary House with a ten-yard garden for her to hang her washing out and for Robbie to do his business. For a while Mum pushes her pram to and from home to the kiosk with goods and takings but with street crime on the rise we all say it's too dangerous. Customers take it in turns to provide an escort home! Everyone urges her to pack it in and one day she announces the kiosk is over - she's a got a position as a clerk with the Board of Trade in The Strand. The money's not great but she's now 9-5 and no weekends, she gets a Civil Service pension and independence from her Old Man's unpredictable lifestyle.

Dad, meanwhile, astounds everyone by announcing he's got a job in Fleet Street - as a doorman on the Daily Telegraph. Exactly how we will never discover but he comes home after his first day in a blue serge suit, with shiny buttons and a peaked commissionaire's hat. Unfortunately for the esteemed newspaper, a few doors along from their office is a William Hill betting shop and their new doorman goes missing at various times in the afternoons. It comes to an end quite quickly. Having not had a meaningful relationship with the taxman for years, he's put on emergency tax. And when he receives his first pay packet he quits, saying it's all an effing liberty and he can't afford to pay the 'Ajax' - the word he uses for income tax.

However he's not giving up on this work malarkey completely. In no time he's got a number with British Rail - as a ticket inspector! This is classic poacher turned gatekeeper. He's spent his life jumping on and off trains, hiding from the clippers and rarely paying his fare, depriving BR of thousands of pounds. Now his job is to apprehend the jibbers.

But there's method in his madness. He's heard that there's a nice little fiddle on the 'rattlers'. At the end of each day he'll have hundreds of collected tickets. Most have been clipped or have a date stamp and he throws these away. But there are scores of 'open' return tickets which he collects from passengers unclipped and which are reusable. At the end of each shift he sells these back to the lads in the ticket office. A nice little earner for all! And it doesn't end there. He gets a cut from another scam - this time from the buffet staff. They smuggle their own loaves onto trains and pocket the cash from anyone ordering toast! Eventually British Rail realise what's happening and ban toast from all trains, citing health and safety from the toasters. And when management start changing the ticketing system so that all tickets are dated, he retires gracefully from the job. For now he's back on the street selling goods from a suitcase.

But there's been huge change in the Hurndall household. Johnny is now married to the lovely Megan after a glitzy wedding at St Giles' Church, where Mum and Dad tied the knot after the war. They had 13 bridesmaids, all dressed in pink, and a page boy - her little brother Tommy who wowed the congregation with his shock of curly blond hair. They were showered with gifts including an expensive-looking cake stand from our aunt Rene purchased from Harrods. The week of the wedding, Megan's brother Michael and I smashed it messing about with a football in the lounge. We carefully pieced it together propped up by the other gifts and various packaging and went amongst the missing for a few days, leaving it for them to discover. Johnny and Megan took residence in a flat above a launderette in Tulse Hill.

Johnny and Megan and me and Mum

Having lost his son, Dad is about to lose his best mate. Robbie, now clinically obese from meat and biscuits, is finding it more and more difficult to move around. Dad takes him to the vet but comes home with just a lead and collar.

'It was more humane to have him put down,' he says, trying not to cry in front of us. But then he drops a bombshell. He's asked the vet to preserve the body so that he can have him stuffed by a taxidermist and live with us in the corner of our new tiny lounge. Mum and I look at each other aghast.

'You must be effing joking,' she says. The row continues through the evening and I hear them in bed still arguing until the early hours. Common sense prevails and Dad drops the idea.

Where there were five in a rented house we are now three in a council flat. Our old home and business is gone. 104 and the kiosk are now memories. Mum has a secure job and Dad continues to ride the wheel of fortune.

And with my O-levels looming I start to think about my own future.

36

Sliding Doors

It's happened to us all - arriving at a crossroad or a seemingly inconsequential moment in our lives when, through accident or design, we choose a path that alters the trajectory of our future. The phenomenon was depicted in the 1998 romantic comedy *Sliding Doors*. Helen, played by Gwyneth Paltrow, is fired from her job as a London ad executive and rushes out to catch the train home. Two scenarios take place. In one, she arrives to find her husband in bed with another woman. She dumps him, finds a new man, and lives happy ever after. In the other, she gets to the platform just as the doors are closing and misses the train by a fraction of a second. By the time she gets home, the woman has left. But her life becomes more and more miserable because of her suspicions about her husband's infidelity.

My defining 'Sliding Doors' moment - the event that will set up my entire life - is about to happen. It's the Spring of 1969. I'm 16, and about to take my O-levels. Following in my parents' footsteps career-wise is a no-no. Being chased by coppers would be a road not taken. No, my dream is to have a career, a profession - to somehow become a journalist. And by sheer chance I'm about to find the golden ticket.

As you know, I attend a sink comprehensive (literally: it will later shut down in shame) in South London. And one rainy playtime I find myself in the dry but deserted refuge of the school library. The librarian, Miss Bray, or 'Boss-eyed Bray' as the kids cruelly nicknamed her, senses I'm only there to keep out of the rain and duly flushes me out.

'Yes, can I help you?' she asks in a tone that means precisely the opposite.

'Maybe,' I reply, desperately thinking on my feet. 'I'm looking for books on how to be a football reporter.' She rolls her working eye to the ceiling. Another dreamer interrupting her mid-morning break. Formal careers advice just doesn't exist here. Once upon a time, Billy Biro had 'careers' on the curriculum - one lesson a week enshrined in the school timetable. But those days are long gone. They have been replaced by an annual Careers Convention at which employers turn up to try to attract the attention of potential recruits. But such is the lacklustre response, the visitors spend most of the day crouched between their banners and balloons, pouring lukewarm tea from flasks, dipping Jammy Dodgers and reading trashy novels.

The Armed Forces are an ever present, particularly the Army, who once even drove a tank into the playground to generate some interest. But this is the era of the Vietnam War, and there are rumours that the US might persuade Britain to join the fray. No chance of us lads from the concrete jungle signing up to fight in the real jungle. We may be wanting academically, but we have our marbles.

Other regulars include some of the High Street banks. But for many of my fellow pupils the only hope of a bank job involves wearing a mask and firing a sawn-off shotgun into the ceiling. And there are always openings in the manor for speedy getaway drivers, numberplate makers, or someone who can hotwire a car. In the distant future the comedian Micky Flanagan will have a routine about careers advice at his own school in the East End of London. The teacher asks the kids what they hope to do when they leave. One lad, Mickey Hutton, draws ridicule from the class when he says he wants to drive a van.

'You dreamer, Hutton,' the kids say. 'Our job won't be to drive a van. It'll be to carry the goods to be put INTO the van.'

The same at our school. Inner London has no dominant industry - no major industrial works, car plants, coal mines, steelworks or the like. Around my way there's only the R. Whites lemonade factory and the place where they make Mr Kipling cakes. Two-thirds of the thousand or so boys will leave school at 15, consigned to a life of manual labour. Most kids, unrealistically, want to be professional footballers, or, failing that, to start earning some dosh as quickly as possible.

Miss Bray no doubt has had her fill of starry-eyed kids asking how they can get on the books of Man Utd or Millwall. And for that matter of dreamers like me who yearn to sit in the stands and report on the action. But before she can utter a word of advice, a bald head appears from behind the aisle of books.

'Who's asking about journalism?' he says.

'Er, me sir,' I reply.

'What's your name, son?'

'Hurndall, sir.'

'What class you in?'

'5L sir.'

'Well, come and see me after school and we'll discuss it,' he says, disappearing out through the swing doors. Miss Bray raises her eyebrows (these, in unison).

'There you go, glad I could help,' she smiles.

That teacher was Harry Dalton (Dalton to me of course) who is Head of English. Now, I should be full of hope and expectation at my appointment later that day. Instead, there's a feeling of dread and trepidation. Uppermost in my mind is the incident mentioned earlier in this book involving that very master in my first week of school but so ingrained in my memory it brings me out in shivers at least once a term. It is of course that day I hit him on the head with a tennis ball.

So, five years on, on my way to this far more cordial encounter, I wonder if he remembers either that incident or the cocky little rascal responsible. I'm certainly not going to mention it - and, thank heavens, neither does he. And judging by his warmth and enthusiasm I guess he must have checked out my English skills with my form teacher. Luckily, it's the subject in which I excel and give my all.

I'd even impressed in journalism working for the school radio - although my 'scoop' was censored. The pop group Love Affair had a hit with Everlasting Love and it was revealed that they didn't play on their instruments during the recording, merely sang over an orchestra track. It created quite a stir in music circles and was a talking point in the media.

Quite separately, my teacher Laycock (he of Sgt Peppers and BBC Radio) ran the school radio station. He invited the rock band leader Manfred Mann (Semi Detached Suburban Mr James) to the school to be interviewed about his career. I was chosen to ask the questions. Now radio isn't my forte. I get quite self-conscious and hate the sound of my own voice. The interview didn't get off to a good start because he started mocking the way I was asking questions, accusing me of putting on a posh voice (which was true!) and I'd blushed considerably. And then I asked him about the Love Affair row.

'A load of nonsense,' he said. 'We rarely play on our records.'

Laycock, monitoring the recording, raised his eyebrows and I realised instinctively that we had a scoop on our hands. However for transmission, Laycock edited the exchange out, saying it would be wrong to embarrass our guest.

Also, I'd written to the football correspondent of The Times, asking for career advice and tips on how to report a match. His name was Geoffrey Green, one of the Fleet Street's finest sports writers. In the year I was born, England had been thrashed by Hungary at Wembley - seen as a watershed for British football. Green had described one goal by the legendary Puskas. The England captain Billy Wright *'rushed out of defence and past him like a fire engine going to the wrong fire'*. Puskas merely dragged the ball back out of his path and put the ball into the back of the net.

Geoffrey Green with England captain Bobby Moore

Green had responded with a three-page hand-written letter. It's in neat handwriting, probably written on a train to a fixture somewhere. He said that if I was serious about journalism I needed to get on the staff of a local paper. Regarding football reporting, he advised me to always keep my eye on the ball, memorising what happens in case it leads to a goal. It may be obvious, but pure gold, nevertheless. I take his letter for granted, but will look back and admire an amazing gesture for a distant, anonymous schoolboy.

Back to my Dalton meeting… at first, he's all doom and gloom. Journalism is an extremely sought-after career and although there are scores of local rags in London, they only take on one or two juniors a year. I would be competing against hundreds, possibly thousands, of people far more academically qualified and far better connected. Editors can choose from university graduates or A level students boasting glowing testimonials from schools and colleges. The industry is also rife with nepotism. In many cases editors take on their sons or daughters, their friends' children, or the proprietor's own family.

'Even though I hate to say it, you've no chance of getting a job,' he says.

My bubble has burst. I think this must be it.

'Except… there is another way in,' he says.

Ah, the backdoor!

37

Opening Doors

Dalton has connections with the biggest news agency in Britain, and one of the most respected in the world. It's called the Press Association, or PA. It is based in Fleet Street, the industry's home.

The home of newspapers

'In the past I've steered a few of our pupils there. The idea is that you stay for a year or two as a runner and learn about news gathering, typing and maybe shorthand. Then, you're far more likely to persuade an editor to take you on.' He reaches inside his jacket for that same posh fountain pen he'd used to fill in that punishment book all those years ago. A shiver goes down my spine. But this time he writes down the name and the address of the recruitment officer at PA, a Mr F. Willet, 85 Fleet Street, London. 'I suggest you write to him. Tell him as much as you can about your yourself, career ambitions and why they should take you on. And let me see the letter before you post it.'

I spend the next week composing my application, ripping up several drafts and starting again. I write that I'm good with people; that I'm about to take my exams but want to leave at 16 to pursue a career as a sports reporter. And I've already been in touch with the industry's top football man.

Dalton seems impressed with the content and my neat italic handwriting, penned with my special left-hand nibbed Osmiroid fountain pen, a Christmas gift from my late Nan. And off the letter goes. I hear back the following week, inviting me for an interview.

Come the day, I'm dressed in the lightweight fawn-coloured suit I'd had made for my brother's wedding, tailored by A. Harris in The Cut at Waterloo from a length of mohair that found its way from the back of a tailor's lorry into Dad's hands. This, with a white shirt (always white, Dad insisted) plus a fashionable 'kipper' tie that I'd bought the old man for Christmas knowing he'd never wear it in a million years. I take the bus - the 45 from Camberwell Road to the Elephant and Castle, along Blackfriars Road, across Blackfriars Bridge, past the Unilever building to Ludgate Circus at the bottom of Fleet Street. For once I even pay my fare.

I sense I'm stepping into history - Dickens' London. Up the hill, I can just make out the Scales of Justice on the roof of the Old Bailey, and the golden cross on the towering dome of St. Paul's Cathedral.

I find the PA building easily enough and notice they share it with Reuters, the famous international news agency. Opposite is the gleaming dark glass art-deco of the Daily Express, then a few doors along, the Daily Telegraph with its Egyptian colonnade façade, where Dad had that brief spell as a doorman. Virtually every big provincial newspaper has an office in this magical boulevard - their names emblazoned on the line of buildings that stretch all the way down to The Strand.

Willet, a greying man with an avuncular smile, has my letter in front of him. He peers over his half-moon spectacles.

'So, you wanna be a scribbler?...'

He asks me to elaborate. Dalton had advised that whatever he asked I should have a point of view. Make sure you converse and don't sit in silence, he'd insisted. At the right moment I produce Green's letter. Willet takes the bait. I reply that the great man had advised me to apply specifically to PA (well, you have to stretch the truth sometimes). The interview's over almost before it's begun. He seems impressed. I will hear by mail in a few days, he says. Sure enough, the letter, embossed with the logo of the Press Association, drops through the letterbox the following week.

Dear Mr Hurndall…

YES! I've got the job! My salary will be £13 a week to start in July.

Stupidly I won't care about my O-levels from this day on, not bothering to revise, and, coincidentally being afflicted for the first time by hayfever which leaves me a shivering wreck, unable to concentrate.

That wet Wednesday at William Penn library not only shaped my future but defined me as a person. It proved to be the luckiest and most important day of my life - a chance meeting that set me up for a career that would take me through hundreds of other sliding doors… into local, provincial and national newspapers and the glamorous world of television. I would travel the globe, meet Royalty, Presidents and prime ministers, Hollywood actors and sports superstars, telling stories via notebook and camera of heroes and villains, triumphs and disasters, lecturing at university and writing books on True Crime.

It would lead to me meeting my wife. Our three children and nine grandchildren walk this earth due to that shower of rain and the helping hand of Harry Dalton, if you get my meaning. My huge regret is that he died before I could ever thank him for sliding open the door that day. Rest in Peace, Harry, my very own Mr Chips. I'm sorry for throwing that ball. And thank you for sparing me a thrashing.

38

A Final Thought

Looking back at my childhood, it's extraordinary to note how things have changed in just half a century or so. As I mentioned in the Preface, whole streets have disappeared; the two schools I attended are closed, consigned to history; the house I grew up in on Camberwell Road is now a petrol station; most of the shops I ran errands to, the youth clubs I attended, no longer exist. The pubs we stood outside as kids with our lemonade and crisps, have been demolished or converted into other uses, such as community centres or places of worship.

And not just bricks and mortar. My parents, my brother, my aunts and uncles, some of my cousins, many of my friends are sadly passed.

Folk move on, others move in, the make-up of an area changes, demographically and culturally. Our former council flat in Boundary House, where we paid a few quid a week rent, is now worth approaching half a million pounds!

Facebook groups reminisce about the 'good old days'. Researching this memoir, so many people told me, 'it's just not the same around here anymore'. But how could it ever be? Time marches on. And so do communities - work, income, attitudes, aspirations, ambitions, tastes... they all play a part.

A song by my favourite band Dire Straits makes the point. Sitting in the front of the tour bus travelling through the American Rust Belt one day Mark Knopfler wondered how it became miles of factories. It inspired his song *Telegraph Road*.

'A long time ago came a man on a track
Walking thirty miles with a sack on his back
And he put down his load where he thought it was the best
He made a home in the wilderness.

He built a cabin and a winter store
And he ploughed up the ground by the cold lake shore
And the other travellers came walking down the track
And they never went further, no they never went back.

Then came the churches, then came the schools,
Then came the lawyers, then came the rules
Then came the trains and the trucks with their loads.
And the dirty old track was the Telegraph Road..."

Camberwell was a *Telegraph Road*. As I noted earlier, it once consisted of rolling green fields where Roman centurions and pilgrims marched through to and from Londonium. No doubt when the manicured lawns was replaced by bricks and mortar those upper class residents in the 19th century also thought the area had changed for the worse.

They didn't own Camberwell. And neither did we. Neither do its present incumbents and nor will future residents. We are all 'men on a track', passers-by on earth's long journey through time.

My family passed through when the borough was labelled one of the most deprived areas of Britain. The dictionary says this means we suffered a 'severe and damaging' lack of basic material and benefits. But that is only half the story. The term is pejorative, bandied about by politicians, academics and social workers.

Deprived?

Behind the counter of that corner kiosk, I got an education that couldn't be bought, serving Woodbines and the Daily Mirror, and taking bets for Dad. I expanded my reading, arithmetic, and got to know hundreds of ordinary folk and even a few chancers. I failed the Eleven Plus but would have got an A Star for social skills.

Deprived?

Thanks to Mum and Dad I developed a strong work ethic, delivering papers at the crack of dawn and standing at the factory gate selling the Late Night Final. My pocket money gave me independence. At the age of seven I could afford - and was afforded - the freedom to go to play out and even make London my playground. Today's kids aren't even allowed to go to the park on their own!

Deprived?

A famous journalist named Nicholas Tomalin once wrote that the only qualities essential for real success in journalism were 'rat-like cunning, a plausible manner and a little literary ability'. That just about summed me up. Serving adults in the kiosk from an early age gave me the skills to weigh people up within seconds - a valuable attribute for a reporter on the street. I learned to think on my feet and develop that 'rat-like cunning' needed for my later life as a journalist, TV producer and filmmaker.

Deprived?

We were certainly short of many of the material comforts of modern life but my childhood was rich in so many other ways and for that I feel blessed.

A MESSAGE FROM THE AUTHOR

Before you go...

Thank you for reading my book. I hope you enjoyed it. Would you be kind enough to post a review on Amazon? Good, bad or indifferent, one or five stars, it doesn't matter. Online reviews are vital to independent authors like myself. They trigger algorithms which help bring the book to the attention of new readers. Just go on the Amazon website and type in my name or the book title. A few lines make all the difference.

Thank you for your support.

ALAN HURNDALL

Printed in Great Britain
by Amazon

60148004R00117